Keiretsu

Keiretsu

Inside the Hidden Japanese Conglomerates

Kenichi Miyashita
David W. Russell

McGraw-Hill

New York   San Francisco   Washington, D.C.   Auckland   Bogotá
Caracas   Lisbon   London   Madrid   Mexico City   Milan
Montreal   New Delhi   San Juan   Singapore
Sydney   Tokyo   Toronto

Library of Congress Cataloging-in-Publication Data

Miyashita, Kenichi.
    Keiretsu: inside the hidden Japanese corporations / Kenichi
Miyashita, David W. Russell.
        p.   cm.
    Includes index.
    ISBN 0-07-042583-3 (HC)   ISBN 0-07-042859-X (PBK)
    1. Conglomerate corporations—Japan.   2. Industrial concentration—
Japan.   I. Russell, David, date.
    HD2756.2.J3M59   1994
    338.8'042—dc20   93-21388
                                                                  CIP

McGraw-Hill

A Division of The McGraw-Hill Companies

1 2 3 4 5 6 7 8 9 0   DOC/DOC   9 0 0 9 8 7 6 5

ISBN 0-07-042583-3 (HC)
ISBN 0-07-042859-X (PBK)

*The sponsoring editor for this book was David Conti, the editing supervisor
was Francis Koblin, and the production supervisor was Donald Schmidt. It
was set in Palatino by Emanon.*

Printed and bound by R. R. Donnelley & Sons Company.

 This book is printed on recycled, acid-free paper containing a
minimum of 50% recycled, de-inked fiber.

Contents

Preface   ix

Introduction   **1**

1. The Keiretsu around Us   **7**

Understanding the Keiretsu Structure   8
Horizontal Keiretsu   9
Vertical Keiretsu   11
Keiretsu Literacy   13
Tracking the Who's Who   14

2. Where It Began: The History of the Keiretsu   **19**

Dawn of the Modern Era   21
The Zaibatsu Are Born   22
The Big Four Zaibatsu   25
Growth of the Zaibatsu   27
The Zaibatsu and World War II   29
End of the Zaibatsu   31
Reforming the Japanese Economy   33

Re-forming the Japanese Economy   34
Birth of the Keiretsu   36
Competition among the Keiretsu   39
Nurturing the Keiretsu   40

3. The Heart of the Keiretsu: Bankers and Traders   **43**

The Main Bank   44
   How a Company Gets a Main Bank   45
   The Power of the Big Six Main Banks   48
   The Primary Functions of a Main Bank   49
The Sogo Shosha   53

4. The Ties That Bind   **61**

Presidential Councils   61
Cross-shareholdings   66
   I'll Buy Yours If You'll Buy Mine . . .   68
Assigned Directors   70
Intragroup Financing   74

5. The Big Six Horizontal Keiretsu   **75**

The Old versus the New   75
Kanto versus Kansai   76
How Big Is Big?   78
Cross-shareholding Trends   81
The Mitsui Group   82
The Mitsubishi Group   88
The Sumitomo Group   94
The Fuyo Group   99
The Sanwa Group   103
The DKB (Dai-Ichi Kangyo Bank) Group   109

6. The Vertical Keiretsu   **115**

The Production Keiretsu   116
   In Japan It's Always a Little Different   118
   Structure of the Production Keiretsu   121
The Distribution Keiretsu   122
The Vertical Keiretsu under Attack   125

7. The Leading Vertical Keiretsu 133

Automobiles   134
    The Toyota Group   134
    The Nissan Group   138
    The Honda Group   140
Electronics   142
    The Matsushita Group   142
    The Hitachi Group   145
    The Toshiba Group   147
    The Sony Group   149

8. Voices from Inside the Pyramid 153

Round Table   154
The Electronics Industry   169
The Auto Industry   176

9. Conclusions: The Past, the Present, and the Future 193

The Original Purpose of the Horizontal Keiretsu   193
Was Keiretsification Successful?   194
Why Do the Horizontal Keiretsu Still Exist?   195
How Are the Vertical Production Keiretsu Changing?   199
How Are the Vertical Distribution Keiretsu Changing?   203
The "Keiretsu Problem"   205
What about American Keiretsu?   207

Afterword   211
Notes   213
Index   219

Preface

In the very short time since 1989 a Japanese word migrated to America, jumped onto the cover of *Business Week,* made a dramatic debut before the U.S. Congress, did a variety of television appearances, and was quickly "naturalized" into the English language. The term *keiretsu* may lack the cultural associations of *kimono* and *geisha* and the upscale image of *sushi,* but it has accomplished something that these other Japanese imports have not: it has joined America's business lexicon. The general subject of Japan's industrial "families" (the various kinds of keiretsu) has become a topic of considerable debate in the United States, in Europe, and even in Asia. Innumerable studies have been undertaken in the United States, from the university to the government level, trying to determine whether to tolerate or castigate the Japanese keiretsu.

Are the keiretsu merely efficient organizational systems for streamlining the Japanese economic machine? Or are they instead exclusionist confederations designed to keep out foreign competition? Are they, perhaps, both? Should the United States allow Japanese keiretsu to operate unchallenged? Should they be allowed to expand their influence in America? Should American firms be trying to emulate the keiretsu in order to improve our elusive "competitiveness"?

Everyone, from columnists to Congressmen, has added to the debate on the keiretsu. Yet the subject of this growing public policy issue is clouded by a lack of information on what the keiretsu are and, more important, how they are understood in Japan. The aim of this book is to provide the foundation for understanding the keiretsu, both horizontal and vertical, and to give the reader some feel for the vital interconnections of Japanese business.

We will examine a number of features that are common to most keiretsu, such as the "main bank," stable shareholding, and interconnecting directorates. We will also look at some features which have no parallel in America, such as a general trading company. We will look at the history of Japan's most famous keiretsu, observe how the government itself promoted the "keiretsification" of the economy, and then visit with workers in the production keiretsu to see firsthand what life is like on the inside. To our knowledge this is the first time that voices from inside the keiretsu have ever appeared in English.

Kenichi Miyashita
David Russell

Introduction

It is a sad comment on the state of U.S. business that our nation was caught off guard just a few years back by the "discovery" of a closed group of Japanese corporate fraternities designed to squeeze blood from their own small industries and shut out all foreign competitors. The explorer who announced this discovery to every journalist he could find was Texas' own T. Boone Pickens. In the middle of a prolonged lobbying effort to win a seat on the board of a Japanese auto parts firm called Koito Manufacturing Co., Pickens implied that Koito was not really the independent firm it appeared to be but seemed to be controlled from above by major shareholder Toyota Motor Corp. Because Koito was a member of the huge Toyota Group, it owed allegiance to that firm rather than to its top stockholder (Boone Co.). In fact, Boone pressed on, most of Japanese industry was a collection of big industrial groups like Toyota.

These "k'retsu" as he called them, were industrial juggernauts that virtually controlled Japanese business and were already preparing to bulldoze their way across the globe in search of new conquests. Although they kept up a fierce level of competition at home, when foreign smoke signals were visible on the horizon, they would forget about their own squabbles long enough to pull the wagons in a circle and fight off the invader (which was exactly what Pickens believed was happening to him).

What was truly surprising about Boone's crusade was not that he was way off the mark—for despite transparently self-serving motives, his portrait of the *keiretsu* (corporate groups) was not entirely inaccurate—but rather, that American executives, many of whom had either been doing business with or competing with large Japanese companies for years, did not speak up early on to put the whole thing in perspective. American corporate managers should have been saying, "Boone, this keiretsu stuff's old hat. Our people have been on top of this thing longer than you've been looking for oil."

Clearly, the reason no one corrected Mr. Pickens and the reason his tirade had such an impact was the total lack of knowledge about one of the most fundamental elements in Japanese business. That this could be true in 1990, after decades of trade, rivalry, and even nightmares about the Japanese buying up our country and renting it back to us, is a shocking statement about how we Americans have come to do business. It would be nice to think that, belated though they may be, our top corporations have begun crash courses to learn the basics of Japanese business structure, strategy, and planning. Unfortunately, there is little evidence for optimism. In spite of Japan's growing economic and political clout, its importance in the minds of many senior executives remains limited by its relative geographic size. Worse yet, the end of the "bubble economy" and the extended recession have led many American executives to "write off" Japan as a major competitor for the next few years. Underestimating the Japanese is such a serious mistake—and one that we have suffered from so painfully in the past—that it would seem unlikely that anyone would make the same blunder again. Yet that is just what is happening today.

A decade ago American managers boned up on their Pacific counterparts by reading about the "Japanese way of management." Books and magazine articles featured colorful stories about the remarkable achievements of Japan, Inc., with pictures of Japanese workers all dressed in spotless company uniforms, exercising together on the factory roof, singing their company song and cheerfully participating in bottom-up management. Some U.S. execs even joined special seminars where they learned how to bow properly, how to exchange *meishi* (business cards), and so on. With this, the companies felt, they had a pretty good handle on dealing with the Japanese challenge. Silly as all the "Zen and the Art of Japanese Management" books and the "You Can Do Business With the Japanese" seminars were, at least they indicated a perceived need to find out more about how Japan functions.

However, with the bursting of the asset bubble that drove Japan's overseas investments, that pressure seems to be gone. People who only a short while ago worried about how they would cope with their Japanese rivals are increasingly adopting a policy best summed up as "Leave it to the politicians." Once again America is returning to a mentality of dealing with problems as they come up rather than building the corporate infrastructure to avoid or resolve them. Not only do we rob our long-term competitive future by accepting the noneducation of our children, we do exactly the same thing in the short term by accepting ignorance as a norm inside our best corporations.

If Americans find Japan puzzling, the Japanese find American approaches to Japan even more so.

In 1983 one of the authors happened to be in a bar in Tokyo's Akasaka district with a middle-level manager at a well-known Japanese general trading firm (*shosha*). As the manager had recently returned from several years in the United States, his division used him as a point man for dealing with English-speaking guests. Like many of his peers who have been "contaminated" by American thinking, he was quick to call things as he saw them rather than sticking to polite but nebulous expressions. We naturally fell into discussing the American clients he had been entertaining earlier that evening. His bewilderment was palpable. "How can anyone come to do business here—or anywhere else for that matter—without having at least a general idea of how a country's business system operates?" he began. "To our way of thinking, what most American companies are doing is simply inconceivable."

When asked if one of his clients had committed some horrendous social faux pas, he laughed. "No, that has nothing to do with it. Nobody really cares whether a client walks on the tatami [straw mats] with his shoes on or presents his meishi upside down or pours his own drink and leaves everybody else's glass empty. Those are only cultural traditions, and every country has them. I'm sure I said and did a thousand things wrong while I was in the States, but people excused me because I didn't know any better. At least in our company nobody cares if none of our clients has bothered to learn a single word of Japanese. We're not getting together to talk about the weather. Our clients have come halfway around the world to talk about business, and we can do that in any language that makes them comfortable.

"What I can't understand, and what most of the people in my firm still cannot believe is that none of our American clients, and only a few of the Europeans, has the faintest idea how our system really works. Some of them don't even know what a shosha is, and they sure don't know how we function." He took another sip of beer. "Of course, that can be a big advantage for us . . ." He smiled and let the idea remain unfinished. "What I mean is, I'm not surprised if a foreign company doesn't spend time studying the languages or customs of their trading partners. That's something we think is important when you go overseas, but they don't. No problem. But when they miss out on the basics, the kind of things you know they'd never slip up on at home, then I'm surprised. That's bad business."

When he was asked to be more specific, he got very specific and ordered another round. Then he leaned forward in his chair and said something like this: "Let's say you're in business, any business, and you're going into a new market. Maybe you just want to set up a hardware store in a small town. You find out there's another hardware store down the street. What do you do? Do you just ignore him? Of course not. You go down to his store first thing to see what his merchandise looks like; you look around and try to find out everything you can about his business. After you look over his stock and his shop, you'd want to find out some basics about how he operates, like how long is he open and how often does he take holidays? Does he work hard or close up early? Who are his suppliers? Are there better ones or cheaper ones? How long has the guy been in business, what's his reputation in the community, and who are his influential friends? If you're smart, you'll find out where he does his banking, who insures his store, and what his credit is like. All this is pretty standard stuff. The bigger the company, the more you want to know, and the more public information is available to you. The companies I dealt with in the States know the firms in their own lines of business pretty well. The domestic ones, that is.

"But when you take the same basic idea and raise it to the level of international business, the whole idea of knowing your competitors inside out gets lost somewhere. Even today, if I'm talking with a top-level American executive, someone who's involved with international trade and who probably understands global financial movements better than I ever will, I can't get over how little he knows about the nuts and bolts of Japanese companies in his sector. Who does business with whom and why? Where does the money come from? If a company gets in serious trouble, who will come to its rescue? What government agencies directly affect a firm's operations, and how far will they get involved? These execs not only don't know, they don't realize that they don't know. It's unbelievable!

"I can't even guess how many people we have worldwide whose main job is to gather information on other companies' business. Then we have a large staff in our headquarters whose only job is to analyze that information and prepare detailed reports for our executives and field personnel to use."

What he was saying about the inner workings of the shosha sounded more like a corporate intelligence agency than a trading company. Asked if this was common, he said: "Listen, to tell the truth, our company has a relatively small operation. Some of the other shosha are much better at it than we are. They have much older and bigger global networks, a lot more staff and a lot more computers devoted to analyzing what's going on with partners and competitors around the world. To some extent or other all the big manufacturers do the same thing. And the city banks, and the big brokers, and . . . Hey, don't look so shocked. It's just business."

About five years later a senior manager of a large manufacturing firm headquartered in Tokyo, who was being interviewed, drove home exactly the same point: "I can draw you a diagram of my top three U.S. competitors' organizational charts," he said. "I can show you where they obtain parts, where those parts are processed, where they are assembled, and how they are delivered to dealers. If I pick up the phone, my staff can easily give me figures on any one of those companies: changes in the number of their employees, their complete salary structure, frequency of labor disputes, product delays, customer complaints, and of course a detailed financial profile. I can already tell you from memory what most of their balance sheets look like, but if I wanted details on any of our big competitors, I could have them in five minutes. Who holds its loans? What's its share price? What do analysts think of its future prospects and why? Most of this is readily available. Certainly those firms' domestic rivals are taking advantage of that information, and of course, so are we."

He was asked about less public information his company had access to as a member of a keiretsu. "Of course, we can obtain a great deal of information on any overseas firm through our shosha. We can find out who they do business with in other markets, who supplies them, what kind of problems they're having, how much they pay for things, where the weak links in their procurement or distribution systems are . . . that kind of thing. We could probably get detailed financial information about them through our bank if it's really necessary, but as I say, we've already got most of that."

What amazed this executive—and the dozens more interviewed—was that so many American companies were not studying Japanese business as thoroughly and systematically as the Japanese were studying them. Even today, with parts of whole industries "lost" to Japan, very few American executives seem to have more than the vaguest idea how Japanese business works. Although a handful of U.S. managers may read up on how to bow correctly before a visit to Tokyo, not one in a hundred is assigned to learn about the structure and influence of the government bureaucracy, the role of the big "city" banks and the trading houses, and the most basic "geography" of Japanese business, the keiretsu.

As that middle-level shosha manager said in the bar years before, not knowing the social amenities of a foreign country is pardonable, but not knowing the fundamentals of how they do business is a sign of carelessness. And to the Japanese, carelessness is one step away from failure.

1
The Keiretsu around Us

We are surrounded by the keiretsu, and we deal with them every day—every time we turn on the TV, pick up a paper, eat at a fast-food chain, or go to work. Quietly, secretly, without warning, keiretsu have infiltrated our daily lives and engulfed almost everything we know. Unbeknownst to most of us, we too have become part of various keiretsu. The word *keiretsu* does not translate neatly into English, and that is the beginning of the problem. The most common Japanese meaning is something close to the English verbs "link," "affiliate with" or "connect to."

In its simplest form, a keiretsu is a group of individual units viewed together, usually as a hierarchical organization. What it is that unites them is not precisely defined, but it usually involves a "flow" (of money, personnel, even personal loyalty) either upwards or downwards in the hierarchy. In the United States, the Columbus Clippers are part of the New York Yankee keiretsu. *Fortune* magazine is part of the Time keiretsu, and Time is part of the Time-Warner keiretsu. Robert Reich is a part of the Bill Clinton keiretsu. If you switch on your TV and watch CNN, you're sampling the product of the CNN keiretsu, which includes all that network's affiliates, all their staff, and all the tiny companies that have anything to do with contributing to their business. There is either a personal or a commercial keiretsu for every kind of organization you can think of: a GM keiretsu and a McDonald's keiretsu, a Harvard University keiretsu, and a Michael Jackson keiretsu.

If this sounds like a pretty broad definition, it is. The term is vague. It merely shows that people or things are connected in some way. Keiretsu are neither good nor bad in and of themselves. Of course, if you dislike the

Yankees or GM or Harvard or Michael Jackson or the President of the United States, anyone associated with them (i.e., their keiretsu) may be fair game for some verbal abuse. But simply to attack the notion of being connected to someone or some organization is self-defeating.

Then why all the fuss about keiretsu?

The answer is that certain large Japanese keiretsu are not merely loose connections between a company and a few of its related firms, but groups of thousands of companies all working for a single large firm. Other keiretsu are made up of dozens of these huge firms (together with their thousands of smaller companies) bound together as gigantic industrial combines. Even this would not in and of itself merit much attention, but against the background of U.S.–Japan trade friction, the term *keiretsu*, replacing the more colorful, but less accurate expression *Japan, Inc.*, has become a label for fraternal collusion to keep foreign goods and services eternally knocking at the door. The U.S. government highlighted these keiretsu in the Structural Impediments Initiative (SII) talks as a target of reproach. Specific accusations (and a number of empirical studies) focus on the closed nature of these huge keiretsu groups, both to foreign investment and to foreign participation, and on their attempts to limit imports to the Japanese market. Although these claims are worth discussing, we will not attempt to answer all the many political questions pertaining to the keiretsu. Our goal is first and foremost to show what the keiretsu are in the Japanese context.

Understanding the Keiretsu Structure

No one knows how many corporate keiretsu there are in Japan. Over 2000 companies are listed on the stock exchanges, and almost all of them have at least one group of subsidiaries and/or affiliates connected to their business. These are all keiretsu. There are probably at least that many firms that are big enough to list their shares but choose not to. Most of them have keiretsu. There is no accurate way to count all the corporate groups in Japan, but the figure must certainly be in the thousands and possibly much higher. Obviously, the great majority of these groups are not our concern here. We will focus only on those keiretsu which have grown to great size and which have become powerful both domestically and internationally. In other words, we will only look at keiretsu whose names might be somewhat familiar outside of Japan. Due to the limitations of this book we will not be able to treat many of the other big keiretsu that are worth examining (the enormous Seibu and Tokyu railroad/real estate/entertainment/leisure keiretsu, for example, or the Daiei and Ito-Yokado retailing keiretsu, to name just a few).

There are various ways to classify keiretsu, but the two most common classifications cover all the groups that we will be looking at. Although the two types of keiretsu are very different, everyone, including Boone Pickens, U.S. trade negotiators, and most of the media, tend to get them confused. The Japanese call them *yoko* (horizontal) and *tate* (pronounced "ta-tay," vertical), and so we will use the words horizontal and vertical to describe them. A *horizontal* keiretsu is a group of very large companies with common ties to a powerful bank, united by shared stockholdings, trading relations, and so on. The Mitsubishi Group of companies would be one example. A *vertical* or **pyramid** keiretsu is made up of one very large company and hundreds or thousands of small companies subservient to it. A good example would be a large manufacturer like Toyota with twin vertical keiretsu within its total "group": one pyramid producing goods and the other pyramid distributing and selling those goods.

Horizontal Keiretsu

When we read about or hear about "the keiretsu" in English without a more specific reference, it is usually the big horizontal groups that are under discussion. The biggest ones all revolve around a financial core, which always includes a major bank. Although mergers are continually shrinking the number of commercial banks in Japan, there are currently 11 large "city" banks, as the Japanese call them, plus three long-term credit banks, all of which have some kind of identifiable group of companies that rely on them as principal sources of finance. However, no one talks about the "14 big horizontal keiretsu" nor even the "11 city bank keiretsu." Only the six largest city banks (Dai-Ichi Kangyo, known as DKB, Sakura, Sumitomo, Fuji, Sanwa, and Mitsubishi) and the leading long-term credit bank, the Industrial Bank of Japan (IBJ), are commonly referred to as the centers of their own industrial groups. In Japanese, the keiretsu led by these six city banks have a special name, the *roku dai kigyo shudan*, or Six Big Industrial Groups. In English, they are simply the Big Six, and we will look at them individually in chapter 5. The IBJ Group, while certainly significant, is a less coherent keiretsu, and we will not examine it in detail here.

The Big Six are the strongest and most representative horizontal keiretsu. One way to think of them is as corporate convoys, large groups of companies that for one reason or another have chosen to travel together and keep an eye on each other. At the center of a horizontal keiretsu there is always a nominal "flagship," which is the city bank. However, there is often another behemoth—a trading company (*shosha*)—which is roughly equivalent to the bank in influence, sailing right beside it. There may even be a third firm, a giant manufacturer, also in this nucleus of the convoy. Around these two or three giants circle the core members, usually three financial firms—a life insurance company, a nonlife insurance company, and a trust bank—and one or two very large manufacturers. Together the financial firms, the trading company, and the group's key manufacturers give the keiretsu its identity.

Around the periphery of these core companies are whole flotillas of firms, some clustering together and some out on their own. At the far edge of this periphery is a scattering of companies, usually smaller ones, but sometimes a few large firms, which choose to remain associated with the group, but at a distance. Toyota is an example of such a firm, officially a member of the Mitsui Group, but operating at the periphery of group affairs. And just to make things interesting, there are a few very large companies that claim allegiance to more than one group. Hitachi is the best-known example of a firm that considers itself above the keiretsu and boldly flies the flag of three different groups.

Although each of the Big Six includes hundreds of firms in its extended group, only a few dozen are considered members of the club. This is the group's inner sanctum, a body of the biggest and most important firms whose top executives meet regularly in a presidential council (*shacho-kai*), where they discuss matters of concern to the group as a whole.

Altogether, only 189 companies account for the entire membership of the Big Six *shacho-kai*. Beyond the official members are scores of closely related firms, and beyond that are hundreds of even more loosely related firms. Outside of the clearly defined limits of the presidential council, the boundaries of the Big Six become fuzzy, which makes it nearly impossible to estimate how far their influence extends, as we will soon see.

There are also many big firms not officially connected with any of the big horizontal keiretsu, firms that like to maintain their image as "independents." This category includes major companies such as Sony, Bridgestone, Nippon Steel, and so on. Much as they strive to remain independent of the big horizontal groups, however, almost all of them have relations with at least one of the Big Six banks and/or IBJ, and significant chunks of their stock are almost always in the hands of the Big Six firms. In the event that any of these independents should ever find itself in a serious business crisis, it would be rescued by one or more of the Big Six or IBJ, and would likely become a member of some bank's keiretsu (a very common pattern we will examine in Chapter 3).

Vertical Keiretsu

Much of the confusion in talking about the keiretsu arises not from the simple distinction between the horizontal and vertical but because the two classifications overlap to a large extent. That is, many of the biggest vertical keiretsu lie inside the borders of the Big Six. Almost all the Big Six companies (i.e., the 189 members of the major horizontal keiretsu) are also the heads of their own vertical keiretsu. Beneath Toyota, Toshiba, Sumitomo Chemical, Mitsubishi Heavy Industries, Mitsui Bussan and all the rest, there are hundreds and thousands of smaller firms. These more or less invisible companies are stacked, wedding cake style beneath the famous big-name firms that lead their keiretsu. Thus, the Big Six are like a collection of icebergs viewed from above. Beneath each member of the horizontal grouping is a giant, unseen mass of smaller companies.

To get an idea of how many vertical pyramids exist in Japanese industry, take a look at a listing of the Tokyo Stock Exchange (TSE), which is divided into two sections of considerably different status. On the more prestigious First Section there are over 1000 companies. These are the largest and most influential firms in the nation, and almost every one of them has dozens or hundreds or, in some cases, thousands of subsidiaries and affiliates extending beneath it. The very biggest companies on the First Section are so large that even their subsidiaries are listed on the First Section (Matsushita Electric has nine such subsidiaries; Hitachi has ten). This is almost unthinkable for most firms, which are lucky to have even one subsidiary big enough to be listed on the lower-ranked Second Section. In short, most of the TSE companies are the heads of their own vertical keiretsu, and a few are very large members of someone else's vertical keiretsu.

It is relatively easy to imagine a horizontal keiretsu, a group of big companies of more or less equal status in orbit around a key bank. But what do the vertical keiretsu look like?

Beneath most listed companies there may be a half dozen or so major subsidiaries. In the case of the manufacturing industry these are usually the first-tier factories producing goods for the "parent" company up above. Below each factory are usually dozens of smaller firms. All of these companies produce some part or subassembly which ultimately works its way up the pipeline to benefit the company at the top of the pyramid. The parent may allow its first-tier subsidiaries to use its name, and if it is quite a large firm, perhaps the second-tier firms as well. In a society as status conscious as Japan, where simply wearing the lapel pin of a known corporation is a symbol of success, this bestowing of the parent's name is often worth more than paying out better salaries.

For obvious reasons, these "vertical keiretsu" are larger and more common in manufacturing industries. They are particularly prominent in the electronics and automobile industries, although almost every other field has its own vertical keiretsu, including advertising, publishing, broadcasting, and other nonmanufacturing businesses. The Japanese tradition of loyalty within a hierarchy has made it very difficult, until quite recently, for subcontractors or free-lance operators to work for more than one organization. For example, an American or British advertising agency might contract a small design studio to do an illustration for an upcoming ad campaign. The design studio might also accept work from several other ad companies. Not in Japan. If you subcontract for Dentsu, the nation's top ad agency, you are effectively in the Dentsu keiretsu, which means you probably don't work for Dentsu's rivals. That's just the way it is. Similarly, if you work in the Toshiba keiretsu or the Nissan keiretsu, you don't offer your services to Hitachi or Toyota. Although the exclusive nature of these vertical keiretsu is beginning to change, the traditional bonds are still very strong, more so for the smaller companies lower in the pyramid.

To really understand the meaning of a vertical keiretsu, we should look at the structure of a giant company, a Hitachi or NEC or Toshiba. The smallest affiliates of these firms are so small that they hardly deserve to be called companies. Some are little more than family operations, perhaps assembling parts for some electronic device in a back room of their home. Some are 10-man machine shops, printing companies, "metal bashing" firms, and the like. Some of them have no idea that the little object they are wiring or assembling or painting will someday wind up in a box marked with a famous maker's name. They take their orders from a bigger company, and that company is working for what it thinks of as a "big company," a larger firm, with maybe 100 to 200 workers. All of these are officially classified as smaller enterprises by the Japanese government. Yet they comprise the bulk of the pyramid (and of all Japanese industry). Above the largest of these small firms is an intermediary, usually a subsidiary of the parent firm.

It is no exaggeration to say that the parent has no idea how far down its pyramid extends. It can see only two or three levels down. Even its main subsidiaries don't see all the way to the bottom. Only people around the middle of the pyramid have any idea how vast the whole thing really is. The president of one firm located somewhere near the middle of the NEC organization estimated that if you include all the little mom-and-pop firms at the base of the pyramid, there are around 6000 companies in the NEC keiretsu. And NEC is only the fourth largest electrical maker in Japan.

Keiretsu Literacy

If we stop to consider just this overview of the keiretsu landscape, it begins to look fairly complicated. There are six large city-bank led horizontal keiretsu, each comprising dozens of very large firms. But beneath almost all of these firms lie vertical keiretsu, some of them containing companies large enough to be listed on the stock exchange, others containing thousands of small companies. How do the Japanese manage to remember them all? The answer is, of course, they don't.

Outside of their own field of business, most corporate managers probably don't know any of the companies in even the biggest vertical keiretsu. And as for the horizontal groups, very few Japanese executives could name all the members of even one of the Big Six, much less their many affiliates. Yet most senior executives would be able to identify the group orientation of almost any major firm if the question were put to them.

How is this possible? The keiretsu affiliations are not formally taught anywhere, and no one sits down and tries to memorize them. The answer is that knowing "who's who" in the keiretsu is essential information for conducting business in Japan. Consider for a moment the Japanese written language, which uses about 2000 *kanji* characters frequently enough so that every literate person must know them, together with their multiple pronunciations. These days very few Japanese can write more than a few hundred from memory, yet everyone can read a newspaper with ease. Why? Because they encounter the *kanji* every day. Not knowing the basics of the written language would make it extremely difficult to function in Japanese society. Similarly, Japanese executives learn and remember the important keiretsu affiliations simply because it helps them to do business. And like the written language, everyone in business expects everyone else to have a certain minimum level of "literacy."

True, most college students, housewives, and even most lower-level company employees don't know whether or not Toshiba is in the Mitsui Group, and really couldn't care less. But ask the president of a medium-sized food-processing company in one of the rural provinces, a man who knows nothing at all about the electronics business, and he'll tell you that Toshiba is part of the Mitsui group. He may know nothing more detailed about the firm, but he knows to which group it belongs. In other words, the core membership of the Big Six and the names of some of the major vertical keiretsu members are taken for granted in Japan. Every executive of every major company knows who does business with whom in the same way that he knows the names of important world capitals: he can't remember where or when he learned them, just that it's important not to forget and that you sound like an idiot if you say that London is in France.

Once again, this information is not formally taught; companies do not give "keiretsu recognition" classes to their new employees and no consultants come around with flash cards to test young would-be executives. But anyone who aspires to rise in any company of any size will gradually learn who's who in business without being told. In a very real sense, this understanding is part of the common, shared background of all Japanese executives. If a foreign visitor were to ask a director of a top Japanese company whether it is important to learn the members of the Big Six keiretsu, he would probably laugh and say it's a waste of time. But he would never for a moment forget that Kirin Beer is a Mitsubishi company or that Itochu is a driving force in the Dai-Ichi Kangyo (DKB) Group.

For the Western reader, however, there is no point in trying to learn all the members of the various groups. What is important is to understand the basic structure of Japanese business, and that requires some understanding of the keiretsu and how they work. Many businesspeople may also want to be able to determine if a company with which they have some contact is a member of one of the big keiretsu, and if so, who else is in that keiretsu and what it looks like.

Tracking the Who's Who

The best single-volume listing of keiretsu membership in English is *Industrial Groupings in Japan*: The Anatomy of the Keiretsu, published by Dodwell Marketing Consultants in Tokyo every two years. This 600-page tome diagrams the Big Six and two lesser horizontal groups as well as many of the vertical keiretsu (both manufacturing and distribution). It also lists a large number of group affiliates together with sales figures. Although its English is often faulty and the analysis of the individual groups is superficial, "Dodwell's" contains an abundance of data on the keiretsu in a clear, easy-to-follow format. Its most useful feature is a list of all the major companies in the Big Six groups, showing their top 10 shareholders and a detailed breakdown of their borrowings from the Big Six main banks, the three long-term credit banks, and foreign banks. This is key information, as lending relationships are vital to determining keiretsu membership. Dodwell's price of $680 is not designed to attract the impulse shopper, but it does contain a wealth of material which can be useful to companies doing business with Japan.

Another English title is more reasonably priced (about $50 for each of its two volumes), but it requires more work on the part of the reader. *The Japan Company Handbook* (JCH), which is published quarterly by Toyo Keizai, Inc., one of Japan's oldest business publishers, is not intended to be a guide to the keiretsu. JCH is the English version of *Kaisha Shikiho*, Japan's business bible, which has been published quarterly ever since 1936 as an aid to stock investment, and is undoubtedly one of the longest-running and best-known series in Japan. JCH covers every company listed on the Tokyo, Osaka, and Nagoya stock exchanges, plus many more. At first glance JCH might seem a bit technical, but it is really much more than a guide for investors. Anyone interested in Japanese business would do well to take a look at it, and anyone contemplating more than a spiritual relationship with Japan should probably pick up at least the first volume.

Like Dodwell's, JCH is long on data and short on prose. Each page gives a capsule description of one company, complete with sales, profit, and dividend data and estimates for the coming term. While the sales breakdowns, share price histories, company finance issues, and mini balance sheets are of interest to investors, they are of little use to aspiring keiretsu detectives. What is far more interesting is the list of top shareholders and bank references in order of importance. Occasionally, where the shareholder information may be confusing, such as when four or five top banks are all major shareholders of some company, the concise notes at the top of the page help to clarify the company's position: "Medium-size steel producer belonging to the Fuyo group. Also has close ties to DKB." That's about all you need to get a picture of where a particular company stands in relation to the major keiretsu.

When such convenient tags are not available, how does one go about determining keiretsu membership? Let's use JCH to illustrate how a company's "family" connections unfold with just a little bit of research into their shareholders and main lender. To do this, we open at random a copy of Volume 2 (Second Section and OTC companies), and hit upon something called Chuo Denki Kogyo (Central Electric Industries), a minor producer of ferroalloys based in Niigata Prefecture. Frankly, we've never heard of Chuo Denki Kogyo, but that makes it all the better for our example.

According to the book, Chuo Denki has about 280 employees and annual sales of around $100 million. Though its name is probably not known outside its own industrial sector, and the firm is not exactly a pillar of Japanese industry, Chuo Denki is at least large enough to be listed on the

Second Section of the TSE. Undoubtedly there is a circle of materials suppliers and product distributors around the company, a collection of bigger and smaller firms that constitutes its own little "group." These several companies probably don't think of themselves as the Chuo Denki Kogyo keiretsu, but in fact that is what they are. Their businesses are highly dependent on Chuo Denki's orders. Chuo Denki probably owns stock in some of them and has appointed directors to some of their boards of directors. They are a very real vertical keiretsu with Chuo Denki at the top.

But who is Chuo Denki? The explanatory note says that the firm is "affiliated with Sumitomo Metal Industries." This tells us that the company is not the orphan it appears to be. Sumitomo Metal Industries (SMI) is a very well known First Section company and one of the most powerful members of the Sumitomo Group. Just how closely is Chuo Denki Kogyo "affiliated" with the Sumitomo keiretsu?

A quick look at the firm's list of major shareholders reveals an interesting pattern. We find that Sumitomo Metal Industries holds about 29 percent of Chuo Denki's equity and that trading house Sumitomo Corp. holds another 13 percent. Sumitomo Life Insurance holds 4.3 percent, Sumitomo Marine and Fire Insurance has 4.3 percent, Sumitomo Trust & Banking has 3.4 percent, and Sumikin Bussan, an unlisted affiliate of the Sumitomo Group, owns 2.1 percent. In all, Sumitomo Group firms make up the top six shareholders and together hold 56.3 percent of Chuo Denki's stock. Do we need to inquire who the firm's main bank is? Of course, Sumitomo Bank is the company's prime credit reference, and the number two bank is Sumitomo Trust. In addition, the company's lead underwriter for stock issues is Daiwa Securities, the top Sumitomo-affiliated broker.

Clearly, Chuo Denki Kogyo is no orphan. Although it has over 3500 shareholders of record, more than half of its equity is tightly held by a single Big Six keiretsu. These firms have slightly decreased their holdings of the company's stock in the past few years, but they are unlikely to sell any large portion of their shares unless there is a serious financial crisis in the group. In short, Chuo Denki is wired into the Sumitomo keiretsu. It never needs to worry about explaining its performance or prospects to its shareholders because they already know the company inside out thanks to information supplied by SMI and Sumitomo Bank. Nor does it give even passing thought to the possibility of a hostile takeover by some outside party. Not only would that party be unable to obtain a majority interest in the firm, but anyone foolish enough to corner shares in the little metals company would have to answer to the management of Sumitomo Bank—a proposition that would make even the toughest corporate raider think twice.

To find out more, we turn to the First Section book and look up

Sumitomo Metal Industries, one of Japan's largest steel makers. The note there tells us that SMI ranks third in crude steel production and is a leading member of the Sumitomo Group. With sales of about $10 billion, over 20,000 employees and three overseas branches, the firm is known to everyone in Japanese business. A look at its list of major investors reveals a familiar pattern: its largest shareholder is Sumitomo Trust, followed by Sumitomo Life Insurance, Nippon Life Insurance (Japan's largest investor and a major shareholder in almost every large company), and then Sumitomo Bank. Its lead underwriter is also Daiwa Securities. SMI is, in fact, one of the three leaders of the Sumitomo Group and one of the 20 members of its presidential council.

Clearly, there is a corporate hierarchy of some kind extending laterally from Sumitomo Bank and its First Section allies, including Sumitomo Metal Industries, then down to Chuo Denki Kogyo on the Second Section, and then on down to the dozens of little unlisted companies that work for Chuo Denki. The connections between Sumitomo Bank, SMI, Sumitomo Life, Sumitomo Trust and the other big guns of the group are part of the Sumitomo horizontal keiretsu, and the line from SMI down to Chuo Denki and then down to its subcontractors and sub-subcontractors represents a vertical keiretsu.

This was only a random search, and an easy one at that. You could pick any major company, look it up in JCH or Dodwell's, analyze its shareholding, and check to see who serves as its main bank. When the main shareholders are not so helpful as to have Sumitomo, Mitsui, or Mitsubishi names, you have to look up the backgrounds of the main shareholders as well. Who are their main shareholders? Who are their main banks? In most cases you will find a keiretsu pattern developing, and if not, you will discover that the company is one of the few true independents in Japanese business.

2

Where It Began:
The History of
the Keiretsu

To look at the keiretsu today simply as large corporate groups with little connection to their respective pasts would delight their public relations departments no end. The three big groups that have proudly retained the names of the privately owned prewar combines (called *zaibatsu*) to which they once belonged—Mitsui, Mitsubishi, and Sumitomo—have no choice but to make the best of it and urge the modern observer to see them for what they are rather than what they were. Many other companies consider themselves fortunate not to have one of those three immediately recognizable names over their front doors, for they wish to forget all about the past.

Some groups have gone to great lengths to "cleanse" their corporate histories of any reference to their zaibatsu heritage. For example, a quick look at the official company history of one major firm leads us to believe that it was nothing more than a small electrical shop started by one individual out in the countryside. The little shop grew larger, and through great good fortune became an electronics giant known throughout the world. The fact that this little shop was started within a well-known zaibatsu, that this zaibatsu failed, was taken over by one of Japan's most aggressive industrialists, and then incorporated into one of the largest industrial combines of the 1930s is likewise omitted. The fact that this firm was an integral member of one of the primary industrial contractors for Japan's war effort, also seems to have slipped through the cracks of the company's corporate history.

Where once a company's zaibatsu affiliation was a sign of achievement, today it bears something of a stigma. Only the elderly remember the zaibatsu at all, and even then only the later corrupted forms which marched off to war. Almost all Japanese today have grown up in the postwar era, where the zaibatsu are seen as symbols of the evils of an earlier age.

The fact that companies like Hitachi and Nissan today bear no resemblance to the industrial beasts that ravaged Manchuria in the 1930s is irrelevant—their PR departments have obviously decided that any reference to something unsavory in the past is not in the firm's best interests. And so, what is left are fairy tales about little electrical shops in the countryside. This tendency is widespread in modern industry. Dozens of Japanese companies are eager to sever their connections, however slight, with the age of the zaibatsu. The word itself has taken on a pejorative ring. Much better, they feel, to emphasize their membership in a modern keiretsu, not that hideous pre-war thing, the unmentionable Z word.

The view of the prewar zaibatsu as an evil that has been put to rest; and, by implication, the view of the postwar keiretsu as a wholly different animal, the source of much good for modern Japan, has long since become orthodoxy. The attitude one finds among many Japanese executives, young and old, could be summed up as: "The zaibatsu are dead and their sins are buried with them. The keiretsu are the product of a free, democratic society born during the Occupation and the free-market capitalism we learned from America." While young Japanese swallow this without so much as a blink, even the most uninformed Western executive does a double take at the mention of Japan's "free-market capitalism," and those who have visited Japan for any length of time have no doubt wondered about its "democratic society." With this in mind, one may be forgiven for being slightly skeptical of current myths about the keiretsu— and about their ancestors of only a few decades ago, the zaibatsu.

As it turns out, the nucleus of today's Big Six keiretsu—the leading city banks—can all trace their lineages to zaibatsu origins. Five of the six are directly descended from banks at the core of the most prominent zaibatsu of a century ago, and the sixth (Sanwa Bank) was formed from an amalgamation of three banks during the zaibatsu-driven merger mania of the early 1930s, and grew by collecting the remains of other failed zaibatsu. The more we learn about the big keiretsu, the more we want to know about their roots. What were the zaibatsu? How did they get so big? How did they die, and how did the keiretsu grow from the same ground?

Dawn of the Modern Era

The arrival of the American navy in the 1850s started a chain reaction in Japan, releasing pent-up political forces which ultimately overturned the old regime. In 1868 this culminated in one of the most dramatic turning points in all of world history: the Meiji Restoration. Japan began an overnight transformation from a government by hereditary shoguns acting in the name of the emperor to a government by elite civil servants acting in the name of the emperor. Where the old feudal government was concerned with increasing the rice harvest and collecting taxes, the new government was intent on building railroads, steel mills, and battleships. This was not modernization for modernization's sake, but a frantic rush to save Japan from what its leaders perceived (not altogether inaccurately) as rampant Western imperialism.

Right next door was the majesty of Imperial China—the source of much of Japanese art, religion, writing, and culture. Yet one of the first things the Meiji officials discovered was that the Western nations were gathering around China like a pack of hungry wolves, each hoping to grab as much as possible. If these powers, the kind of people who had sent Perry with his ships of war to Japan, could simply carve up China like a Christmas turkey, the Japanese islands, defended by brave young men with swords, would fall overnight.

This is what the new Japanese government sought to avoid at all costs. And so, in a display of adaptability that would stand them in good stead for the coming century, the Japanese officials decided to emulate the societies they feared. They would do what China had failed to do: build a Western army and navy, equip them with Western weapons, and support them with a strong Western industrial base. To the Meiji government, this was Priority One. And it was in this fertile ground of rapid social change and breakneck industrialization that the seeds of the zaibatsu sprouted and grew.

Fortunately, the shogun's government had already paved the way for a policy of learning everything of importance from the West in the shortest possible time, sending students to the United States as early as 1860 to learn the customs of that strange land. The Meiji leaders expanded this approach, sending missions to all the major Western powers to study, absorb, and report back on what they had seen. Industrial developments overseas were regularly relayed to Tokyo where they could be evaluated and, where feasible, copied. It is important to remember that this intense observation of the West was not founded in idle curiosity. The driving motivation for almost every major government policy during the nearly half century of the Meiji era was fear. The government constantly pushed the new nation to "catch up" with the Occident, for only then could it demand its right to sovereignty.

The Zaibatsu Are Born

The Japanese leaders noted that in the capitalist nations they studied wealth was often concentrated in the hands of a few families. Not just the old aristocracy, but nouveau riche industrialists and financiers, families such as Krupp and Thyssen, Rothschild, Rockefeller, and Morgan. These families controlled vast empires of oil, mining, steel, railroads, and finance. If this was the way the Europeans and the Americans built up their industrial might, the Meiji leaders reasoned, there must be something to it. Unfortunately, many of Japan's wealthiest merchant families had not successfully navigated the transition to the post-Restoration world, although there were still some thriving businesses. Obviously, all that was needed was to establish a few key industries, then encourage some of these wealthy families to invest in and manage these businesses and Japan would have created its own Rockefellers. In time, the families would profit from their new businesses, while the state would acquire the industries it needed for economic expansion and military development.

The problem with the plan was that the wealthy merchant families were led by uneducated men who had made their fortunes under the old regime. They had no understanding whatsoever of modern industry, little interest in risky, new investments, and no particular skills at managing the few in which they did invest. The following story perfectly illustrates the failure of the government to turn cautious merchants into a new industrial elite, and how ambitious entrepreneurs with ideas of their own, succeeded in their stead.

The Japanese leaders knew that controlling their commercial shipping lanes and being able to deliver troops quickly to distant locations were two essential factors in strengthening the power of the state. All shipping to and from Japan and all passenger transport was handled by two foreign firms, one American and one British. This was not merely a national embarrassment, but a strategic weakness. As a first step toward rectifying this situation, the government formed YJK, the Japan National Mail Steamship Company, using government-owned ships, government funds, and also some money coerced from a number of wealthy merchant families. But these well-to-do families had neither experience nor interest in operating such a venture. They fought among themselves constantly. As managers, they could not even handle intercoastal shipping, much less dream of running international routes.

In 1874, Japan prepared to launch its first modern military expedition, against Taiwan. It had the army it needed, but there was no navy to deliver them overseas. That had been one of the purposes of establishing YJK's shipping service. The government "requested" YJK to ferry its men to Taiwan. The management declined. This was an awkward position. Here was Japan's first opportunity to give the impression that it was a strong nation, ready and able to stand up for its interests anywhere in the Pacific. What would the Western nations think when they heard that the Japanese army was camped out near Yokohama harbor, all dressed up with nowhere to go?

Enter a brash young man named Yataro Iwasaki a low-ranking samurai. Before the Restoration he had worked in Osaka as an agent for his lord's domain, and he was accustomed to doing business with both Japanese and foreign merchants. In 1871 his patrons turned their business into a private operation with Iwasaki as the head. In a short time he had borrowed enough money to buy out the business and set up a new firm with some other ex-samurai. He moved the new company to Tokyo and renamed it Mitsubishi Steamship Co. (the name, meaning "three diamond shapes," came from the old logo of his previous business). This Iwasaki was not from a prestigious, well-established merchant family, not the kind of man likely to become a Krupp or a Rockefeller. He was young, cocky, and eager to expand his new business. And his business was ships.

Out of desperation the government offered him a commission. Iwasaki accepted immediately, and Mitsubishi-flagged ships carried Japanese troops to Taiwan and back again. A partnership was born. The next year when the old YJK shipping concern fell into serious financial difficulties, Meiji officials looked the other way as the firm sank, leaving privately owned Mitsubishi the undisputed ruler of Japan's domestic shipping business.

Iwasaki took over several government-owned ships, which he then chartered back to the government for handsome fees. He also obtained public funds to develop his business. Just one year after receiving its first commission, Mitsubishi Steamship began to challenge the Western carriers. Within another year, the upstart Japanese firm had forced both its American and British rivals to abandon the Yokohama-Shanghai route. Both the Meiji officials and the Mitsubishi managers—for different reasons—were overjoyed.

During the next decade the government continued to set up numerous industries on its own, and paid handsomely to acquire industrial plants and equipment, all out of the public treasury. It built silk factories, cement factories, and glass factories, established shipyards and coal mines, and hired foreign experts at extravagant fees to operate them.

Most of these businesses did not fare well, and soon enough the government coffers were running low. The result was a massive government fire sale in the early 1880s. But capital was short in those days. The only people in a position to buy were the nouveau riches of the modern era, self-made men like Iwasaki at Mitsubishi, Soichiro Asano of Asano Shipping, and Ichibei Furukawa of Furukawa Mining. One other buyer stood out from the rest, a very old, well-to-do merchant family that had somehow managed to win the trust of both the old government and the new, a family called Mitsui.

Badly in need of funds and eager to have concerned management at the helm of its fledgling industries, the government sold cheap. Mitsubishi acquired one of Japan's three shipyards; Mitsui picked up an important new silk factory (silk being Japan's major export) and a major coal mine; Asano bought a large cement plant; and Furukawa obtained important copper mining interests. Two other prominent families of the era, Sumitomo and Yasuda, did not join in the bargain hunting, and as a result spent the next several years trying to catch up to their rivals.

While the officials' main goal was to raise funds and guarantee the continued development of these key industries, the government's actions produced as a side effect the foundations of exactly the kind of wealthy industrialist families that these officials had heard about in Europe and America. Once the government had improved its financial situation, it could afford to be quite generous with subsidies, tax incentives, and official dispensations to help the newly privatized businesses grow. With increasing demand from the surging economy, these family businesses were assured of tremendous growth. And with a rapidly expanding banking system ready to lend capital against the output of a mine or the anticipated revenues of a shipping business, the founders were able to diversify into other fields. Not only Mitsui, Mitsubishi, Sumitomo, and Yasuda, but Asano, Furukawa, Shibusawa, Okura, Fujita, and several others grew into multifaceted businesses, most of which remained the private property of their founders.

By the turn of the century, Japan had given birth to several groups of widely diversified companies, each owned and operated by a single family. As these few families' wealth continued to expand, they became the nation's new aristocracy, the "financial cliques" or *zaibatsu*. Although there is no absolute definition of a zaibatsu, it is generally understood to be a diverse group of large industries controlled by a single family, usually through a central holding company. Without family ownership and control, a zaibatsu is nothing more than a large industrial combine. Over the years the term *zaibatsu* came to be loosely applied to all the new groups even if they were closer to combines than family-run zaibatsu. In time even the oldest, archetypal zaibatsu no longer qualified as such, as we shall see shortly.

The Big Four Zaibatsu

We do not have space here to go into the background or development of the individual zaibatsu, although many of their stories are fascinating. For example, the founder of the Asano zaibatsu came to Tokyo with a grand total of ¥33 in his pocket. He had to sell firewood and charcoal to stay alive. Several years later the Asano holding company alone was capitalized at ¥35 million, and through it he controlled Asano Bank, Asano Savings Bank, Asano Cement, Asano Trading, Asano Shipbuilding, Asano Steel Works, Asano Kokura Steel, Oriental Steamship, and a multitude of other major companies. There are many stories that parallel this rags-to-riches tale among other zaibatsu founders.

The majority of the zaibatsu were started in the early years of this century and grew to prominence around the time of World War I. However, there were four major groups that stood head and shoulders above the rest. They began earlier, grew faster, and had more political as well as commercial clout than did their rivals. These were the "Big Four" zaibatsu of the late nineteenth century:

- *Mitsui.* One of two old, pre-Restoration families to form a zaibatsu, the Mitsui were originally successful textile merchants who came to manage tax revenues for the Shogun's government. The family became moneylenders on a grand scale and were later allowed to issue both currency and government bonds. The Mitsui Bank opened in 1876 and dominated Japanese banking for decades. In the same year it also founded a trading company, Mitsui Bussan. Within a few years the latter had offices in New York, London, and Paris, a remarkable feat at the time. Bussan almost single-handedly wrested control of Japan's international trade from the foreign merchants, which won it even more friends in government circles. The firm bought a huge coal mine at the government tag sale in the 1880s, and this powerful triumvirate—the bank, the trading company, and the mine—became the foundation of the Mitsui zaibatsu. By the 1930s Mitsui was probably the largest corporate group in the world.

- *Mitsubishi.* We saw before how an entrepreneur named Iwasaki turned a single government contract into a huge government concession. But early in Mitsubishi's history it temporarily lost its political backing.

Iwasaki and his brother were forbidden to establish a bank, so they arranged to buy a bank. They also bought an important shipyard, plus several coal, gold, silver, and iron mines. In short order they were competing with the much older House of Mitsui on all fronts. Using its long-standing connections with foreign merchants, Mitsubishi even established its own trading operation. A couple of decades hence, the family dominated shipbuilding and heavy industry, and was a major player in mining, shipping, trade, brewing, insurance, and banking.

■ *Sumitomo.* Like the Mitsui, the Sumitomo family have a long and proud past. A Sumitomo married into a copper business in Osaka, became a prime contractor to the Shogun's government, and was then selected to operate the country's largest copper mine. At the time of the Restoration, Sumitomo officials did some fast talking and were able to make the mine their own property. The family used this income to help launch a shipping concern and warehousing business. Sumitomo should have been second only to Mitsui in growth, but its conservative leadership kept the family out of modern business until almost the end of the century. Once the family's elder statesman stepped down, however, the Sumitomo zaibatsu jumped into banking and other businesses, although it always remained close to its roots in mining and metals.

■ *Yasuda.* The Yasuda were old-fashioned moneylenders who became financiers, like the Mitsui. The Yasuda Bank opened just four years after the Mitsui Bank. The family business grew rapidly, investing in mines, shipping, railways, warehouses, construction, and so on, but it had little feeling for such industries. As it grew, the Yasuda zaibatsu came to specialize in finance, controlling an important bank, a major trust bank and two big insurance firms.

To these Big Four we should add a fifth group whose lineage will reappear in our examination of the Big Six: Shibusawa. Eiichi Shibusawa was a one-man commercial dynamo during this same period. In addition to founding the Tokyo Stock Exchange, and being instrumental in setting up both the Dai-Ichi Kokuritsu Ginko (First National Bank, later renamed the Dai-Ichi Bank) and the Bank of Japan, he helped to establish well over 100 companies. It was no wonder he was chosen to head the Tokyo Chamber of Commerce—the companies he founded plus the bank's clients comprised a good-sized chamber of commerce by themselves. By 1905 his Dai-Ichi Bank was ranked second only to Mitsui Bank as the top financial institution in the nation. His own group, the Shibusawa zaibatsu, was never as powerful as the Big Four, but it was extremely influential and widely respected all the same.

Growth of the Zaibatsu

During the early years of the twentieth century the zaibatsu were big only in Japanese terms. Relative to the much larger scale of American and European industry, the Japanese industrial groups were still insignificant. All of that began to change in 1914. World War I provided a brief window of opportunity for the zaibatsu to begin growing. Japan supplied munitions and other goods to the Allies, who were also losing ships in the war. Japan doubled its merchant marine fleet in just four years and saw total freight income rise 10 times in that period. Without competition from European companies, which at that time dominated many world markets, Japanese firms were free to expand internationally. Exports jumped 266 percent in five years and domestic industrial production grew at almost double that rate. A nation which had only a short while ago been completely dependent on imports of foreign goods was suddenly running a trade surplus.

Growth was not limited to the Big Four zaibatsu. Many of the second-tier groups, including Asano, Furukawa, and Fujita, did so well that they used their profits to start their own banks. Other successful entrepreneurs grew so fast that they sought to copy the bigger players and establish their own zaibatsu. A crafty Osaka stockbroker named Nomura (relying on information obtained from Mitsui Bussan) bet heavily from the outset that the war would be a plus for the Japanese economy. As the stock market boomed, he made a fabulous fortune that became the foundation for his own zaibatsu. The Suzuki zaibatsu in Kobe grew from nothing to become one of the richest conglomerates in the world almost overnight. The Okura, Kuhara, and Iwai zaibatsu mushroomed.

The Big Four zaibatsu expanded their financial businesses, establishing insurance companies and trust banks. Mitsui and Mitsubishi ventured beyond mining into the iron and steel business. But it was international trade that really marked the growth of the zaibatsu from important domestic players to world-class operations. The leader in this field was indisputably Mitsui. By the end of the war, the group's trading arm, Mitsui Bussan, had 57 foreign branches, business was booming (including critical third-country trade in which the firm acted only as middleman for non-Japanese trade), and profits jumped nearly 10 times in just four years. Bussan trained its people well and made sure they could operate effectively in the countries to which they were assigned. The Japanese government hardly needed to establish a foreign intelligence service, for it already had one of the best information-gathering and analysis networks in the world operating under the Mitsui logo.

One famous story tells of how, in the midst of the wartime boom,

Bussan's top executives concluded that trouble was ahead. They realized that sooner or later the war would end, American and European companies would come back to the markets, and the demand rush that was fueling Japanese growth would collapse. Consequently, Bussan began lowering its transaction volume even before the armistice was signed. The other trading companies thought this was a golden opportunity to rush in where overly conservative Mitsui managers feared to tread, and the postwar recession hit them like a bulldozer. Even well-connected firms such as Mitsubishi Trading went into the red, although they managed to survive. Most of the others were crushed.

By the end of the twenties, the better-capitalized Big Four (and Shibusawa) were stronger than ever, while the older second-tier players, such as the Asano, Okura, and Furukawa zaibatsu, were severely weakened. A few of the new groups (e.g., Nomura) thrived, but many of the small, would-be zaibatsu simply vanished. Nor was their demise always due to natural causes. Zaibatsu rivalries helped to push some of the groups over the edge, such as when the old Mitsubishi and Mitsui zaibatsu joined forces in a "run" on the Bank of Taiwan, the main financial prop for the Suzuki zaibatsu. Under this pressure, the upstart Suzuki group collapsed and disappeared without a trace.

The Big Four did more than merely survive. They continued to diversify into a variety of industries, and they used this time (and the failure of their competitors) to strengthen their key banking businesses. By 1930 the Big Four banks controlled over 20 percent of all deposits, roughly 14 percent of all loans, and over 25 percent of all securities in Japan. It is a common perception today that the zaibatsu banks were the financial engines of their groups. In fact, most of the zaibatsu banks did relatively little lending within their groups. This was partly due to growing public criticism of the closed nature of the zaibatsu, and partly because many of their group members were already big enough that they no longer needed bank financing.

By the 1930s, all of the older zaibatsu were in the hands of second- or even third-generation management. Where the founders had been for the most part rough-hewn, aggressive entrepreneurs, the new heads of the families were college-educated and refined. They were the very definition of high society rather than the arrivistes their fathers and grandfathers had been. But something more important had changed. Where the original zaibatsu were challengers to the older merchant families and grew by boldness and daring, a generation later they had become the Establishment, and they wanted to be sure that they would remain so.

In other words, the zaibatsu grew wealthy much as an individual grows wealthy. When they were young, they were adventurous, but as they matured, they became more interested in preserving their wealth. They used their substantial resources to assure their continued, if less dramatic, growth and monopolized large segments of their respective markets so that up-and-coming rivals would have little chance to challenge them.

The Zaibatsu and World War II

To later observers, the 1930s were the heyday of the zaibatsu, a time when they reigned supreme in the Japanese economy. By taking advantage of the military's demand for even more rapid industrialization to support the growing war effort in China, the zaibatsu gleefully plundered Japan's colonial possessions in search of raw materials and wartime profits. While this view is certainly not unfounded, it misses some critical perspective. For example, as we have already noted, the biggest zaibatsu were already growing somewhat conservative by the 1920s, less willing to gamble their assets and more concerned with preserving the empires they had built. To put it in modern terms, the zaibatsu had become risk averse. They remembered well that their heady profits from World War I did not stem from the war, but from staying out of the war and enjoying the benefits of increased international trade.

Thus, in the 1920s, the most powerful zaibatsu (the same ones which the Occupation forces would later accuse of being the root cause of Japan's militarism) used their influence with the political parties to put the brakes on Japan's single-minded military expansion. In 1925, Prime Minister Kato (whose party had been financed largely by Mitsubishi funds) slashed the military budget by 25 percent. The Army alone lost four divisions—an insult for which the General Staff would never forgive Mitsubishi. This blatantly "unpatriotic" move inflamed not only the military, but the press and the intelligentsia, most of whom railed against the zaibatsu. The Marxist intellectuals accused them of being rich, self-serving industrialists with no concern for the common man (which was true enough), while the right-wing radicals accused them of interfering with Japan's "imperial destiny," which from their viewpoint was also true. Within a few years, the zaibatsu found themselves caught in an ideological no-man's-land, attacked from both the left and the right for being corrupt and unpatriotic.

The irony is that the zaibatsu founders considered themselves the greatest "patriots" of their generation, the men who had built modern Japanese industry, both for profit and for the glory of the nation. Their descendents inherited this "What's good for Mitsubishi is good for the nation" mentality, and most of their senior managers were proud nationalists. But they were also loyal to the interests of the zaibatsu families that employed them. Political sentiments aside, all of the zaibatsu desired the prosperity that was guaranteed to flow from their continuing dominance of domestic business and their growing influence overseas. Compared with this, the extremely risky prospects of military adventures in Asia were foolhardy.

The public outcry against such a selfish stance on the part of the nation's leading business combines grew stronger year by year. In 1932, following vicious newspaper attacks against the Mitsui group, a right-wing assassin killed Takuma Dan, the zaibatsu's senior executive. The murder sent shock waves through all the zaibatsu. It was obvious that popular violence would soon be directed at the others as well—and that the police and the Army would be quietly rooting for the assassins. The zaibatsu immediately began drastic internal policy shifts to reorient their family-held combines towards a more public, more socially acceptable image. They made public "conversions" (*tenko*), proclaiming their true "patriotic spirit," and implied support for the military and for Japanese expansionism.

Despite this apparent conversion to more "politically correct" thinking, the old zaibatsu's sudden promilitary attitude did not fool the hard-core right wing into believing that they were truly going to support the war in China. The military wanted companies that would not merely develop the new territories it was opening up, but would also do as they were told. The zaibatsu were still cautious about new ventures, however, and though they wanted to appear to side with the military, were not about to put their combined resources at the whim of the hotheads who were gaining increasing control of the Imperial Army. Thus, when the zaibatsu did try to develop new business on the continent, the Army actively interfered. Instead, the military and their bureaucratic supporters granted exclusive rights to expand in Japan's new territories to a group of new, more cooperative combines: the "new zaibatsu."

The new zaibatsu were a handful of large business combines that sprang up from the late 1920s through the 1930s. Although controlled by central holding companies, they had no family business at their core, making them more like modern conglomerates and not true zaibatsu. Most important, many of their businesses centered on heavy industries rather than finance, which was exactly what the military wanted. Thus, it was these "new zaibatsu" rather than the Big Four that were allowed to charge into China, establish mining operations, build railroads, and take whatever profits they could find. The largest of these groups was the Nissan, or Nippon Sangyo (Japan Industries), combine. Born from the remains of a bankrupt second-tier zaibatsu, the Nissan group took advantage of growing military demand to transform itself into an industrial giant. (When Nippon Sangyo was broken up after the war, portions of its business became the separate companies known today as Nissan Motors, Nissan Chemical Industries, Hitachi, Hitachi Shipbuilding, Nippon Mining, and several others.) Despite their auspicious start, the new zaibatsu were inexperienced and lacked the strong financial base of the old zaibatsu. Most of them expanded too quickly, and by the end of the decade, they found themselves strapped for funds.

By this time the old zaibatsu had geared up their own heavy industries—compared to which the new zaibatsu were lightweights—and took over support for the snowballing war effort. By the outbreak of the Sino-Japanese War in 1937, heavy industry accounted for roughly two-thirds of all factory production. This was an era of mergers, not between groups, but within the various zaibatsu, and it produced many of the firms whose names are familiar today. Where a single group might have had two or three similar businesses, it combined them into one; Sumitomo Copper and Steel and Sumitomo Steel Works became Sumitomo Metal Industries; Mitsubishi Shipbuilding and Mitsubishi Aircraft became Mitsubishi Heavy Industries, and so on.

The wartime record of the zaibatsu is already well known. In particular, the Mitsubishi group's contributions, including Japan's biggest battleships and the infamous Zero fighter plane (both built by Mitsubishi Heavy Industries) made that group's name familiar to every soldier in the Pacific. Although it was Mitsubishi that put the muscle in Japan's military advance, the other zaibatsu also contributed mightily to the war effort. Even in the 1940s, when conducting the war without the full cooperation of the Big Four zaibatsu would have been unthinkable, the military still viewed them as unprincipled capitalists and found ways to strike back at them even as they placed orders for more equipment.

End of the Zaibatsu

The initial purpose of the U.S. Occupation was to assure that a former enemy would never again become a threat to world peace. To do that, it was deemed necessary both to disband the military and to eliminate the industrial forces that had supported it, that is, the zaibatsu. MacArthur's Basic Directive from the Joint Chiefs of Staff instructed the Supreme Commander for the Allied Powers (SCAP) to supervise the dissolution of "large Japanese industrial and banking combines." Although SCAP's officers made an initial effort to do just that, their success was extremely limited.

There was no doubt in anyone's mind about the power of the zaibatsu, especially the older ones. By the end of the war half the nation's financial system and a third of its heavy industry were controlled by just the Big Four groups. These had to be dealt with. From SCAP's perspective, the zaibatsu all had one thing in common: central control by a single bloodline whose legal incarnation was the family-owned holding company. Without these holding companies, it was assumed, the zaibatsu ties would be greatly loosened. If General Headquarters (GHQ) eliminated the holding companies, the many firms held "captive" would be technically free to go their own way.

The Allies reasoned, however, that even if the holding company "command centers" were destroyed, the zaibatsu family members could still continue to exercise the same degree of control over their respective groups by virtue of their executive positions at the most important group subsidiaries. Instead of a holding company, all the family would need to do to run the zaibatsu would be to gather the presidents of all the important group companies at informal meetings. Moreover, if, once the holding companies were broken up, and the remainder of the zaibatsu shares were traded freely, the group firms also bought large blocks of each other's stock, the elimination of the holding companies would have little real impact.

To prevent this, MacArthur's GHQ ordered the 15 largest zaibatsu to freeze all their assets for inventory and reallocation. SCAP ordered members of 56 designated zaibatsu families to give up not only their honorary titles and executive positions in the subsidiary companies but their personal assets as well. The family members were forbidden to take up any management position in their old zaibatsu companies. Then, to permanently eliminate the threat of zaibatsu power, SCAP ordered a purge of the top management of many of the major subsidiary companies.

That the Americans would eliminate all traces of family control was considered inevitable by the Japanese. That the holding companies would be wiped out and their stockholdings scattered was also taken for granted. But to eliminate the corporate elite that ran the zaibatsu companies was going too far. After all, these men were relatively apolitical, hard-working products of Tokyo University and other top institutions, no different from their old classmates who were now running the Ministry of Finance and what would soon become the Ministry of International Trade and Industry (MITI). When SCAP purged a small number of bureaucrats, it left these two elite ministries more or less alone. From the Japanese point of view, the senior corporate managers should have been left alone as well. "Why should the zaibatsu executives suffer simply because they were forced to associate with those idiots on the Army General Staff?" is a reasonable summation of the thinking at the highest levels of the Japanese bureaucracy at the time.

The result of such thinking was obvious. The Japanese bureaucracy through which SCAP chose to operate decided to take things into their own hands. They would cooperate with the Americans to their faces, but do everything possible to delay or ignore those directives which seemed too harsh or misguided. Thus, when SCAP ordered all "standing directors" of zaibatsu firms to be removed, Japan's pivotal postwar prime minister, Shigeru Yoshida and his colleagues intentionally misinterpreted the order to mean all "managing directors," thus eliminating only a small fraction of zaibatsu executives, leaving the real managerial talent that had made them so strong still intact.

Reforming the Japanese Economy

In April, 1947 the Japanese legislature passed the SCAP-devised Antimonopoly Law (AML). Article 9 of the new law made holding companies illegal. The purpose was to eliminate the last forces holding the hundreds of zaibatsu companies together so that they could become independent businesses. To its surprise, SCAP found that many, if not most, of the old zaibatsu firms wanted to stick together. The real binding force of the zaibatsu, it turned out, was not the holding companies, which had grown much weaker over the years, nor the founding families (which had effectively given up executive control of most of their companies), but rather, the extensive personal relationships and sense of loyalty to an intangible corporate identity, an identity represented by the old zaibatsu name.

Had the holding companies in fact run their gigantic corporate empires and had the families actually run the holding companies, the Occupation reforms would have truly crippled the zaibatsu. Without executive leadership or the family directors to whom they owed loyalty, the group companies would have lacked direction. They might have become the discrete and independent units they were intended to be in the American democratic vision of 1946. But this was not the case. The holding companies had little power as such, and the family members were only titular executives of the subsidiaries. The real power lay in the staff of each separate firm. When a portion of their managers were actually purged, this merely provided opportunities for new executives—all steeped in the firm's traditions—to step forward.

GHQ, for all the good that it did in enacting land reform, educational reform, women's suffrage, and so on, proved incapable of dismantling the Japanese industrial machine. Part of the problem was the constant sabotage of their efforts by the bureaucracy, and part was a sudden change of heart in Washington.

When the Occupation started, its job was to secure Japan so that it could never again become an aggressor. By the end of 1947, global political realities were beginning to change. Communism was spreading in both Europe and Asia. By 1948, the Pentagon began to see Japan as a strategic buffer between the United States and the Communist mainland. At the same time other American interests—both commercial and political—began attacking SCAP's attempt to implant New Deal idealogies in a country that needed a strong industrial base more than trust busting. The end result of this complex debate was a growing consensus that what America needed was a strong Japan rather than a weak Japan. From 1948 onwards, the new theme was rebuilding the economy, both to ensure the continuation of a democratic (i.e., non-Communist) government and to make the country safe for foreign investment. In sum, fewer than two dozen of the several hundred zaibatsu companies originally targeted for dissolution were ever broken up.

The most important point in the remaining years of the Occupation is SCAP's empowering of the bureaucracy to do what the Japanese military had failed to do—that is, put the bulk of the Japanese economy under central control. And that central control comprised only a small portion of the bureaucracy: MITI, the Ministry of Finance, and the Bank of Japan, all of which originally acted as proxies for the Occupation officials. In some ways it was a return to the 1880s—the economy was weak, industry was in a shambles, urban unemployment rising, and the need to catch up with the West was stronger than ever. But there was an important difference: in the early zaibatsu days the Japanese government had aided industry with an eye toward fostering military development. The new government was prohibited from building a strong military. It needed only to rebuild industry. With the Army and the zaibatsu families out of the picture, the politicians as docile as ever, and the ex-zaibatsu companies hungry for work, the bureaucracy found itself exactly where it always knew it should be—in de facto control of the nation's future.

Re-forming the Japanese Economy

In the Antimonopoly Law, SCAP created the Fair Trade Commission (FTC), a "watchdog" to keep an eye on Japanese business and to make sure that zaibatsu-like activities would never again occur. Had the FTC been allowed to do its job, the Big Six keiretsu would not exist today. The FTC originally had seven members, all appointed by the prime minister for five-year terms. Its job was (and still is) to scan the Japanese economy for signs of collusion, cartels, price-fixing, and so on. From its very beginning, the FTC's raison d'etre was to do all the things that the American government saw as necessary to keep Japanese business fair; the Japanese bureaucrats saw its restrictions as leg irons in an economic marathon. In MITI's eyes, the FTC was a symbol of well-intentioned but dim-witted American intervention in an economy it didn't understand. If they had any sense, they would take it home with them.

Early in 1952, as the Occupation forces were packing their bags, MITI pressured a group of textile makers to limit their production and stick to official quotas. This was exactly the kind of production cartel that had been common among the zaibatsu companies before the war. The FTC responded just as it was designed to, denouncing MITI's organization of a government-run cartel as illegal and improper under the Antimonopoly Law. "Not so," replied the bureaucrats, "We issued no orders. We merely gave the industry a little friendly advice. The law doesn't say anything about giving advice, does it?" It is indicative of the times that this ridiculous sham carried the day.

From then on the ministry's "unofficial" but unequivocally imperative "administrative guidance" became a principal tool for reorganizing the economy and forcing uncooperative firms to get with the program. And the program MITI (among others) had in mind aimed at exactly the kind of results the zaibatsu had produced: a rapid development of big industries supported by an army of smaller, cooperative subcontractors. The old zaibatsu companies got the message—no more holding companies, no more bothersome family members on the board, no more threats of violence just because they were making money, but otherwise business as usual.

Chalmers Johnson, in his landmark exposition of the growth of industrial policy after the war, *MITI and the Japanese Miracle*, tells what happened to the Antimonopoly Law: "As soon as the occupation ended in April [of 1952], MITI introduced in the Diet two laws ... both of which authorized MITI to create cartels among small businesses as exceptions to the Antimonopoly Law. They were the precedent for many such laws to come—and for the revision of the AML itself in 1953, the first such revision by an independent Japanese government. . . . MITI's position, according to its annual reports, was that it respected the intent of the original AML but had found that in practice it led to the excessive fragmentation of industries and stood in the way of capital accumulation in order to enhance international competitiveness. In its proposed amendment to the AML, MITI asked for the power to approve 'cooperative behavior' (*kyodo koi*, the new euphemism for cartel). . . . On September 1, 1953, the Diet amended the AML . . . to permit so-called depression and rationalization cartels, and it also abolished SCAP's Trade Association Law."

In the next few years the bureaucracy enacted dozens of laws diametrically opposed to both the spirit and the letter of SCAP's policies. One of the key ordinances that MacArthur had aimed directly at the zaibatsu was the Law Prohibiting Excess Concentrations of Economic Power. This was abolished by the bureaucrats in 1955. The FTC was rendered powerless. With almost the entire government and all of big business united towards a common and unassailable goal—reviving the national economy—how could anyone presume to stand in the way? The last straw was an outright attempt to eliminate the FTC altogether and to publicly certify the existence of a new order. During the winter of 1957–1958, MITI set up a high-level committee to consider the future of the Antimonopoly Law. Its final conclusions included what is perhaps the clearest statement ever made with regard to Japan's economic policies during the postwar period: the public interest is not best served by the legal maintenance of a free competitive order.

Only a few years after the last SCAP officer packed his files and closed his office, the most basic laws aimed at permanently eliminating zaibatsu-like power had either been thrown away or were under attack. The watchdog that was supposed to guard the system from abuses by private industry was muzzled by other government agencies that were encouraging, in some cases forcing, industry to abuse the system. And the officials in charge of the development of the economy stated that free competition—the cornerstone of SCAP's commercial reforms—was not in the public interest.

The Antimonopoly Law was never wiped off the books, nor was the FTC eliminated, but both were completely housebroken. Ultimately both served a useful purpose, for they could always be held up to show outsiders that Japan was run along liberal, democratic lines thanks to the lasting influence of the American Occupation.

Birth of the Keiretsu

One of SCAP's accomplishments had been to outlaw the use of the old zaibatsu names. Never again, they thought, would Japanese industry be dominated by firms called Mitsui, Mitsubishi, Sumitomo, or Yasuda. The big zaibatsu banks, for example, were forced to change their names. Mitsubishi Bank became Chiyoda Bank, Yasuda became Fuji Bank, Sumitomo became Osaka Bank, and Mitsui and Dai-Ichi banks, which had been merged during the war, were separated again, and Mitsui retained its wartime name, Imperial Bank. As soon as the Americans were out the door, the law against using the old clan names was abolished.

To the hundreds of fragmented firms created when SCAP broke up the biggest zaibatsu companies (such as the trading houses), the old zaibatsu names were symbols of their former power and prestige; they meant unity and cooperation among firms in a cooperative group—all the things SCAP wanted to eliminate and the new government wanted to promote. As one Japanese scholar succinctly put it, "No sooner had the Occupation ended in 1952 than the former zaibatsu restored their outlawed company names and began picking up the pieces and re-assembling themselves. . . . Even their human networks were reestablished in the form of executive clubs where company presidents held regular meetings."

Once their old names were restored, encouraging the old group industries to come back together was easy. In order to help those companies regroup, merge, and put on some muscle, they would need solid financial support to develop their production capacity and experienced organizations to export their products overseas. In other words, they needed the old group banks and the old group shosha—two types of firms that were in the nucleus of all the biggest zaibatsu.

Reassembling them proved a challenging task, for SCAP had done a confoundingly good job of decimating the trading companies in particular. For example, Mitsubishi Shoji was broken up into over 170 separate trading companies. After the Occupation shipped out, all the pieces began reorganizing, forming ever larger subgroups, until by the end of 1952, the bulk of the companies had merged into four large trading firms. One of those bore the name Mitsubishi Shoji. In 1954 it was agreed that the four would merge into a single unit, and, with considerable support and pressure from the other Mitsubishi group companies, it was decided that the new parent should be Mitsubishi Shoji. The new company increased its capital more than fourfold, and the members of the Mitsubishi Group were allotted shares in the new firm as compensation for their efforts to bring about the merger. This was the first instance of one of the ex-zaibatsu groups establishing cross-shareholding relationships within its group—something which had also been illegal until the previous year, but which the Japanese bureaucracy now saw as necessary.

By 1953 MITI was already calling for the "keiretsification" of industry. The ministry even paired up manufacturers and shosha when the former had no fixed outlet for exporting. Within a few years it organized and encouraged mergers of literally thousands of small shosha to form about two dozen powerful traders.

The banks were a larger, but in a sense a simpler, project thanks to SCAP's ineptitude. In typical bureaucratic fashion, the GHQ divisions in charge of antitrust activities and management of the banking system were separate and did not have overlapping jurisdiction. Thus, the Antitrust Division was free to go after the zaibatsu combines, but it could not touch the zaibatsu banks. They came under the jurisdiction of the Finance Division, which had no interest in trustbusting. Thus, the old banking system was still very much in place when the Occupation shipped out. Although there were several government-related banks that could supply the budding keiretsu with funds, it was deemed most efficient to use the old zaibatsu banks as they already had extensive knowledge of the key companies the government wanted to resurrect. The Bank of Japan supplied them with funds which they then funneled to the nation's cash-starved industries.

For this reason, industries naturally began to gather around the banks, and institutions such as Mitsubishi and Sumitomo banks naturally gave preference to companies they knew well, their old zaibatsu colleagues. Of the Big Four zaibatsu banks, only Yasuda thought it best not to return to its old name, and to this day is still known as Fuji Bank (although its other core financial firms retained the Yasuda name). While Mitsubishi, Mitsui, and Sumitomo banks set about regrouping their old zaibatsu partners, Fuji became chief lender to a number of important firms that had survived the Occupation when their zaibatsu were destroyed. Sanwa Bank, which was formed early in the 1930s during the zaibatsu merger mania, had already made a name for itself as a home for zaibatsu strays, picking up several members of the defunct Suzuki zaibatsu as members of its own circle. After the war it continued this tradition. And the core of the old Shibusawa zaibatsu, Dai-Ichi Bank, became once again the financial center for that old group of firms as well as other companies with little or no previous zaibatsu affiliation. These six banks became the hubs of the Big Six keiretsu.

The result was the steady rise of the commercial ("city") banks to positions of tremendous power. For better or worse, bankers determined the future of Japanese business. Even more so than in the old zaibatsu days, the status of working for a big bank was comparable to working for one of the elite ministries. The lapel pin of any of the big city banks conferred upon its wearer a level of social standing that continues to this day. It also instilled in Japanese bankers an inflated view of their own importance which shows no signs of disappearing in this century.

Competition among the Keiretsu

Viewed from our perspective in the 1990s, the formation of the Big Six horizontal keiretsu during the 1950s was inevitable. The government made it difficult for business to raise the funds it needed from any source other than the banking system, and at the same time it encouraged the city banks to lend to important industries. It rewrote the laws to make it legal for the banks to own stock in their clients (contrary to the Antimonopoly Law), silenced the government watchdog assigned to monitor such activities, and overtly called for the keiretsification of industry. The only real surprise is that the keiretsu didn't grow even faster than they did and that there weren't more of them.

In retrospect, had there been a Sanwa-led shipbuilding keiretsu, a Mitsubishi-led steel keiretsu, a Sumitomo-led chemicals keiretsu, and so on, organized around a single bank, the bureaucrats' job would have been infinitely easier. Each cartel would then have interconnecting shareholdings and directors who would meet regularly in a shacho-kai (presidential council) to discuss business relevant to their own industry. Even by Japanese standards, that would have been remarkably efficient. Unfortunately for MITI, this was impossible. The government had chosen the most expedient route of encouraging the old zaibatsu companies to reform as modern corporate groups. The structural paradigm for the zaibatsu was a pattern called *Ichi gyoushuu, issha taisei*, meaning "one firm in each major industrial sector"; this allowed the group to become a semi-autonomous economy unto itself. Even the keiretsu that were not based on a well-established zaibatsu (e.g., the Sanwa Group) accepted this structure as axiomatic. Thus, the keiretsu that came together after the war were heterogeneous, not cartel-like.

The zaibatsu usually included a strong bank, a shosha, and a mining or heavy industrial firm at the center, and the postwar groups followed suit. By definition there was now a large bank at the center, but in many cases the nucleus of the keiretsu would also include a trading company and a big manufacturer. There would also be a trust bank, a life insurance firm, and a nonlife firm, so that together with the bank and the shosha, most of the group's financial needs could be met internally. Then there would ideally be one key company in each important industrial sector, including chemicals, construction, steel, electricals, cement, paper, glass, oil, autos, shipping, warehousing, and nonferrous metals (by the time the DKB Group was being formed in the late 1970s, this pattern was out of date and DKB pulled multiple firms from the same sectors into its keiretsu).

When a new sector became prominent, all the keiretsu would jump into it, whether there was room for six big firms or not. The result was intense competition, much more so than in the good old days when the zaibatsu could privately carve up markets among a few strong players and close everyone else out. Now that the government was in charge and identifying the industries to be developed, the growth of certain sectors was assured and all the keiretsu wanted to be part of it. While the bureaucrats established official cartels in almost every important category, their efforts to limit production only intensified the competition among the keiretsu.

Nuturing the Keiretsu

It should be evident that the Big Six keiretsu did not simply drift together, nor were they assembled according to some master plan formulated by MITI. The government prepared the ground that allowed the Big Six to emerge, then nurtured their core companies, steered them, and protected them from outside competition. But the actual formation of the keiretsu and much of their activities were left up to the groups and the individual companies. The driving motivation in these groups was not nation building, nor was it an international game of economic "catch-up," but the old drive to expand a company farther and faster than its rivals, to generate profits, and become the leader in a particular industry. In other words, the motives were neither better nor worse than those in the old zaibatsu days, and the means were often much the same.

The only kind of competition that the big companies did not have to fear was international. With the Japanese economy in a weakened state throughout the 1950s, foreign takeovers, especially in new growth fields such as electronics, would have been relatively easy to execute. The first wave of postwar cross-shareholding was the corporate response to that threat, but this alone was not sufficient to shelter Japanese industry. The real reason that some of the key keiretsu companies were not hijacked by American rivals (who were already buying into or buying up European firms) was the protection offered by the government.

The keiretsu's domestic markets were protected by import restrictions (so much so that by 1960 international organizations were already demanding that the Japanese markets be opened to free competition), and the companies themselves by similar restrictions on foreign capital. Not only could foreign firms not buy a Japanese company without permission, but they could not even take a controlling interest in a joint venture with a Japanese firm. If somehow a foreign firm did effect capital participation in a Japanese firm, there were limits on how many directors it could have on the company's board and what their voting rights could be. Even with all these measures (many of which lasted into the 1970s or 1980s), there were still foreign companies that got around the system.

One of the biggest and most threatening was IBM. A major industrial target for Japan in the 1960s was to develop a computer industry. However, it would be impossible to do this without cooperation from IBM, which virtually dominated the business. IBM had already established a local company, and there were signs that IBM Japan was planning to develop the Japanese market for itself. Perhaps no one at IBM had thought much about how the firm might share its technology with companies like NEC, Hitachi, and Fujitsu and help to create a powerful Japanese computer industry with which to share the expanding pie. These concerns no doubt vexed MITI officials.

The man in charge of helping IBM to understand its duty to nurture rather than crush the nascent computer industry was the straight-talking head of MITI's Heavy Industries Bureau. As Johnson explains in *MITI and the Japanese Miracle:* "IBM held all the basic patents on computer technology, which effectively blocked the development of a Japanese computer industry. [The MITI man] wanted IBM's patents and made no bones about it. In as forthright a manner as possible, he made his position clear to IBM Japan: 'We will take every measure possible to obstruct the success of your business unless you license IBM patents to Japanese firms and charge them no more than a 5 percent royalty.' . . . IBM ultimately had to come to terms." It sold its patents and accepted MITI's administrative guidance over the number of computers it could market domestically as conditions for manufacturing in Japan.

With MITI acting as a bureaucratic "godfather" to watch out for keiretsu interests, both immediate and future, there was no need to worry about foreign intervention. Both the Japanese markets and Japanese firms were protected until about 1970, when the first wave of liberalization began. Around that time General Motors was trying to buy a sizable share of Isuzu, a move which seemed ominous to the policymakers in Tokyo. It was in December of that year that the MITI minister, a man by the name of Kiichi Miyazawa (who rose to the post of prime minister in 1991) told the Japanese legislature that the most important task facing the nation was to preserve the independence of Japanese management in the face of an invasion of foreign capital. Miyazawa noted that Japanese firms could block foreign takeovers by holding each other's shares. "It is not necessary to employ holding companies to carry out this stable cross-shareholding strategy," he advised, "for it is quite possible through the cooperation of related financial institutions."

Simply put, as late as 1970 the head of MITI was recommending that the keiretsu main banks fulfill the role once played by the zaibatsu holding companies in defending Japanese industry from the threats of the free international marketplace. By the 1970s, the Big Six had already achieved the government's goals of building up Japan's heavy industries to internationally competitive levels. By the 1980s, as cries were being raised around the world for Japan to open itself up to free competition, the keiretsu no longer needed protection, although vestiges of it remained for years in many sectors and some are still intact today.

Successive waves of liberalization and deregulation followed, and are still continuing, primarily because there is no need for the government to protect most industries and because other nations are finally demanding it. Not surprisingly, the influence of MITI, that all-powerful overseer of Japanese industry, has declined as well. These days, when MITI suggests that a key keiretsu company should reduce production or cooperate more with rivals in the same field, the company just nods politely and goes back to doing whatever it had planned in the first place. The companies themselves have grown considerably, and they are much more concerned with how rivals in their own industry will react to policy changes than what the blue-suited officials in the bureaucracy might think.

3

The Heart of the Keiretsu: Bankers and Traders

There are certain elements that are common to all large horizontal keiretsu, including of course the Big Six. The most important elements are the two kinds of companies in the nucleus of the largest groups, companies which do not have counterparts in the United States. These are the main bank and the general trading company (*sogo shosha*). Other important elements, such as cross-shareholding relationships, assigned directors, intragroup financing, and intragroup trade, are examined in Chapter 4.

Not surprisingly, a main bank is a financial institution that keeps money flowing to a group of industrial concerns. But if this were all a main bank did, the United States would be chock-full of bank-led keiretsu. A main bank in Japan does much more than simply make loans. It is also the central clearinghouse for information about group companies and the coordinator for group activities. It monitors the performance of its group, holds equity in most of the major companies, and provides management assistance when it deems necessary. In the worst case, if one of the group firms is in serious trouble, the main bank is expected to step in with both financial assistance and a whole new management team selected from among the bank's executives.

A trading company is obviously concerned with commerce, and in a horizontal keiretsu it has the vital role of coordinating trade, not only within the group, but among different groups and even with foreign customers. Three of the Big Six groups (Mitsui, Mitsubishi, and DKB) have shosha in the nucleus of their groups, functioning as coflagships together with their respective main banks. The shosha also hold equity in many of the group firms, provide financing (though in different ways than the banks), and like the banks, send directors to oversee member companies' management. By combining the information gained from the shosha, which deals with many group members on a daily basis, with that gained from the main bank (which examines the firm's accounts), the nucleus of the keiretsu can form an amazingly detailed and accurate picture of what is happening inside each company in the group.

The Main Bank

In the United States and in Europe, corporations have commonly used a variety of means to fund their operations, including both bank lending and equity-linked financing. Until quite recently, Japanese companies did not have this range of options. Throughout its early history the Tokyo Stock Exchange (TSE) was little more than a roulette wheel and only began to gain some respect as a vehicle for corporate financing before the war. The TSE was closed after the war, and when it reopened in 1949, it looked as if someone had turned the clock back 50 years—speculators ran wild, long-term investment meant anything longer than a week, and the economy's seesawing up and down was not designed to instill confidence in investors.

As a result, the TSE was not a company's first choice for fund-raising. Because the government wanted to control the limited flows of capital in the economy, the Ministry of Finance also devised strict regulations to make sure that the stock market would not mature and rival the banks. Thus, as we saw before, the government helped to build and shape the new bank-led keiretsu and the banks became the source of funds for postwar industry. This primacy remained essentially unchallenged until the late 1980s.

Banks are so important in Japanese business that every company, large or small, eventually develops a close relationship with at least one bank to whom they turn for funds, advice, market information, protection, and in a crisis, management assistance. The biggest firms might have two or three such special banks, but they are seldom entirely equal. There is almost always one that is recognized as the company's "main bank." The concept is ubiquitous in Japanese business, and there are even books listing which banks are considered main banks for which corporations. However, the term has no legal meaning. A main bank is really nothing more than a special relationship that exists between a corporation and a commercial or long-term credit bank, and that relationship is governed only by the tacit bonds between the two parties, not by law.

How a Company Gets a Main Bank

Let's consider a case of main bank formation involving a fictional firm, Dai Nippon Widget. DNW is a medium-sized manufacturer that wants to increase its capital investment, double its production capacity, and export like crazy to widget-hungry countries in North America. In its early stages DNW borrowed from small, local banks, but now that its operations are growing, so is its need for cash. Initially, DNW is lucky and is able to secure small loans from a number of different city banks. The banks prefer it this way because spreading out the lending means they can also spread out the risk, and companies like DNW like it because it keeps them independent of any single bank. Let's say Dai Nippon Widget begins by borrowing very small amounts from Sumitomo, Mitsubishi, and Dai-Ichi Kangyo (DKB).

As Dai Nippon Widget grows, it does not buy its new equipment equally from firms belonging to all the various keiretsu. Nor does it export through the trading companies of all the groups; nor does it insure its goods with several different insurance companies. Simply in the process of doing business, DNW finds that it is developing stronger business connections with certain firms, and those firms are affiliated with certain groups. Let's imagine that it buys most of its raw materials and ships some of its finished products through an arm of Mitsubishi Shoji, the general trading company of the Mitsubishi Group. That firm may point out to the company's management that the kind of equipment they need to improve widget production is available, perhaps at a significant discount or with a better service package or whatever, from Mitsubishi Heavy Industries (MHI), one of the country's biggest machinery makers. Perhaps DNW's management was not planning to invest in equipment as sophisticated as what MHI has to offer. To do so would entail increasing its loans, which its bankers have indicated they are not prepared to do right away. For a time, Mitsubishi Shoji might extend loans to the firm, using its finished goods as collateral. But DNW needs substantial financing over the next few years if it is to grow into a world-class widgetmaker.

Most of the city banks take relatively little interest in smaller businesses on the way up, but aggressive Sumitomo is a conspicuous exception. After a thorough review of the company's technology as well as its financial profile, Sumitomo Bank may offer to increase its loans to DNW. The management may be pleased with these advances by one of the nation's biggest banks, or they may not. Among other things, they know that Sumitomo will not like the idea of financing a purchase from MHI in the Mitsubishi group. They may "strongly recommend" that DNW purchase its equipment from either Sumitomo Heavy Industries, Sumitomo Precision Products or some other group-related firm.

DNW's management thinks about the pros and cons of the situation. Perhaps they mention Sumitomo's offer to one of the Mitsubishi Shoji people the next time they are talking. He pulls a little notebook from his jacket pocket and makes some notes. The next day he calls to say that if DNW is absolutely sure they want a bank loan, a loan review could be arranged with Mitsubishi Bank. Needless to say, the trading house would prefer to handle the little company's financing by itself, but if the firm comes under Sumitomo's wing, more than just a financing opportunity will be lost. Before long, DNW has talked with loan officials at Mitsubishi Bank and they see good reasons to support the firm's plan for a five-year capital investment binge. That a majority of the company's future transactions will remain with Mitsubishi Shoji and MHI is understood.

Before the president makes up his mind what to do, representatives from Sumitomo and DKB contact him separately. Does he want to become a "subsidiary" of the Mitsubishi Group, the bankers ask. Has he built up the company with his own hands just to give it away? At the very least, they say, DNW should keep its borrowings from various banks approximately equal and maintain its independence. Both are willing to increase the firm's loan ceiling within reason and can help to arrange any kind of equipment purchases it might need. Of course, each bank hopes eventually to bring DNW within its own sphere of influence, but the first step toward that end is not to be "demoted" on the company's list of borrowers.

Now DNW is in a difficult spot. At this point it may decide that it wants to avoid being pulled into any one group, and so spread out its bank loans and take advantage of the rivalry among the big banks. But DNW is not a very large or influential firm, and the managers know that trying to play off keiretsu banks against one another is not a game for small, unlisted companies. Sooner or later one of the banks will put conditions on further loans, and DNW will be forced to jump one way or another. And all the time that the little firm is trying to remain independent, other companies with whom it does business will be trying to steer it subtly toward one bank or another.

The management meets several times to discuss the problem, but the answer seems obvious. They want to keep their independence, but they also want to keep their long-standing relationship with Mitsubishi Shoji, and there is a good chance they will buy the equipment offered by MHI anyway. Taking a larger loan from Mitsubishi Bank and supplementing that with smaller loans from the other two banks seems the wisest course. Although the company still sees itself as completely independent, it is coming to realize the advantages of having a powerful main bank and in doing business with a related group of companies. While DNW's executives don't suddenly start drinking Kirin Beer, toting Nikon cameras, or driving Diamantes, it is not so very long before the company is looking at employee health insurance policies from Meiji Mutual and talking to people from Tokio Fire & Marine about insuring the new equipment they intend to buy. No one forces them to do this, of course, and the management may stoutly refuse to do such a thing for a few years just to show its independence; but little by little the company decides that it makes more sense to go along with the group idea than to be overtly uncooperative.

A few years down the road, DNW is profiting handsomely from its investment. It has become a global force to reckon with in the artificial intelligence-controlled widget market. About 10 to 15 percent of its annual sales are now made to Mitsubishi Electric and other group companies, another 30 percent go to a variety of Japanese firms, and the rest are exports. Both its domestic and international sales are handled by Mitsubishi Shoji. The firm's new plant has equipment from several makers, but a significant part of it is from MHI. As its borrowing has increased steadily year by year, Mitsubishi Bank has sent an executive to join DNW's board, although only in the low-profile position of Auditor. The president was not initially pleased with this move, but the other directors pointed out that cementing ties with what has become their main bank is a smart move.

As DNW's sales rise steadily, brokers come knocking on the president's door almost daily to explain the potential profits—both corporate and personal—of taking his company public. He discusses the matter with someone from the bank, and his bankers agree that an over-the-counter listing would not be unwise. They also recommend which broker should be the lead underwriter. Before the company makes its initial offering, however, it agrees to sell 2 percent of its shares to the bank on a private basis (banks are forbidden by law to hold more than 5 percent of any commercial firm). The bank has no need to pressure DNW to do this. The company has grown substantially thanks to the bank's help and it wants to remain a valued client.

Until he retires nine years later, the president of Dai Nippon Widget maintains that his company is 100 percent independent. But everyone, from his employees to his rivals, labels DNW a "Mitsubishi company." The year after he departs, the bank asks to put a regular director on DNW's board.

What does it mean for DNW, or any company, to have a main bank within a horizontal keiretsu?

As we have seen, the keiretsu members have traditionally encouraged small firms with whom they are dealing to do business with
other group members. This is one of the ways in which a main bank—the
official leader of each group—will try to influence its clients (though some
banks are more active in this respect than others). Loan clients will be
asked to buy products and services from within the group, sometimes in
excess of their real needs. Similarly, the bank may press them to continue
borrowing funds long after their funding needs have been met. The bank
may also demand that the company establish accounts at one of its
branches in return for making new loans. Once a special relationship
develops, as it has with DNW, the firm would normally move its principal
accounts, especially its payroll account, to the main bank. Its employees
are paid each month through direct transfers to their various banks, but all
transactions would henceforth originate at the main bank. Once a company has developed a main bank relationship, it is quite common for the
firm's employees to keep their personal savings accounts there. (Some
banks have been known to open an account for every employee automatically and tell the company to encourage its employees to use them.) Twice
a year employees receive a "bonus," which is actually part of their regular
salary. Again, they will be encouraged to leave a large part of this bonus on
deposit with the main bank. If the company is an especially good client, the
bank may provide its employees with preferential rates for housing loans.
Bankers are happy to do this because they have already assessed the
client's risk, and as the client is the de facto guarantor of its employees'
mortgage loans, the company must also become a credit examiner. The
companies are willing to do this because (1) the salaries of most of their
staff will rise at a fixed level with age, so the employee's ability to service
debt is a known factor, and (2) when a 28-year-old employee arranges a
30-year loan through the good offices of his company, he or she is highly
unlikely to consider jumping to another firm.

The Power of the Big
Six Main Banks

In one study, which covered all the 873 nonfinancial firms listed on the
First Section of the TSE, four banks stood out dramatically as main banks
to industry: Mitsui, Mitsubishi, Sumitomo, and Fuji. Each serves as the
main bank to over 100 firms. In other words, roughly half of the major
companies in Japan use one of these four institutions as their main bank.
The other two of the big keiretsu banks, Sanwa and DKB, account for about
70 and 50 companies, respectively. In total, the Big Six banks act as main

banks for approximately two-thirds of the top companies in the nation. (If we add the 50-odd firms linked to the Industrial Bank of Japan, the seven most important banks cover about 70 percent of Japanese big business.) For those who find it hard to believe that history and tradition play much of a role in the contemporary Japanese economy, it is instructive to note that the four main banks that stand head and shoulders above the rest are the banking arms of the Big Four zaibatsu, all industry leaders since the 1890s, while the other two banks are ranked in chronological order of their formation as keiretsu.

The Primary Functions of a Main Bank

Lender. The most important role of the main bank is that which originally led to the growth of the companies in its group—supplying funds. In most cases we can identify a company's main bank simply by examining how much it borrows from various institutions over a period of time. In the study cited above, the main bank was the primary source of borrowing for over two-thirds of Japan's 873 biggest nonfinancial firms, and the secondary source of funds for another 17 percent. In sum, the main bank is either the primary or secondary lender to approximately 85 percent of Japan's top companies. For smaller companies, the figures would be even higher, since the main bank is by definition a small firm's leading supplier of loan capital. In the case of smaller, unlisted companies, many of their main banks would not be city banks, but much smaller regional banks.

Stockholder. It is well known that large Japanese companies tend to hold each other's stock in a pattern known as *stable cross-shareholdings* (a pattern we saw developing in Chapter 2 and which we will examine more closely in Chapter 4). The big city banks are among the nation's largest shareholders and certainly among the best-known stable shareholders. In the study above, the main banks proved to be the number one shareholder for over 16 percent of the companies examined, the number two shareholder for over 22 percent, and the number three shareholder for about 15 percent. In sum, main banks are among the top three shareholders for more than half of the major listed companies in Japan. Here again, the banks would be even more conspicuous as shareholders of smaller firms within their groups, usually ranking number two or three behind another group member.

Credit Monitor. Professor Paul Sheard, of Australian National University who has made a close study of the Japanese main bank system, concludes that the banks can be viewed as "a substitute for the kind of screening and monitoring institutions that are prevalent in other capital markets, such as bond- and credit-rating institutions and security analysis institutions." Why? In general he says, corporate accounting and disclosure in Japan have never developed as they have in other nations. For instance, "until recently, there had been virtually no use of consolidated accounting, despite the fact that large Japanese firms are renowned for having extensive networks of subsidiaries and affiliates. Similarly, the Western system of external auditing is poorly developed in Japan, and assets are typically recorded at their historic rather than current value in corporate balance sheets, making published accounts of firms . . . of dubious value." As a result, the nation's top banks have become a kind of agent to monitor corporate performance and evaluate risk. While independent monitors of industry are well established abroad, the half-dozen bond-rating agencies in Japan are new arrivals and still fighting an uphill battle to gain acceptance. Many institutional investors (who make up the bulk of the market) have access to "inside" information on corporate performance, management problems, and future prospects via their corporate ties. Why should they pay an outside agency to provide risk or performance analysis based on far less detailed information?

At the same time, partly because it takes responsibility for knowing the state of its group companies, the bank is liable for a considerable amount of risk should one of its clients take a turn for the worse (see below). In the past, when a big company was in difficulty and could not repay its debts, there have been several cases where its main bank has shouldered a greater share of debt write-offs than its loan total would seem to warrant.

Venture Capitalist. Professor Ken-Ichi Imai of Hitotsubashi University, one of Japan's leading authorities on the keiretsu, sees another role for the main bank, one that does not benefit all the companies in its group, but is of huge importance to those that can take advantage of it. He points out that the main bank is not merely a lender, but also a well-informed, risk-averse venture capitalist. Because of the kind of information-gathering necessary to perform its roles as lender, stockholder, and credit monitor, the bank knows the companies in its group intimately. Among other things, it is familiar with technical developments and the progress of R&D at its more high-tech group firms. Thus, when a client firm stands to make major progress through heavy investment in a certain technology, the company does not need to go hat-in-hand to its bank to make a presentation for a new loan, talking around the technical details that bankers don't understand anyway. The main banks are already very well informed about the technology of their group firms and their potential for growth. In special cases, the main bank is prepared to make extraordinary loans to help push that technology to a higher competitive level, whereas an "outside" bank would need many months of study just to understand the proposal.

Imai cites as an example NEC's huge investments in semiconductor production technology in the 1970s, which "set the stage for a breakthrough by Japanese industries into the age of microelectronics. These were not technologically radical, but economically as well as organizationally radical." In fact, NEC outspent most of its rivals in semiconductor plants by roughly two to one over a six-year period in the late 1970s. The reason, says Imai, is the solid backing the firm received from its main bank. Sumitomo Bank understood the importance of this new technology and realized that massive capital investment could put NEC in the forefront of semiconductor production. The company relied on external financing for up to 85 percent of its total capital in the 1970s, and as a result of the bank's recommendation, Sumitomo group companies provided about one-third of all its loans. Imai concludes: "Information exchange was the key for innovation and investment. . . . The main bank . . . monitors a borrower's corporate performance and transfers this information to other lenders, taking on the responsibility of overseeing the company's circumstances. The advantage of the main bank system lies in the opportunity for banks to play an active, long-term strategic role in creating mutual benefits and assisting in the coordination of networks. This system has contributed considerably to innovative financing in Japan."

Company Doctor. There is a well-known adage in business circles, one that Japanese executives are fond of quoting to foreign visitors: "Japanese companies do not go bankrupt." Of course, this is nonsense. Many thousands of companies fail every year, but almost 100 percent of them are smaller firms and their failures are regarded as insignificant. What the phrase means is that big, important companies do not fail. This, too, is a minor exaggeration, but at least on the very rare occasions when big companies do fail, they don't go bankrupt in a big, messy way as they do in other countries. Japanese readers are never treated to headlines saying "Yamaichi Securities Belly-Up," "Heiwa Sogo Bank Goes Bust," or "Itoman in Chapter 11." According to government officials, such unseemly behavior would weaken confidence in the system (i.e., it cannot be permitted).

The result is a tacit understanding that private industry will take care of itself in the direst of cases, such as when one of its number is about to go under and create a "lack of confidence" in the system. If a company is big enough, or the causes of its failure are scandalous enough, someone must step in and clean up the mess before market confidence is shaken (or the truth leaks out about massive corruption, possibly involving the main bank).

One might expect the cash-rich life insurance companies to come to the rescue of a sinking firm, but in practice the responsibility has come to lie squarely with the banks. This is reasonable in light of what we have noted above. The main bank is responsible for watching over its group's business operations and, in effect, relaying credit information to other firms. Thus, the main bank should be better informed than anyone else about a potentially dangerous situation at one of its group firms. It is commonly assumed that if a company is in trouble, its main bank probably saw the problem coming long ago, tried to steer the firm to a safer course, and had its advice rejected. In other words, the bank has known the ship was sinking for some time and has been preparing the pumps for the inevitable bail-out.

This brings up another reason why the insurers are not called upon to help a firm in distress, and that is the nature of the remedy: money is usually not enough. Of course, the banks must take financial steps to improve the condition of an ailing firm: extend new loans, reduce interest on old debt, even write off debts completely if that is necessary. But in a number of instances the situation has gone far beyond the point where a mere injection of new capital or debt forgiveness will be enough to save a firm. In such cases the company's management team must either be replaced or redirected, and the impetus for such change usually comes from the main bank. The bank will send in anywhere from one to several directors with managerial authority to help run the ailing company. Often one of the bank's senior executives will become the client firm's new president. For all practical purposes, the company has been thrown into receivership: the bank is running its business at arm's length through its agents inside the company.

From the Japanese point of view, this is neat and orderly. The government is not involved, the courts are not involved, and the free market is not involved. This arrangement avoids the unseemly publicity and legal complications of bankruptcy procedures in the U.S. model, or the functions of an appointed receiver in the British model. It also avoids the headline-grabbing exploits of takeover artists on the prowl for distressed companies they can buy up and sell off piece by piece. During the merger and acquisition boom of the late 1980s, an American investment banker in Tokyo shook his head in disgust at the difficulties of plying his trade there and said, "The concept of 'break-up value' doesn't even exist in Japan."

The large Japanese banks are the only institutions that have the capital, the information, and the human resources to perform this function adequately. In many cases, the bank can do no more than make a firm's demise relatively quiet and dignified, such as the failure in 1977 of Ataka and Co., a large trading company. Ataka's main bank, Sumitomo, not only swallowed a lot of the firm's debt but also arranged to have part of its client's business taken over by rival shosha Itochu, partly to allay customer fears.

In some cases, the bank can help to stabilize a firm and keep it afloat even in fiercely competitive markets. Examples include Mitsubishi Bank's long-term aid for Akai Electric and IBJ's ongoing coordination of support for Fuji Heavy Industries (maker of Subaru cars). Both companies have gone from deep wells of red ink to spurts of black. Sometimes the bank's intervention actually leads to a major turnaround for a sinking firm, not merely bringing it back to fiscal health but helping it to become a major player in its market again. Examples here include IBJ's resuscitation of Nissan Motor and Yamaichi Securities and Sumitomo's support for Toyo Kogyo (now Mazda Motor). Banks like Sumitomo and IBJ have acquired reputations as exceptionally skilled "company doctors" for their proven abilities in this area.

These are not all the functions of main banks, but they are at least the most important ones. They lend funds, hold equity (and coordinate stable shareholding within the group), monitor company performance, act as a venture capitalist for firms with special market situations and, in the worst case, as a safety net for companies in trouble. An employee of a firm in a bank-led keiretsu knows that his company may fail, and the top management may even lose their jobs, but the firm will not end up being eaten by wolves. It will fall into the arms of its main bank, which will do everything possible to keep the company alive and together and will sometimes do better than the previous management in bolstering its profitability.

The Sogo Shosha

The other kind of firm that is vital to the operations of the keiretsu is a uniquely Japanese institution, the general trading company or sogo shosha. There are hundreds of small and medium-sized shosha, but only nine of them are big enough to take notice of. And even among those nine, the top six are disproportionately large (the number six firm is more than twice as big as number seven). If the number six sounds coincidental, it's not. There is one giant shosha in each of the Big Six keiretsu. In three of the groups the shosha is considered so important that it is part of the nucleus of the group together with the main bank, and in the Mitsui Group the shosha was traditionally more influential than the bank. In all six groups the shosha play the same critical role, helping to coordinate group activities through every aspect of commerce. Clearly, the sogo shosha is no ordinary firm, and the definition "general trading company" gives us a very poor idea of what it does. In *The Invisible Link: Japan's Sogo Shosha and the Organization of Trade*, authors Michael Yoshino and Thomas Lifson explain the phenomenon as follows:

> A sogo shosha is like no other type of company. It is not defined by the products it handles or even by the particular services it performs, for it offers a broad and changing array of goods and functions. Its business goals are equally elusive, for maximization of profits from each transaction is clearly not the major goal, at either the operating or philosophical level. There are really no other comparable firms, although important business and government leaders in the United States and elsewhere have become convinced that there should be. The six [major shosha] affect the lives of most participants in the world economy. From the oil used to cook french fries at a local fast food restaurant to the subway cars running beneath our streets, products passing through their hands are all around us. Collectively they are the largest purchaser of U.S. exports in the world, accounting for 10 percent of our total overseas sales, 4 percent of world trade, and influencing the jobs and fortunes of tens of millions of people all over the world.

A decade ago the shosha still clung to the slogan that they dealt in everything "from noodles to missiles." Times have changed and that image is no longer fashionable, but the description is still accurate. If something is bought or sold anywhere in the world, from iron ore to textiles to oil, autos, jumbo jets, or nuclear power plants, the chances are a Japanese trading company is involved at some stage. They not only handle direct imports and exports to and from Japan, but they also handle "third country trade." Third-country trade means that the shosha is involved as a middleman even though the transaction has nothing to do with Japan. For example, every year a huge quantity of American goods and services are brokered by these traders, often when the seller and the buyer are both U.S. firms. How can a Japanese company act as a middleman for American business? That is precisely what a trading company does—insert itself between buyer and seller and show them good reasons to use a well-connected, well-financed middleman.

. In fact, the shosha have many roles. They procure raw materials and sell finished products throughout the world. In the process, they serve as the eyes and ears of their major clients (both Japanese and others), providing them with global market information and analysis. They help smooth out the rocky road their clients would otherwise face in dealing with foreign languages, foreign currencies, and foreign governments. They not only buy and sell but also invest overseas, particularly in fields that promise a steady supply of critical raw materials (such as mining and oil and gas exploration) and in large-scale industrial projects where few other companies have the resources to compete with them.

In Japan, they distribute what they import, and they ship and store what they buy. This puts shosha near the top of the ladder of the domestic distribution chain, which is one reason why many a foreign firm has looked to the shosha as the easy way to access the Japanese market. The shosha are also hungry for profit, which is one reason why many foreign firms have looked elsewhere. On the whole, the shosha make very little profit on their business, although this was certainly not the case in the past. However, as the structure of Japanese industry has changed radically over the last decade or so—exporting more semiconductors than automobiles— and as Japanese companies have grown larger, expanded overseas, and found they could manage to do business on their own, there has been less and less need for the variety of services the shosha offer. Many of the larger corporations have found they can often do without another middleman in their operations. Giant firms such as Toyota have even set up their own shosha to service their own corporate group.

As a result of all these changes, the traders are operating on rice paper–thin margins these days. The six biggest firms regularly report tens of billions of dollars in sales, but in reality the figures represent the value of their customers' products being traded rather than their own sales. For example, in its fiscal year ended in March 1992, Itochu (formerly called C. Itoh & Co. in English), the number one trading house in terms of sales, recorded over $160,000 million in sales, but only around $80 million in net profits, an apparent final margin of 0.05 percent. Obviously, the profits for playing middleman (while maintaining hundreds of offices and an army of staff worldwide) are slim. However, the shosha view every new transaction, no matter how small or how minuscule the profit, as a way to develop a long-term relationship with a prospective customer and boost their total "sales" figures (which is how the traders are ranked in the industry).

The shosha play an extremely important financial role in Japanese business by providing credit for small- to medium-sized companies. Without the shosha to act as financial intermediaries, these firms would have to deal directly with the giant city banks, which do not have a reputation for bending over backwards to accommodate small business. Not surprisingly, the big banks abhor the risks involved in making loans to thousands of small companies, vetting each firm's business performance and future prospects, checking collateral, and so on. The banks are much happier to extend credit to the giant shosha, and in most cases the smaller firms are happier to deal with them instead of the banks. In their book *The Financial Behavior of Japanese Corporations*, Ballon and Tomita explain as follows:

> For a bank to lend to a trading company that is financing an enterprise is much less a default risk than a direct loan to the enterprise, because the trading company can, if necessary, absorb the loss . . . A meaningful advantage is that smaller firms can borrow from trading companies at more favorable interest rates than at the banks and without compensating balance. If receivables are in jeopardy, the trading company can come to the rescue with much less adverse publicity than if banks are involved. For the trading company itself, because its popular image and ranking in the industry is determined by sales volume and because the trading company is not subject to the governmental checks and controls on financing that restrict the banks, its financial operations are a direct contribution to sales. As a result [shosha] are able to contribute substantial integrative power to the keiretsu, both vertically and horizontally.

This helps to explain why the shosha are so critical to the operation of the big keiretsu. In essence, they pick up where the group's main bank leaves off. Whereas the main banks in a sense "insure" the business of the top level of their group companies, the shosha "insure" the thousands of fringe firms, both inside and outside their own group, via trade credit. And trade credit is particularly important in Japan. One study showed that the average amount of trade credit outstanding for the manufacturing sector was more than double the level in the United States. The difference is largely due to the operations of the shosha, which act as intermediaries in a wide variety of transactions, many of which the two principals in the transaction could apparently handle on their own. Yet both sides want the shosha to participate. This also helps to explain why there is a much higher ratio of wholesale to retail transactions in Japan than in the United States or Europe. Part of the reason is the repeated "middleman" transactions handled by the shosha.

Exactly how the trading companies perform this function is shown in the accompanying illustration (see page 57), which is based on a diagram in an article by Paul Sheard in the *Journal of the Japanese and International Economies*.

The shosha here acts as an intermediary between a buyer and a seller. The goods involved could be anything from chopsticks to rolled steel. The process looks like this: The buyer places an order and the seller delivers the goods on credit, perhaps knowing nothing about the buyer, but knowing

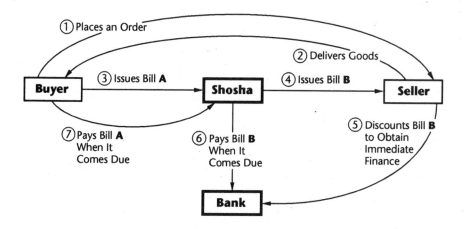

that a "name" shosha is handling the deal. The buyer then issues a bill *A* to the shosha, which in turn issues its own bill *B* to the seller. The seller can obtain immediate cash for this transaction by taking the shosha's bill *B* to any bank in the country (something he could never do with a note from the buyer). The shosha must pay its bill *B* when it comes due at the bank, and collect payment from the buyer for his bill *A* when that comes due.

By intermediating the transaction, the shosha eliminates the need for the seller to extend credit to some tiny firm it has never heard of; instead, it extends credit to a giant trading company. Similarly, the buyer is in debt not to the supplier but to a large, well-connected trading company which can manage the risk much better than the seller.

Convoluted as this system may sound at first, it has enormous impact on the ability of small Japanese companies to do business smoothly. Where small firms would have to pay in cash, possibly by putting up collateral for short-term loans, or take large risks in dealing with companies whose financial status they know little about, instead they buy and sell freely and obtain the goods they need immediately on credit. Nor are the merits limited to small firms. The banks, which would normally have to perform innumerable credit checks on thousands of small companies, can relax and expand their guaranteed loan base because the shosha has done all the credit checking in advance and so assumes the risk itself.

Note that the trader's role in this kind of transaction is not to trade but simply to supply trade credit. The shosha does not normally function as a commodity broker—it does not generally buy and sell on its own account. The price for the goods is determined between the supplier and purchaser, and the trader merely intermediates between the two by supplying credit. It is interesting to note, however, that if Bill A and Bill B are of the same duration, the shosha is not even supplying credit. Why then would the transaction partners deliberately involve a middleman? Because the shosha is still performing an insurance function, insuring the seller against default by the buyer and thus making the transaction practical for both parties. It is for this role that the shosha receives a commission (a small percentage of the transaction value), and it is for this reason that observers call the shosha "a kind of quasi-insurance agency."

Professor Sheard also highlights an interesting aspect of this insurance-without-trade function: "In effect, intermediation by the trading company serves to break a single physical transaction into two separate financial components. In many cases, the physical delivery of goods takes place directly from supplier to purchaser; the trading company does not take delivery of goods or play any active role. An extreme, but by no means uncommon, case is where the plants of the supplier and purchaser are located adjacent to one another in the same industrial complex with direct feedthrough of materials, and yet the trading company earns commission income as a financial intermediary in the transaction."

This whole system hinges on the concept of insuring two parties against the possibility of default. But how serious is the risk of default? The answer is, very serious. In 1985, for example, there were over 15,000 cases of companies whose transactions with banks were suspended because of defaulting on their bills. Many of these were exactly the kind of small firms that might be involved in a transaction with another small company and default on their debts, possibly bringing down the creditor firm as well. True, the shosha sometimes make money for doing nothing. But every year they have to write off hundreds of millions of dollars in bad debts to cover defaults by their customers.

The worst-case scenario, however, is not the default of small- or even medium-sized clients, but the default of a trading company. Of course, the failure of a major trading company is just as unthinkable as the failure of a major bank. And, as it usually does, the unthinkable happened. Back in 1977 a major trading house went under. Needless to say, a full-scale bankruptcy would have sent shock waves throughout Japan. Although Ataka & Co. was only the tenth largest shosha, it was reportedly doing business with around 35,000 companies at the time. Something had to be done to prevent a "loss of confidence" in the market. This is the point in the script when the company doctor makes his appearance, and as we saw earlier, Ataka's main bank, Sumitomo, stepped in to clean up the mess. Significantly, none of Ataka's manufacturing creditors lost a single yen when the company disappeared.

The sogo shosha obviously require enormous sums of cash to continue operating their worldwide networks and to handle their numerous financing operations within Japan. So while they are invariably close to the main banks in their respective groups, none of the top shosha can get by with loans from a single bank. They all finance through several banks and so, in one sense, are the largest firms in their groups to consistently cut across keiretsu lines. The shosha must borrow funds wherever they can find them and go after new clients wherever they can find them, even if it means digging in someone else's backyard.

The U.S. government paid the shosha the ultimate compliment during the Structural Impediments Initiative talks by charging that they control imports and distribution to such an extent that they limit the entry of American goods to the Japanese market. Indeed, the biggest shosha probably do have enough power to do that if all six bitter rivals decided to cooperate to shut out American products. While the results of further U.S. government investigation will be interesting, instinct says that the rising yen means that the import of cheaper U.S. goods and their sale inside Japan at comparatively high prices would provide a guaranteed high-margin business, something no shosha would be likely to turn down.

4
The Ties That Bind

In addition to institutions such as the main bank and the shosha, there are other common structural features of the big horizontal keiretsu. These include presidential councils, cross-shareholding, interlocking directorates, and intragroup trade patterns.

Presidential Councils

Each of the Big Six keiretsu has a special committee called the *shacho-kai* ("presidents' assembly"). In fact, it is not limited only to group presidents. In the interests of democracy, the chairman of each member company is also eligible. The important thing is that one man or the other will always appear to represent his firm at these monthly sessions. There are usually a number of other groupwide meetings for general managers from each company, but the shacho-kai are special. Membership determines the "inner" group of companies from the "outer" group of a keiretsu. For example, Mazda Motors and Matsushita Electric are both close to the Sumitomo Group. But neither president sits on Sumitomo's shacho-kai so neither is officially a member of that group. There are similar examples in every keiretsu, large companies with strong financial ties to the group's main bank and often large cross-shareholdings of stock, but insufficient historical background or inclination to become members of the club.

One question that the Japanese seem never to worry about (perhaps because the answer is obvious to them) but foreigners inevitably ask is "What exactly do these presidential councils do?" The very need to ask such a question provides an interesting light on the shacho-kai. Not only is membership very exclusive, but the proceedings themselves are kept secret. Yoshinari Maruyama, a Japanese scholar who has studied the Big Six for years, points out that the minutes of these meetings are kept in the strictest confidence. In some groups, members are not even allowed to take notes during the meeting to assure that no unauthorized written records of the proceedings exist. Thus, no outsider really knows what goes on inside the shacho-kai. Nor are the members given to discussing it on late-night talk shows. Of course, over the decades a few members have commented to the effect that nothing of any great importance is discussed, but there is no way to verify such claims.

The Mitsubishi Group's shacho-kai is called the *Kin'yokai*, and its head is the president of Mitsubishi Shoji (Mitsubishi Corp.). Professor Maruyama points to the writings of a former president of that firm to elucidate the functions of this famous shacho-kai.

> In 1976, Fujino Chujiro, who was head of the Kin'yokai at the time, wrote ... that the club aims to cultivate group solidarity.... The club's most important role is to determine group strategy and to plan group actions vis-à-vis external parties. It deals with the question of whether the group should move into new industries, such as nuclear energy, deep-sea development, space development, or biotechnology. The group's interests with respect to other [keiretsu], affairs of the business community, and dealings with the government are also examined at club meetings. Its second role is to mediate between group member companies. In this connection it should suffice to mention the important role that the Kin'yokai played at the time of the merger that reconstituted Mitsubishi Corp. as a general trading company....
>
> The third role of the club is to obtain adjudication and approval from the top executives of group member companies. For example, in 1972 there arose a factional dispute among the chief executives of Mitsubishi Petrochemical Co., Ltd., over who would become the next president. The Kin'yokai passed judgment on this matter, and it was a rare example of such a decision being reported to the mass media.

Determining group strategy, supporting group solidarity, mediating intragroup activities and settling intragroup squabbles. All of that seems fairly simple. Except perhaps the first part about "determining strategy and planning group actions vis-à-vis external parties." That sounds very much as if the shacho-kai might be functioning as some kind of planning agency for the group as a whole, and that is exactly the impression the Big Six want to avoid. If even a few of the keiretsu were seen to be meeting regularly to carefully plot future strategies for their group companies, their image would suffer and there might be more of a cry to get the Fair Trade Commission to investigate the situation. At least that is the fear inside the Big Six groups.

So everything is kept secret. Although the fact that over a hundred chief executives of Japan's biggest firms are meeting privately every month is public knowledge, the question of what these meetings are all about has been left up to their groups' public relations offices. The PR people's comments provide ample evidence that the Japanese are not, as is sometimes charged, lacking in creativity. The executives enjoy having lunch together once a month, it is said, and talk about the state of the economy. They hear stimulating lectures from contemporary writers, artists, and so on, including topics such as modern Japanese literature. One study reported that the alleged major topic of conversation at their presidential council meetings was golf, and that, according to its sources (presumably Japanese executives), the shacho-kai rarely discussed strategy or operational decision making so as not to violate the Anti-Monopoly Law. Anyone familiar with the contempt that Japanese executives feel for that law, and the Fair Trade Commission which enforces it, would be amused at this explanation.

And yet, the claim is made that once every month the presidents or chairmen of all the groups' senior companies arrange not to be overseas on business, not to be sitting in committee meetings at one of the innumerable organizations to which they belong, and not to be entertaining some bureaucratic vice-minister in charge of monitoring their industry, all so that they can dine together, swap tall tales about their golf scores, and listen to talks about modern art. Remember that every month the Sanwa Group must gather its most important 44 top executives in a room; the Mitsubishi and Fuyo Groups must each call the roll for 29 CEOs; Mitsui has 26 and Sumitomo 20. Even without the DKB Group (which meets only once every three months), that is a total of 148 of the top executives from the most important companies in Japan coming together every four weeks ostensibly to take part in programs of social and cultural enrichment.

Undoubtedly, one of the primary reasons for having a presidential council is simply to allow the group's decision makers to meet regularly. As is often pointed out, Japanese society places a high value on face-to-face meetings, even when there is no apparent reason to be meeting. Any foreign executive who has sat through interminable committee meetings with a Japanese joint-venture partner and wondered why so much time is "wasted" talking about nothing of consequence can testify to this. Sometimes the reason for meeting is simply to meet. Nothing in particular needs to be "accomplished." Undoubtedly when the leaders of Japan's top companies get together they do talk about the state of the economy. They do talk about golf. And we know that they do invite various outsiders in to give speeches on cultural topics, current events, and so on. The truly cynical might say that it would be impolite to talk about anything serious while everyone was still eating, so some "entertainment" would be almost a necessity before closing the doors and getting down to—Well, that's it, the only reasonable conclusion is that they do talk about business. If almost 189 top executives, whose firms control a very, very conservatively estimated $2 trillion in sales each year, went to such trouble to meet regularly and did not talk about business, something would be very odd.

Consequently, the question is not "Do they talk business?" but "What kind of business?"

As the former head of the Mitsubishi Group noted, entry into new commercial fields would be one natural topic for the assembled top execs to talk about. So would proposals to cooperate with other groups, either domestic or foreign, in projects involving a number of different group firms. Discussion of extending the use of the group name and/or registered trademarks to affiliated firms would also qualify. So would general discussions of upcoming changes in government policies affecting business, changes in the tax laws, and similar legal and regulatory matters. In short, anything that affected a large number of group firms would be a natural topic, including anything that might threaten the group's stability. Is it even conceivable, for instance, that the U.S. government charges (or more recently, the German government's charges) about the keiretsu were not on the agenda at every one of the Big Six meetings?

But the question remains, do these presidential councils function as real decision-making organs for the Big Six keiretsu? On one extreme there are those in Japan who say unquestionably yes, including a number of academics. Professor Maruyama puts it this way: "Why would you gather together the only men in a company who have the legal right to make decisions for their companies if not to make some decisions? The shacho-kai members are the men who control the *daihyo-in* [the legal seal of a company, necessary for signing any important legal document, contract, etc.]. Why bring such men together just to talk about golf?" On the other extreme are the Big Six groups themselves, which maintain that these meetings are completely social, fraternal, and innocent.

Our feeling lies somewhere in between. That is, the shacho-kai are indeed social gatherings, but social gatherings of businessmen. It is unthinkable that they are not talking about the very thing that brings them together in the first place. Because of their limited time to meet, the existence of parallel working-level councils, and the fundamental nature of Japanese organizations (i.e., to discuss matters informally outside a formal gathering rather than to debate them openly), we do not believe that the presidential councils are regularly used for strategic planning, policymaking, and decisionmaking. However, there is ample reason to believe that they could be used for those purposes at any time if a crisis loomed or the individual groups so desired.

After the Occupation ended and the zaibatsu companies began to re-form as keiretsu, the presidential councils were undoubtedly strategy and policy meetings first, and social functions second. Also, during the 1950s and 1960s most of the groups were led by strong individuals who embodied the group identity and whose comments had the force of policy statements. During this period, the keiretsu needed to coordinate their activities in a fundamental way: How would they respond to MITI calls to foster the chemical or the steel or the auto industry? How would they respond to bureaucrats granting them permission to form cartels in various fields? Who would coordinate group exports and who would prepare foreign exchange budgets to show to government officials? While these and many similar discussions must have taken place outside the shacho-kai as well, it seems likely that during the keiretsu's formative years the monthly meetings were used to discuss, to debate, and to decide group policy. To think otherwise just doesn't make sense.

By the 1970s and 1980s, however, the keiretsu were well established and group policy was pretty well set, so there was less need to use the shacho-kai so actively. The only time it would be necessary to discuss policy in such a group context would be to bring up points of diversion from group policy. For example, executives of Mitsubishi Bank once reportedly considered abandoning the "three diamonds" logo that is synonymous with the Mitsubishi name; pressure from other group members, all of whom use the logo, forced the bank to rethink that plan. This kind of situation might well have been discussed openly at the Kinyo-kai meeting.

In addition, the advent of new technologies raised new topics not covered by the old policies, including the entry of the keiretsu into fields such as computers and telecommunications. But the big difference in the 1970s and 1980s, according to informed sources, was the lack of leadership. The strong voices which had guided the keiretsu during their early years were no longer there. This brought about a fundamental change, at least in most of the Big Six. Without strong leadership the presidential councils became something much closer to club meetings. And the sudden growth of several group companies to the status of world-class competitors meant that these firms were now much larger and less dependent on the main bank and the shosha for guidance. The meetings thus became more of an open forum and less of a directed planning session.

Despite commentary in the Japanese press to the effect that some activities of the Big Six shacho-kai violate the spirit if not the letter of the Antimonopoly Law, it seems highly unlikely that these meetings are used to do the kinds of things that we fear most: setting prices, arranging cartels, planning how to keep foreign business out of their markets, and so on. While such discussions are not inconceivable within the shacho-kai, it is far more likely that if they were held, it would be at lower levels, either in a working-group meeting or within the various companies directly concerned with those particular issues.

Cross-shareholdings

Perhaps no aspect of the keiretsu is as well known as the fact that the groups like to commingle their equity. This is not a new phenomenon. Some of the giant prewar zaibatsu did not merely put all their shares in group subsidiaries into holding-company safes. Some of them, such as Sumitomo and Mitsui, were already selling shares in group companies to other group companies back in the 1920s. But what we now think of as strategic shareholding developed after the war. Until the end of the Occupation, former zaibatsu companies were forbidden to hold each other's stock. Within a very short time after SCAP packed its bags, the laws were changed and a policy of intragroup cross-shareholding developed. This trend gathered steam rapidly in the high-growth period of the late 1950s and early 1960s.

By the late sixties, as the government began slowly to relax the system of regulations on foreign capital entry, there were growing concerns about possible takeovers of Japanese firms by their larger and more powerful Western counterparts. In *The Financial Behavior of Japanese Corporations*, Ballon and Tomita explain as follows:

> When the Japanese government began to liberalize foreign capital entry into Japan, management became increasingly concerned about the thin capitalization of Japanese companies in general, which seemed to offer too ready a temptation for takeover by foreign capital. It was a challenge altogether different from the technological lag faced by industry in the earlier postwar period. In order to acquire foreign technology, licensing had been practiced on a grand scale. When foreign interests demanded management participation as a condition for the transfer of technology, the result was an increased number of international joint ventures. . . . But the vulnerability resulting from heavy dependence on borrowed technology was only compounded by the new threat—takeover—now possible because of the "free" entry of foreign capital. The solution to this problem was "stable shareholders," who would not allow shares to be acquired by foreign interests planning a takeover.

By the late 1960s firms like Sony, Matsushita, and Honda were exporting large volumes of increasingly better-quality products to the United States and other markets. Such companies and dozens of other up-and-coming firms would be attractive targets for a large American buyer with global ambitions and a bit of long-term vision. Or, at least, that was the fear that spread through Japanese business in 1969 when General Motors let it be known that it was contemplating taking a sizable stake in Isuzu Motors. Shock waves rippled through the Japanese business world. Was this the beginning of the foreign invasion that had been successfully avoided back in the 1950s?

The GM-Isuzu negotiations took years—not because the two companies could not agree, but because the Japanese government was scrambling to find a satisfactory way to cope with the situation. This was the time when MITI minister Miyazawa declared that banks and other keiretsu financial institutions could do just as good a job as the old holding companies in keeping Japanese shares out of foreign hands. At the time, MITI still had tremendous influence over the industries it supervised. In 1971, the ministry helped to arrange the GM-Isuzu transaction along lines that eased the fears of Japanese business. The American firm could buy as much as 35 percent of Isuzu's shares, but only if most of the remaining shares were placed with stable Japanese shareholders.

GM agreed to buy a 34.2 percent stake in Isuzu, but had to guarantee that the company would not try to increase its holding, and under no circumstances would it try to buy a controlling interest in the firm. In addition, MITI asked over 400 Isuzu shareholders not to sell their shares, particularly not to GM. Institutional shareholders were asked (a polite term) to sign over their Isuzu shares to a special consortium of trust banks. In this way, a stable shareholding could be maintained, the best-known company in America could be permitted to buy a stake in a listed Japanese firm, and an outright takeover could be prevented.

Industry got the message. Major firms in every sector began taking steps to increase their stable shareholding ratios, and the keiretsu solidified shareholding arrangements within their groups. Not long after, a wave of takeover attempts by Japanese (not foreign) speculators and corporate raiders only increased management's sense of vulnerability and the conviction that stable shareholding was the best defense. Even more than in the 1950s, keiretsu membership became synonymous with protection. Not an ironclad guarantee against a corporate raid, but protection in the sense of group support. When the Osano group cornered around 30 percent of the shares in Mitsui Mining, members of Mitsui's shacho-kai stepped in and bought them back. When the Sasagawa group did the same to Nakayama Steel (a member of the Sanwa Bank Group), Sanwa led a five-bank rescue team to buy back the shares.

I'll Buy Yours If You'll
Buy Mine . . .

As a simple illustration of cross-shareholding, let's look at Sumitomo Trust & Banking, the number two banking arm of the Sumitomo group. Of its 1.24 billion shares outstanding, 11 different Sumitomo companies own more than 1 percent of the firm's equity and several more own less than 1 percent. The largest block resides with Sumitomo Life Insurance (4.17 percent), followed by Sumitomo Corp. (3.45 percent), Sumitomo Bank (3.38 percent) and NEC (2.92 percent). Other shares are in the hands of Sumitomo Marine & Fire Insurance, Sumitomo Chemical Ind., Nippon Sheet Glass, Sumitomo Metal Industries, and Sumitomo Warehouse. Conversely, Sumitomo Trust owns 2.3 percent of Sumitomo Bank's stock, 5.6 percent of Sumitomo Marine & Fire, 6.1 percent of Sumitomo Corp., 4.4 percent of Sumitomo Chemical, 7.2 percent of Nippon Sheet Glass, 5.2 percent of Sumitomo Metal Industries, 6.1 percent of NEC, and 7 percent of Sumitomo Warehouse (life insurance companies are not allowed to list in Japan, or the bank would own a big chunk of Sumitomo Life as well).

If the main banks simply held shares in the principal group companies, it would be easy to see a pattern of bank dominance through equity participation. However, when the companies truly have mutual shareholding, the situation becomes more complex. The keiretsu have a system not of mutual dependence, but of mutual interest. In other words, being a member of a large horizontal keiretsu means being financially linked to most or all of the key firms in a group, and vice versa. This also means that everyone has a very real stake in seeing that all the group firms increase or improve their business in the years to come.

The merits of cross-shareholding within a group are obvious. No one company in the group needs to buy a large percentage of the stock in any other group company, yet each of the group firms could easily find 20 to 30 percent or more of its equity residing safely with other member firms. This not only helps to ward off would-be takeover artists, but cements relations with the rest of the group. Mutual shareholding thus becomes part of the "glue" that helps to hold the group together. Moreover, with fewer "outside" shareholders, the company's management has much greater freedom to act without concern for short-term consequences.

Viewed from this perspective, one of the primary reasons for the much-discussed Japanese practice of "long-term planning" is not a unique corporate strategy but a unique ability to get away with it. Japan's infamous 15-minute shareholders' meetings are a direct result of this situation—and one that any American CEO can immediately appreciate. Another point about all this massive intercorporate stockholding is that it is self-perpetuating. Equity assets (and real estate assets as well) are kept on a company's balance sheet at book value, which for many of them is a ridiculously tiny fraction of market value. These are the famed "latent assets" (*fukumi*) that stock analysts in Japan constantly refer to in discussing a company's real worth. Selling these shareholdings would result in instant realization of these assets at market prices, and whopping big capital gains taxes as well. But holding them on the books costs next to nothing—especially since the dividends from these massive holdings are surprisingly low and the tax rate on corporate dividends (providing the shares were not financed with loans) is minimal.

One more point is worth noting about cross-shareholding by hundreds of listed companies in all the big keiretsu. When such activity is carried out across the economy on such a large scale, it naturally reduces the number of floating shares on the stock market, and thus increases the value of each company's equity portfolio, stable and otherwise. In addition to direct cross-shareholding by the keiretsu, which accounts for roughly 25 percent of all Japanese shares, a little under 50 percent is in the hands of institutional investors—mainly banks, trust banks, and insurance companies, the bulk of which have keiretsu connections. The result is that only a little more than one-fourth of the outstanding shares of Japanese stock is available for trading, a factor which definitely helps to squeeze prices upward whenever an economic boom increases demand. Of course, keiretsu partners would not sell their stock in other group firms simply because the stock price was rising, but they are free to use their huge stock portfolios as collateral to borrow other funds for investment (as many companies did during the "bubble" years of 1987–1989).

In real disaster scenarios, even "stable" shares are not considered sacred and may be sold off—if the transactions are handled correctly. In times of financial distress, companies will dispose of their shares, usually on a private basis, rather than at the market, and then only after consultation with the firms involved. To return to the example of the bankrupt trading house Ataka & Co. (discussed in Chapter 3), its considerable shareholdings were sold off. But not by Ataka. The sale was managed by its main bank, Sumitomo. In such cases the bank's right to sell a client's "stable" shares to offset its own write-offs is understood. After all, the bank is acting as a kind of "damage control" agency, swallowing bad debts so that the effects of its client's sudden demise do not ripple outward and cause problems for the business community at large. Interestingly enough, the sale of these securities was handled quietly and the principal motive was certainly not profit (the sale yielded less than 10 percent of the portfolio's market value). Instead, the majority of shares wound up in the hands of Sumitomo Group firms and other friendly companies, obviously at minimal cost. Why let stable shares wander outside the group?

Even then, some of the firms in which Ataka had maintained holdings could not allow their shares to be sold so easily, even by a main bank acting as receiver for the firm. Since Japanese companies are not allowed to buy their own shares, some of these companies had to negotiate with their own main banks, insurance companies, and other stable shareholders to buy up their shares rather than allowing them to come on the public market or be absorbed by Sumitomo Group firms.

We can see that the rather simple idea of stable cross-shareholdings becomes somewhat more complex in practice. The whole system presumes the "stability" of one's shareholders, and that in turn, rests on the close cooperation and support of at least one main bank. During the stomach-wrenching stock market slide of 1990–1992 even the giant city banks pared down some of their massive stock portfolios to raise cash. Industry leaders were hardly surprised, for they have known all along that stable cross-shareholdings are not guarantees that no shares will be sold, only that sales will be handled prudently. On this point, former Toyota chairman Taizo Ishida no doubt spoke for a majority of executives when he said of his own firm's shares, "Even financial institutions are not stable shareholders in the strictest sense. So we have an arrangement whereby if for some reason they sell their shareholding they will let us know beforehand. In such a case we want the Toyota group to take over the shares."

Assigned Directors

Traditionally, the most powerful companies in any group—the main bank, shosha or other core firm in a horizontal keiretsu, or the parent (top) firm in a vertical keiretsu—have dispatched their own executives to serve on the boards of directors of smaller firms with whom they are doing business. There are a number of reasons for this. The least important, but certainly the most typically Japanese function, is simply to farm out excess personnel. Because of the rigid seniority system, every year in every company a group of executives rises to a position just below the director level. Those who have stepped on few toes and are also good at the important things in management (such as mah-jongg and golf) are likely to rise to the uppermost echelon of the company, where they will generally have little to do and comfortable chairs to do it in. But what does a company do when it has, say, a dozen or two dozen candidates for director every year? Of course, a few of them will get seats on the board, but only a few. So a lot of the would-be directors are held back. Then, next year there are twice as many. The following year you have even more. It is plain to everyone (especially their subordinates) that these "managers" have risen as far as seniority will carry them and are stuck in a perpetual holding pattern outside the boardroom.

The traditional in-house solution to excess managers was to give most of them token jobs, 'desks by the window' as they are thought of in Japan, where they can while away the hours, read the newspaper, and ease into the shock of retirement. A few others could be shuffled around to semiresponsible jobs in whatever the company viewed as useless divisions where they could do little harm. Until about a decade ago, the personnel department was a favorite "preretirement" spot for companies with excess staff, and the international department was an even bigger dumping ground (which helps explain the frustration felt by many a foreign firm in the past which sent their top people to Tokyo to set up a joint venture, only to find that the heads of the international division at their Japanese partner were of little help in running a business.

The most "politically correct" solution, however, is to reward those nondirectors who have reached the appointed age by making them directors—of another company. Especially in the vertical keiretsu, where larger firms inevitably have a hierarchy of subservient smaller firms beneath them, it is simple enough to "promote" a senior manager to another firm's board of directors.

A much more important reason for dispatching an executive to another company (especially at the upper levels of the vertical keiretsu and throughout the big horizontal groupings) is for a large firm to send one of its dozens of directors to a related firm as a visible sign of the relationship between the two firms and as a conduit for information. In some cases this may also be a kind of "outplacement" for unwanted personnel, but for the most part directors are sent to other firms for the services they can provide, not to get them out of the house.

In the Big Six keiretsu, directors are most often dispatched horizontally from the nucleus—the main banks, shosha, and other key firms—to other core companies. These firms in turn send directors downwards into their own vertical keiretsu, and within these, directors (and others) may be sent further on down into the pyramid. The most important player in this game is the main bank. They send directors for years, sometimes many years and sometimes permanently, to sit on the boards of companies whose welfare is important to them, especially those who owe the bank money. The logic of the system is hard to argue with.

For example, let's say you are the CEO of one of the nation's largest commercial banks—we'll use Fuji Bank and its group as an example. One of the electronics makers in your group is Oki Electric. Oki Electric is a large, healthy company with strong sales ties to NTT (the national telephone semimonopoly). It is also a major borrower from Fuji (to the tune of about $150 million a year) and an important member of the Fuyo Group. Are you going to ask Oki's management to send you reports every month about the company's financial status, its current and pending deals with major clients, and a detailed summary of the firm's business strategy? Not likely. And if you did, would you feel absolutely confident that the company would report to you even the slightest internal problem before it began to grow into something serious? Probably not. And if you did hear of some minor problem and started to make inquiries, wouldn't you be inviting friction with Oki's management? Much simpler instead to send a director or two to participate in the firm's management. Then everything is open and above board.

Needless to say, these assigned directors are there to help the company, not to spy on it. However, it is no secret that they will keep the bank informed about Oki's business performance, client relationships, new product development, overseas expansion, labor problems, threats from gangsters, attempts by stock speculators to greenmail the firm, and a variety of other relevant information. If there are any problems in the firm, someone at the bank is responsible for knowing about them. Of course, the bank would not act on this information except in the most extreme circumstances, but bankers always sleep better when they know what color socks their borrowers are wearing each day.

What are the advantages for Oki? Considerable. For one thing, it never needs to negotiate credit with its main bank, nor with its number two bank, Yasuda Trust (also a member of the Fuyo group), because all the information on the company's creditworthiness is already available at the bank. If the firm needs an unusually big loan to develop, say, a major new cellular phone plant overseas, someone at the bank whose responsibility includes watching over Oki Electric will be able to recommend that the project is sound, that it has been in the works for some time, and that it will add substantially to the company's bottom line within a certain period.

There are other, less tangible benefits from having a direct relation with a bank. For example, if a firm is having trouble in dealing with another member of the group, a word from the bank may be all that is needed to smooth things out. If the firm is having trouble with its clients, whether inside the group or not, a visit from a senior director of one of the largest city banks will have far more impact than a visit from someone representing a middle-ranked telecom manufacturer. In this sense, the pipeline to the bank is a two-way flow. Granted, the bulk of the information is flowing up to the bank, which monitors both its investments and the group's activities closely. But there are also times when the bank's resources—and not only financial ones—come to the aid of the group companies. In other words, receiving a director from the bank can help to bring about all the benefits that accrue from having a main bank. The dispatch of a director thus formalizes one firm's commitment to another. It is for this reason that many smaller firms, particularly those in vertical keiretsu, actually request to have management personnel sent, either from a bank or from a parent firm. And in some cases the latter refuse to do so, because sending in a director would imply a commitment that the larger firm is not yet willing to make.

However, it is standard operating policy for the Big Six banks to post executives to their most important clients. Since we used the Fuyo group as an example, we might note that beyond Oki Electric, where the bank has placed both a managing director and an auditor, Fuji Bank executives serve as president of NSK, vice president of both Marubeni and NOF Corp., senior managing director of Nissan Motor, Taisei Construction, Showa Denko, NKK, and Showa Line Ltd.; managing director of Keihin Electric Express Railway; and auditor at Sapporo Beer, Nichirei, Yokogawa Electric, and Toho Rayon. Fuji has a royal flush at Tokyo Tatemono, where the chairman, president, vice president, and one director are all bank alumni.

But assigned directorships do not stop there. Just to firm up ties in the group, Yasuda Fire & Marine has sent a senior auditor to Tokyo Tatemono, NKK has sent a director to Showa Line, Nishin Flour Milling has sent an auditor to Tobu Railroad, and Nisshinbo has supplied a chairman, president, senior managing director, and auditor to Toho Rayon. Does that seem like a lot of personnel playing musical chairs in the corporate boardrooms of the Fuyo Group? In fact, these are only a few of the Fuyo companies that have received executive transfers from other group firms. All told, the group (again, mostly the bank and other core companies) provided a total of 31 chairmen and vice chairmen, 74 presidents and CEOs, 35 vice presidents, 264 senior and managing directors, 319 directors, and 180 auditors to related firms. When all advisers and other executive staff are included, at last count the Fuyo Group had over 900 senior personnel on loan to other firms in the group. The Sanwa Group had even more, and the DKB group had close to 1200. Altogether, in 1992 the Big Six keiretsu had posted over 4000 board members to other companies, including over 400 presidents or CEOs. And this counts only firms listed on the stock exchanges— if we counted personnel sent to unlisted firms, the numbers would rise dramatically.

Intragroup Financing

In Chapter 3 we looked at main banks, and we saw that their primary role
was as lender to their group firms. But the main banks make up only one
arm of a keiretsu's financing operations. Although the main bank is usually the group's top lender, its services are supplemented by the group's trust
bank, life insurance company, nonlife insurance company, and shosha.

The importance of this ability to self-finance much of the group's
activities should not be underestimated. One of the reasons that Japanese
firms have grown so rapidly in both size and global market share in the
past three decades is capital investment. On a per capita basis, Japan out-
invests the United States by more than 2 to 1. Even as a portion of GNP
Japan has outinvested the United States for the past quarter of a century.
Since the middle of the 1950s, Japanese firms have borrowed heavily to
invest in their own futures, and that investment has paid off handsomely.
Through almost all of the postwar era, financing has been done first and
foremost through group firms. The most visible function of the Big Six
keiretsu, and the most tangible benefit of membership, has always been
access to funds.

If we examine the Big Six in terms of average levels of intragroup
financing, we will find that the Sumitomo group, which is famed for its
strong group identity, is usually at or near the top of the list. Of 16 listed
firms' total borrowing in FY 1990, on average, 34.8 percent of the funds
came from the group's prime lenders (Sumitomo Bank, Sumitomo Trust &
Banking, Sumitomo Life Insurance and Sumitomo Fire and Marine Insurance). Across the entire Sumitomo group the average of intragroup
financing was 21.5 percent. But averages can be deceptive. Looking at
specific companies, we note that large, capital-rich firms such as Sumitomo
Corp., the group shosha, borrowed only a little over 15 percent from other
group members. For the smaller firms in the group, the story is different.
Sumitomo Warehouse raised over 67 percent of its capital from group
firms; for Sumitomo Construction the figure was 56 percent, Sumitomo
Coal Mining was 45 percent, and four other firms were about 37 percent.
In other words, a large part of the Sumitomo group borrows more than
one-third of its necessary capital from other Sumitomo companies.

The Mitsubishi and Mitsui groups, which like Sumitomo were
formed earlier than Sanwa, Fuyo, or DKB, both average roughly 19.5 percent for total in-group financing. Sanwa was about 18.2 percent and Fuyo
17.4 percent. Newcomer DKB's in-group average is only about 12.5 percent. Clearly, the older the group, the tighter its connections and the more
it reinforces those connections with loans as well as directors.

5
The Big Six Horizontal Keiretsu

The Old versus the New

The biggest and best-known keiretsu are the Big Six: the Mitsui Group, the Mitsubishi Group, the Sumitomo Group, the Fuyo Group, the Sanwa Group, and the Dai-Ichi Kangyo Group (which, like the bank it is named after, is abbreviated as DKB). At least the names of the first three are probably familiar to a large number of people outside of Japan. Mitsubishi, Mitsui, and Sumitomo are even the best-known groups in Japan. Why? In part, because their group identities are very strong. Most of their member companies bear the group name and use the group logo, while the other three groups are comparatively loose affiliations and almost none of their members shares a name or logo with any of the others.

This brings us to a distinction that is lost in all the literature on the keiretsu: the Big Six groups are not equal in the eyes of the public nor in the eyes of Japanese businessmen. They each have an "identity" or "personality" connected with their age, their background, and the reputation of their main bank. The most common distinction is the one we just made between the famous three and the other three. This is usually presented as a distinction between the "old" and "new" groups. In a strict historical sense this is inaccurate. It is true that the Mitsui and Sumitomo businesses are older than the rest, but the Mitsubishi zaibatsu, the Yasuda zaibatsu (the core of today's Fuyo Group), and the Shibusawa zaibatsu (what became the Dai-Ichi Bank group and the core of today's DKB group) are all of about the same age. It is only the establishment dates of their formal shacho-kai that can be so neatly divided into old and new.

And yet, the age distinction persists. Worse, both Western and Japanese scholars often call the Mitsui, Mitsubishi, and Sumitomo groups the "zaibatsu-centered" or "prewar" keiretsu and the others the "bank-centered" or "postwar" keiretsu. This is even more ridiculous, for as we have seen, at least five of the six groups were zaibatsu-centered before the war, and all six were bank-centered after the war. Inaccurate as these terms may be, we will use the less objectionable former distinction between old and new, and occasionally refer to the Mitsui, Mitsubishi, and Sumitomo groups as the Old Three and the Fuyo, Sanwa, and DKB groups as the New Three.

The main difference between the image of the two groups is certainly historical: whereas Mitsui, Mitsubishi, and Sumitomo are thought to have helped build modern Japan a century ago and followed it into war half a century later, Fuyo, Sanwa and DKB came together in their present form only after the 1964 Tokyo Olympics (the unofficial starting point for contemporary Japan in the minds of many Japanese), and to some extent they are still evolving today. If nothing else, this "modern" image, especially for the Fuyo Group (the core of the old Yasuda zaibatsu), testifies to the value of a great public relations job. The Old Three are generally thought of for their emphasis on steel, shipbuilding, chemicals, and other smokestack industries. Businesspeople respect them for these same qualities, but to most Japanese they convey an image of old-fashioned heavy industry. It is often said that housewives are happy to bring beers named Kirin and Asahi into their homes, but sales would drop sharply if the companies changed their respective labels to "Mitsubishi Beer" and "Sumitomo Beer."

Kanto versus Kansai

There is another distinction among these industrial groupings, and it, too, is historical. Unlike the matter of a group's age, which is immediately comprehensible to foreign businesspeople, this other distinction is one of "feeling" and is understood more on a visceral than an intellectual level by everyone in Japanese business. If you were to mention a certain keiretsu in conversation, no one would think, "Ah, yes, that's the second-oldest of the Big Six." Instead, they would respond to the group's image, the "feeling" they sense about its background. And much of that has to do with the group's ties to other businesses, to different parts of the government, and last but not least, to one of the two major urban centers of Japan, either Osaka or Tokyo. To the Western mind this last point may seem a rather trivial geographical distinction, yet it sparks rivalries going back hundreds of years. The Kyoto-Osaka-Kobe area, known as Kansai, was for over 1000 years both the home of the Imperial family and the commercial center of Japan. It was the shoguns who eventually set up in the Kanto area, and after the overthrow of their government in the 1860s, the Emperor was moved to Tokyo, which had become the de facto political capital. Gradually the commercial axis shifted as well and the once-dominant city of Osaka became the Chicago of Japan: great in its own right, but forever regarded as the Second City.

To many a foreign observer, this would all seem to be ancient history. The waning influence of Osaka and the ascendancy of Tokyo began hundreds of years ago. Surely any jealousies from those days should be long gone by now.

Think again. In fact, the extent of the ongoing rivalry between Kanto and Kansai is surprising. The two areas have very distinct identities, and very strong feelings about themselves and about each other that are self-perpetuating. It may seem odd for two cities only about as far apart as New York and Boston to have such a long-standing rivalry, and anyone who has never been to a Yankees–Red Sox game might expect them both to grow out of it sooner or later. Insiders know better.

On a business level, of course, Osaka-based companies do business with Tokyo-based companies every day, and both have extensive operations in each other's home territory. Yet both sides have a very strong sense of "turf" and both are acutely aware of their members' historical connections in their area. For example, the ongoing relationship between Nomura Securities and Daiwa Bank springs naturally from their common roots in prewar Osaka. And both firms have helped to make Tokyo a center of world finance because, like it or not, they know that it is Japan's financial capital. But, like almost all old Kansai companies, they keep their headquarters in Osaka, the real center of commerce.

It is one small indication of how deep the Tokyo-centric prejudice runs that until very recently the chairmanship of the Federation of Bankers Association of Japan, the organizational arm for the world's largest banking industry, traditionally rotated among the heads of Japan's biggest banks—that is, Japan's biggest Tokyo-based banks. Banks such as Sumitomo and Daiwa could be prominent members, but they never qualified to chair the bankers' association simply because they are not based in Tokyo. It may be only the slightest exaggeration to say that neither of these firms, nor Sanwa Bank, Nippon Life Insurance, Matsushita Electric, Suntory distilling, Itochu or Marubeni trading, nor any of a few dozen other Kansai firms would be crushed if the long-awaited Tokyo earthquake should someday restore Japan's balance of power overnight. Broad though this generalization may be, it is nonetheless true, and woe be the Western executive who prepares to do business in Japan without this background in mind.

How Big Is Big?

The Japanese love to rank things, and corporations are no exception. The vocabulary of business is cluttered with collections of the Big Nine shosha, the Big Four securities houses, the Big Three computer makers, even the Big Two auto makers, and so on. But when it comes to the "Big Six" keiretsu, for once the adjective is well deserved. These six horizontal keiretsu are not merely big, they are absolutely enormous.

How big are they? The only honest answer is no one really knows. Toyo Keizai (which publishes the *Japan Company Handbook* mentioned in Chapter 1) produces an annual survey entitled *Kigyo Keiretsu Soran* (Overview of the Industrial Keiretsu). It provides copious data on the Big Six groups, including comparative figures for previous years. Based on its data for fiscal year 1990, the Big Six groups accounted for over 17 percent of the total paid-in capital, over 15 percent of total assets, and over 15 percent of aggregate sales for all companies in Japan. These figures alone are impressive. What makes them more impressive, however, is that Toyo Keizai's data cover only those firms that are official members of each group's presidential council. So these figures do not represent the real strength of the Big Six at all, only their core companies, which comes to 189 firms out of over two million registered companies in the nation. Even so, these 189 firms alone comprise roughly 15 percent of the entire Japanese economy.

The Fair Trade Commission, that independent investigative body of dubious distinction described earlier, also makes periodic surveys of the Big Six. The FTC examines not only core companies in each group but also subsidiaries and affiliates. Thus, its data cover all firms in which core companies or their subsidiaries hold at least a 10 percent equity stake, which expands the data sample to about 12,000 firms. Not surprisingly, the picture of the keiretsu's role in the economy expands as well. In its 1989 survey (based on data for fiscal 1987), the FTC found that total capital in the hands of the Big Six was in excess of 32 percent, their gross assets were almost 27 percent and sales topped 25 percent of Japan's entire output. These are staggering figures. Six groups of companies account for roughly one-third of the paid-in capital in Japanese enterprise and one-fourth of both assets and sales.

Mind-boggling as such numbers may seem, they still don't tell the real story. Difficult though it may be to believe, the truth is that they are deceptively low. Here are four reasons why:

1. In the first place, the FTC figures do not include any financial institutions. That means none of the assets of the huge city banks that lie in the nucleus of each of the Big Six are counted. Nor are those of any of the Big Six trust banks, the life insurance companies, or the nonlife companies. While there are usually good statistical reasons for leaving these firms out of economic calculations, in this case it leads to a view of the Big Six that is much too narrow.

2. The FTC survey (in fact, all studies of the keiretsu) relies on a strict definition of core companies to determine Big Six membership. In other words, to be considered one of the Big Six keiretsu, a firm must be a formal member of one of the six shacho-kai or have 10 percent of its equity owned by a firm that is. Any company that does not meet these criteria is simply ignored. In the interests of compiling neat sets of data, this formula makes very good sense. But if the FTC were really trying to get to the bottom of how much influence the Big Six exert on the economy, it would certainly include dozens of other firms that have very close ties with a particular group but do not have formal membership in a presidential council. Needless to say, this gets into somewhat of a "grey" area, undoubtedly one that the FTC (and other keiretsu-watchers) would much rather avoid. For example, both the Shimadzu Group and the Morimura Group (two small collections of fairly large companies) are widely considered to be part of the Mitsubishi Group although they are not formal members of its shacho-kai.

Look at Honda Motor Co. Honda's main bank is Mitsubishi (from which it borrows heavily), one of its three "outside" directors is from Mitsubishi Bank, and its largest stockholder is Mitsubishi Bank. In fact, its top three shareholders are all core Mitsubishi Group companies. But because of Honda's independent management stance, it is not viewed as part of the Mitsubishi Group. Cases such as this make it difficult to draw the line, and make the presidential-council-only rule that much easier to live with. However, this attempt to simplify the data results in a distorted picture of the subject under investigation. There are many companies that are not as "grey" as Honda.

For example, Mazda Motor Corp. is very close to Sumitomo Bank (its president, one vice president, a managing director, and director are all from the bank), but because its number one shareholder is Ford Motor Co., Mazda will never find a chair waiting in Sumitomo's executive council. Nor will Kajima Construction, one of Japan's leading general contractors. Kajima's primary source for lending is Sumitomo Bank, its number one and number two stockholders are Sumitomo Bank and Sumitomo Trust, and its only private-sector director comes from Sumitomo Bank. However, since it is not an official member of the group, neither that firm (with sales of about $16 billion and total assets of over $20 billion) nor its scores of subsidiaries are counted in the total figures. Even more important are the "invisibles," things such as clout within a specific industry (where Kajima is tops), political connections (even better), and influence over related industrial sectors (considerable). None of these can be adequately expressed in quantitative terms, but they are all part of what a firm such as Kajima adds to the Sumitomo Group's power and prestige. However, neither Kajima, Mazda, Honda, nor any of a dozen other prominent firms is included in the statistical surveys of the Big Six keiretsu. If their contributions were added, the figures in every category would rise substantially.

3. Not only are the FTC figures misleading with respect to some of the largest companies affiliated with each group, but they completely miss the bottom end of the spectrum as well. As with the definition of core companies, the use of the 10 percent figure is easily justified: it is a common benchmark for labeling a firm an affiliate. However, when our goal is not to conform to standards but to search for an accurate picture of the keiretsu, the 10 percent shareholding rule is sadly inadequate. There are numerous instances of Big Six group firms owning less than 10 percent of a smaller company's stock yet controlling it as if it were a fully owned subsidiary. There are many cases in which the "parent" firm owns no stock at all but manages dozens or hundreds of "affiliates" by controlling its order flow for parts or assembly procedures. This is an element of the vertical keiretsu structure that we look at more closely in Chapter 6. But we should note at this point that almost all of the small manufacturing firms that are ultimately "affiliates" of giant vertically integrated makers are also, in the "macro" sense, part of one of the Big Six horizontal groups.

In short, the total number of companies surveyed by the FTC falls far short of the true number. The 1989 report found only 6875 firms that could technically be termed affiliates (10 percent shareholding). However, some of the larger vertical keiretsu have several thousand small companies working within their own vertical "pyramids." Within the Big Six there are a few dozen firms large enough to have that kind of subcontracting base. A little simple arithmetic shows that the FTC's estimate that the Big Six keiretsu account for a grand total of about 12,000 companies is off by a wide margin. Of course, the vast majority of the uncounted companies are quite small, some no bigger than a handful of staff. But if we push the total number of companies up closer to 100,000 companies, the real outline of the Big Six keiretsu in the Japanese economy begins to take shape.

4. Even for the very biggest companies within the Big Six, the FTC numbers are misleading. The term *total assets* is a measure of what each

company reports as its assets. However, as anyone who has ever looked at the Japanese stock market will tell you, most corporate balance sheets belong on the shelf labeled "fiction." Assets, including stocks and real estate, are held at book value, not real market value. Consider that most of the leading keiretsu firms have held each others' shares since Eisenhower was in the White House and much of the land was purchased only a little more recently. In the interim, urban real estate has appreciated by roughly 30–40 times and the Nikkei stock index has climbed by almost as much.

To cite an extreme example, Mitsubishi purchased much of the land in the Marunouchi district of downtown Tokyo in the late 1800s, and it is still carried on company books at its original cost: less than ¥1 per square foot. No realtor can give you any meaningful appraisal of what that land is worth today, but it is surely among the most valuable property in the world. So much for book value. How can we assign an average figure for true asset value to the 189 core companies in the Big Six? Would it be a multiple of 10 times their stated value? 20 times? 50 times? What would be an appropriate multiple for the assets of their subsidiaries and affiliates? No one knows. The only sure fact is that the figures stated by the companies are nearly meaningless.

We began with official estimates of the Big Six's total capital, assets, and sales as roughly one-third, one-fourth, and one-fourth, respectively, of all Japanese companies. Clearly, these numbers are inadequate. Unfortunately, there is no possible way to estimate, much less to measure, what the real figures should be. For want of more revealing data, we can only "guesstimate" that the Big Six horizontal keiretsu, including all their component firms, comprise no less than one-third of the total Japanese economy. And that is a rather conservative guess.

Cross-shareholding Trends

If we examine the Big Six in terms of cross-shareholding, we find a familiar pattern: the Old Three have much higher average ratios (roughly, Mitsubishi: 35 percent; Mitsui: 19 percent; Sumitomo: 27 percent) than the New Three (Fuyo: 15 percent; Sanwa: 16 percent; DKB: 12 percent). This is one area where the distinction between so-called old and new has some validity. The three firms still flying their zaibatsu colors are more coherent in terms of historical membership than the other three. Although the core of the Yasuda zaibatsu was preserved in the Fuyo Group, the rest of the group is a hodgepodge of zaibatsu leftovers that came into Fuji Bank's orbit in the 1950s. Sanwa is slightly more coherent, and DKB, which had a very tight core group around the old Dai-Ichi Bank, lost its coherence when it merged into its current form (which we will discuss momentarily). Thus, the Old Three group members were closer to each other and had a stronger tradition of cross-shareholding to begin with, while the New Three had to develop "friendly" cross-shareholding ties over the years.

Is this a weakness of the newer keiretsu? Certainly not. With a combined average cross-shareholding ratio of approximately 14 percent, these groups would seem to have more than sufficient holdings in their key group firms. On the contrary, the Old Three, with a combined average of 27 percent, would seem to be sitting on unnecessarily large piles of group-company stocks. Although the threat of a hostile takeover, domestic or foreign, of a Mitsubishi, Sumitomo, or Mitsui firm seems extremely remote these days, the groups hold onto their portfolios. In a sense, the cross-shareholdings have outlived their original, strategic purpose and now serve merely as one of the common bonds that help to unify the group. And yet, the Old Three, with the longest history, the strongest traditions, the most personal ties, and the least need of "glue" to keep their members together maintain the higher levels of cross-shareholding. If anyone needed to indicate their loyalty to the group and to each other, it would be the New Three, who lack all these historical advantages. Yet the New Three show no signs of upgrading their mutual shareholdings; in fact, their ratios have all declined slightly during the past decade.

Both groups have been gradually decreasing their group portfolios over the past few years, but only marginally. Since the stock market plunge of 1990–1992, the Old Three have been selling off small fractions of their holdings, most likely to raise cash at book-closing time, but their total sales have not amounted to anything substantial. The New Three, too, have been trimming their holdings, but also in small increments. In all likelihood, both groups will keep shaving their average cross-shareholding levels for years to come, but not dramatically. Some observers have suggested that the newer keiretsu will bring their average level down to around 10 percent, which is all they feel they need to maintain their business connections, while the old zaibatsu groups will keep theirs quite high simply because that is the way they have always done things.

The Mitsui Group

Profile. The prewar House of Mitsui was the quintessence of a zaibatsu. Its family members became the new aristocracy, its managers the new business elite, and its main companies the role models for others to emulate. But immediately after the war, with the pillars of the zaibatsu

---

SNAPSHOT: The Mitsui Group

Executive council: Nimoku-kai

Founded: October, 1961

Membership: 26 companies

Average cross-shareholding ratio: 19 percent

Number of affiliates (10 percent equity ownership): 171

---

destroyed, the group foundered. The bank, always an aristocrat in its own eyes, was slow to shift to the idea of retail banking, and when it did, the public did not flock to put their savings in what had been the Imperial Bank during the war.

Perhaps the Group's two most important assets were the redoubtable Mitsui Bussan, which regrouped during the 1950s and in most respects took over as group leader, and the one thing the Allies couldn't take away from Mitsui, its prestige. Before the war the Mitsui clan was the most prominent family outside the Imperial Palace, and its status has changed little despite the vast changes in Japanese society since that time. Even in recent years, when the Imperial princes came of age, likely candidates from within the Mitsui family were inevitably among the first to appear in the Tokyo press as the most suitable matches for any forthcoming marriage.

What does having a family lineage suitable enough to ally with that of the Imperial Household have to do with a modern keiretsu? In a word, everything.

There is an old saying about the three industrial zaibatsu groups, one to which we will refer often: For people, Mitsui; for organization, Mitsubishi; for unity, Sumitomo. Simple though it sounds, it tells a great deal about how these enormous keiretsu are perceived, and even today it still explains much about how they actually operate. "For people, Mitsui" has a double meaning. From its earliest days, the Mitsui zaibatsu was famous for hiring "the best and the brightest" from the nation's top universities, adding a little polish, and producing sophisticated, internationally minded top executives. Mitsui companies still hire some of the cream of the best schools (as do the other keiretsu) and quite a few from upper-crust families. But this is not the real meaning of "For people, Mitsui." Rather, it refers to a business empire built in part through impeccable social credentials.

If the expression "It's not what you know, but who you know that counts" is still true in our own society, it is three times as true in Japan.

Illustrations in Chapter 5 are by Jeffrey Klein.

Main Members of the Mitsui Group

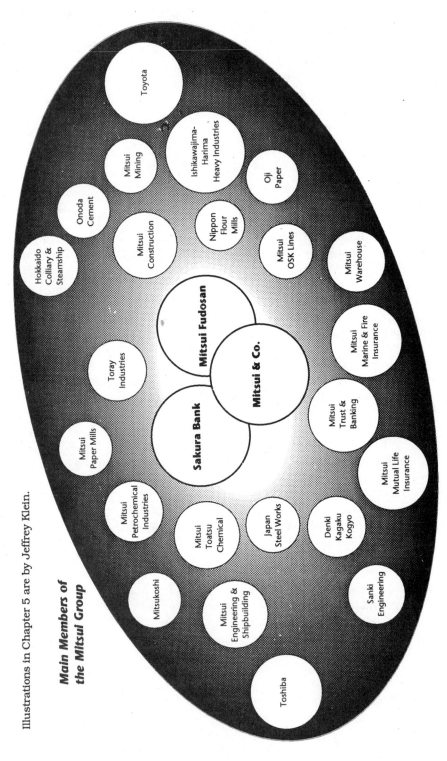

Senior Japanese executives have only two assets: their experience in managing their companies and something called *jinmyaku*, or a network of personal connections. Jinmyaku is what we would mean by "the best Rolodex in Tokyo," and top Mitsui managers are famous for it, at home and abroad.

To run a company well in Japan, one needs high-placed contacts extending throughout the business world, the government bureaucracy, into national and local politics, and even overseas. A familiarity with the Imperial Household is not a handicap. Despite the "democratization" of Japan, there is still a place in Japanese business for people with good social credentials. And no name in the country still symbolizes social standing, high-level connections, and a solid foundation in business like Mitsui.

The Main Bank.   The clearest sign of the Mitsui Group's fate in the postwar years is the poor showing of Mitsui Bank. Precisely because of its patrician, government-connected Imperial Bank image, the bank did not prosper in the way that its ex-zaibatsu rivals did. Its eighth place ranking among the Japanese city banks was an ignominious position for what had once been the ultimate powerhouse among Japan's financial institutions. In 1990 the bank finally managed to regain some of the importance, if not exactly the stature, it had lost long ago, but doing so required an even greater sacrifice of Mitsui pride. In April of that year Mitsui merged with another middleweight, the Taiyo Kobe Bank (itself the product of a merger many years before) to form the second largest bank in the world. In April, 1992 it mercifully renamed itself Sakura Bank. The loss of the prestigious Mitsui name was no doubt a blow to group pride, but not being counted among the top banks in the nation was a far greater insult to bear. These days Sakura Bank is second only to DKB in fund volume, and when combined with the group's trust bank, Mitsui Trust & Banking, leads all other groups in lending. Moreover, the Mitsui connections behind the new cherry blossom logo are still well understood throughout the Japanese business world.

The Shosha.   With the bank's power eclipsed in the postwar era, group leadership fell to its old rival, Mitsui Bussan (Mitsui & Co). Bussan had dozens of offices around the globe before World War I, and its international prowess has always been one of the group's main strengths. Today it has 160 offices and almost 500 subsidiaries and affiliates overseas, plus hundreds more in Japan. Although it is ranked fourth in sales among the top six shosha, Bussan is a major player in every field. It leads all traders in areas such as chemicals and steel, and is strong in developing liquefied natural gas—an increasingly important energy source for oil-starved

Japan. Bussan has close ties with Unisys Corp. (U.S.); together they set up Nippon Unisys, which uses Bussan's services to import and distribute computers in Japan. In addition, Bussan represents aircraft maker McDonnell Douglas and Bell Helicopter (Textron). One of the firm's old divisions was spun off back in the 1920s as a separate trading house, Tomen. Though completely independent of Bussan and allied with a smaller city bank (Tokai), Tomen still maintains ties with the Mitsui Group.

Presidential Council. The Group's top executive round table is called the *Nimoku-kai* (Second-Thursday Club), and consists of 26 core companies. With cavalier disrespect for its name, it meets on the first Thursday of each month. In addition, there is a larger conference, the *Getsuyo-kai* (Monday Club) which meets on the second Monday of each month. This lower group, which is a working-level meeting to supplement the presidential council, is open to the executive managing directors of 78 group members and affiliates. The official chair of the Nimoku-kai rotates among three firms: Mitsui Bussan, Sakura Bank, and Mitsui Fudosan (real estate). At present, 12 of the group companies use the Mitsui name, notably less than in the other two of the Old Three. This is sometimes taken as a sign that Mitsui is less interested in keeping up the old-style keiretsu image. Not so. Two years ago, one of the core companies, Taisho Marine & Fire Insurance (Japan's third largest nonlife firm), changed its name back to Mitsui Marine & Fire. One interpretation of this is that the group has decided that giving the appearance of a "loose" keiretsu, such as Sanwa or DKB, is not the way it wants to go. As long as it has the Mitsui name and has regained one of the top spots in Japanese banking, it might as well make the most of its heritage.

The looseness of the Mitsui Group has worked to its advantage, however. One of the distinctive features of this group has been its ability to attract powerful "outside" members, that is, companies that have no formal Mitsui connections but behave like regular group members. Some very powerful companies that are not Mitsui "blood relations" have strong ties to the Group. For example, Toyota Motor, one of the largest companies in Japan, and the head of its own enormous group, is a full member of the Nimoku-kai. The common rationale for its alignment with Mitsui is that the group does not have another car maker under its umbrella (Mitsubishi has both its own offspring, Mitsubishi Motors, plus an adopted son, Honda; Sumitomo has Mazda; Fuyo has both Nissan and Subaru; Sanwa has Daihatsu, and DKB has Isuzu). All the same, any of the other keiretsu would gladly make room for Toyota, and if it chose, it could sit in with multiple keiretsu, as does Hitachi. Toyota prefers to stay where it is.

Another giant under the Mitsui roof but somewhat distant from the core of the company is Toshiba, a firm that had Mitsui financial backing almost a century ago. Toshiba adds a much-needed high-tech card to Mitsui's hand, which is a bit too flush with smokestack industries. Toshiba participates in MISCO, the Mitsui Information System Conference, a decade-old consortium of 80 companies, not all of them Mitsui Group firms, that works to promote advances in computer technology and networking.

Another important player in this image-enhancement role is Sony. Although not a member of the Mitsui Group, either as a core company or peripheral firm, Sony has long been close to Mitsui Bank. During the Occupation, when the chairman of the bank was forced to give up positions in all family-owned firms, he became chairman of the board at the little electronics firm. Even a decade ago Sony was borrowing heavily from Mitsui Bank. Today the company is large enough to finance through the capital markets, although when it borrows, Sakura Bank is its primary lender in the Big Six. Sakura and Mitsui Trust together still own about 7.5 percent of Sony's shares, and two Sakura Bank directors serve on Sony's board.

For all of Sony's proud independence, it takes advantage of its Mitsui connections when the need arises. For example, when the old "video wars" were raging and Japanese electronics makers had to take sides with either the Beta or VHS camp, Sony found itself short of friends. As one maker after another lined up on the VHS side, Sony encouraged Mitsui member Toshiba to support it, and Toshiba (much to its later regret) did so, producing Beta video equipment for several years before switching sides. It is interesting to see how far group "loyalty" can be stretched, especially when two firms are rivals in the same field and the one asking for assistance is not even an official member of the group. It also makes one wonder how much the upper echelons of the Mitsui Group would like to pull market-leader Sony into at least some kind of "observer" status in the Nimoku-kai that they agreed to use their influence with Toshiba to help their old friend out of a jam.

Summary. The Mitsui firms no longer have the kind of Midas touch that the family name imparted generations ago, but the core companies' ability to open the right doors is still remarkable. However, all its superb personal connections have not helped the group to avoid a series of unfortunate problems. First, it invested in a disastrous petrochemical project in Iran (destroyed, rebuilt, and destroyed again in the Iran-Iraq War); then it had to rally support for group member Toshiba when one of that firm's subsidiaries was caught in violation of COCOM trade regulations and despite the parent firm's ignorance of its subsidiary's transactions, the "Toshiba incident" erupted in the United States. Then the president of the Mitsukoshi department store was caught up in a scandal involving improper use of company funds and had to step down. In short, it has been a difficult decade for the Mitsui Group.

On the positive side, the Sakura Bank merger was not only a big plus for the group, but the post-merger indigestion (a syndrome that can last for decades in unfortunate cases) seems to be less severe than expected. There is also considerable talk of a merger between Mitsui Petrochemical and Mitsui Toatsu Chemical, two large firms in their own right, which would yield a major chemical power with international clout. Following the recent merger of Mitsui Oil and Mitsui Liquefied Gas and the retrogressive name change at Mitsui Marine & Fire Insurance, there are unmistakable signs that Mitsui is moving to reinforce its group identity. The next decade will determine whether or not the Mitsui keiretsu will ever see its strength and influence return to their past glory.

The Mitsubishi Group

SNAPSHOT: The Mitsubishi Group

Executive council: Kin'yokai

Founded: 1954

Membership: 29 companies

Average cross-shareholding ratio: 35 percent

Number of affiliates (10 percent equity ownership): 217

Profile. The reason people constantly use the Mitsubishi Group to illustrate points about the keiretsu is simple: more than any of its rivals, Mitsubishi epitomizes the old-style Japanese horizontal group. It is the largest industrial keiretsu in Japan; it has a very high level of equity cross-shareholding; directors are routinely exchanged among group companies (97 percent of shacho-kai members have directors loaned by other member firms); and the group itself has an unusually high degree of internal organization. Almost all of its 29 core companies sport the Mitsubishi name and the group's ubiquitous three-diamond logo. The Kin'yokai members alone have about $1 trillion in combined assets, and total group sales for

Main Members of the Mitsubishi Group

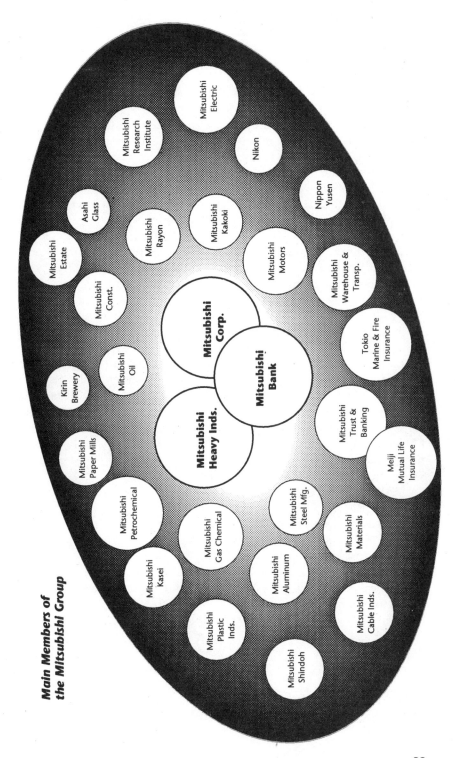

fiscal 1990 came to approximately $360 billion, a little over 3 percent of the total for the entire nation.

Like the other industrial zaibatsu, Mitsubishi profited from the government's emphasis on heavy industry in the postwar period. Things went fairly smoothly as long as its key group firms could depend on both government demand and steady orders from Japan's biggest firms. But things changed suddenly in the 1970s. Oil prices skyrocketed, Japanese industry went into a tailspin, and businesses big and small began to talk of "restructuring." The result was the low-energy consumption, high-tech manufacturing boom of the 1970s and early 1980s. This was a good period for innovative manufacturers aiming for overseas markets, young companies like Sony and Honda, but lean times for the stodgy, old smokestack industries that had been the backbone of the Mitsubishi Group. Many of the group companies had to undergo radical changes during this period, even laying off staff and severely trimming operations.

The middle of the 1980s brought better times, however, backed by a strong yen, cheap oil, and tremendous capital investment throughout Japanese industry. Mitsubishi Heavy Industries (MHI) became a favored stock during the wild bull market of the late 1980s, the number one defense contractor (Japan has one of the world's biggest military budgets), as well as a maker of rockets for Japan's space program, automobiles (one of its divisions became Mitsubishi Motors), and a wide variety of industrial equipment. By the end of the decade, the group was trying to change its conservative image, in part through the internationalization of its interests. Mitsubishi Real Estate, one of the least aggressive of Japan's big property firms, struck a much-publicized deal with the Rockefeller Group, and newly independent Mitsubishi Motors tied up with Volvo.

All the same, Mitsubishi's greatest strengths are mostly in rapidly aging industries, and people still generally think of the group in terms of oil, steel, chemicals, machinery, and so on. True, none of these businesses is going to disappear tomorrow, but the group is beginning to work together to develop a slightly more high-tech image for the Three Diamonds. In 1985 the entire Kin'yokai membership formed a cooperative venture called Space Communications. A few years later it launched its first telecommunications satellite. If Mitsubishi's hopes were already in orbit, its "heavy" industrial image brought them crashing down. Space Communications' second satellite never got off the ground, and the first one malfunctioned and was shut down. Mitsubishi will be back in the game, of course, but to observers the setback is symbolic.

The Main Bank. Mitsubishi Bank is the archetype of the Japanese financial institution—large, international, and a tad stodgy. Though only the fifth-largest bank in terms of fund volume, Mitsubishi is undoubtedly the most respected among the Big Six. In an era when bank scandals seem to occur with depressing frequency and other corporate scandals often point back to complicity by a firm's main bank, Mitsubishi has somehow managed to stay clear of the flying mud. It is old and somewhat conservative, which is one reason why its assets and profitability trail the industry leaders, but it has maintained a surprisingly clean image for an institution of that size.

Needless to say, the bank has tremendous clout in the marketplace, and its personnel selection is tops in the Mitsubishi Group. It is not only one of the most sought-after placements for elite college grads, but also a favorite spot for Ministry of Finance officials to steer their sons. A little over 20 years ago there were serious plans for Mitsubishi to merge with the even older Dai-Ichi Bank, but when the plan was leaked to the press, it became the focus of bitter internal strife at Dai-Ichi and was dropped (Dai-Ichi did pull off a successful merger a few years later to form what is now DKB). That incident is now well in the past, but it must irk some Mitsubishi managers that the bank missed a golden opportunity to expand overnight into the world's largest bank. Then there is the extensive keiretsu that Dai-Ichi Bank would have added to the Mitsubishi fold, another lost opportunity.

Mitsubishi Bank would still like to grow, but none of the smaller, unattached city banks are all that attractive. There is perennial talk that it will someday form an alliance with the Bank of Tokyo (BOT), once the nation's exclusive foreign exchange bank and still an unofficial extension of the Ministry of Finance, but BOT is strong in Third World lending, something any bank already saddled with mountains of bad debt at home would do well to avoid. If Mitsubishi does effect a tie-up with any domestic institution in the coming few years (which seems unlikely), it will probably be with one of the better regional banks.

A few years ago, Mitsubishi became the first Japanese bank to list on the New York Stock Exchange. This is something few of the other city banks will rush to do, as it means issuing regular reports in line with SEC regulations—a far cry from Japanese banks' policy of releasing as little information as possible about the state of their financial health and doctoring much of that until the last line of their annual reports should read, "and the depositors lived happily ever after."

The Shosha. The Mitsubishi Group's trading house is Mitsubishi Shoji, or Mitsubishi Corp. in English. Shoji, like bussan, means something like "commerce," and there are thousands of companies big and small with one or the other term in their names. But just as "Bussan" alone inevitably refers to Mitsui Bussan, "Shoji" when used alone points to Mitsubishi. Although firms such as Itochu (formerly C. Itoh) attract more attention due to their lead in overall sales, Mitsubishi Shoji is by far the largest firm in terms of operations. It has about 450 subsidiaries and affiliates in Japan and another 375 overseas. Total consolidated assets at the end of fiscal 1991 were roughly $80 billion, of which the parent firm accounted for about $58 billion (about 25 percent higher than the figure for Itochu).

"For organization, Mitsubishi" goes the saying, and Shoji's power as an organizer of group business is tremendous. It buys over 20 percent of all goods and services produced by the Mitsubishi Group companies—an awesome feat in itself—then acts as distributor, exporter, and agent to bring these products to market. Of course, the raw materials and finished goods it brings into the group are also a key part of its business. Group firms account for roughly 10 percent of Shoji's sales.

The firm also likes to play the role of a key coordinator for group activities, although it sometimes winds up with egg on its face in the process. Shoji was instrumental in putting together the tie-up between the Mitsubishi Group and Germany's celebrated Daimler-Benz A.G. Group. The accord was announced with great fanfare in March of 1990, when the two groups said they would be looking into the possibility of tie-ups in 11 areas, including electronics, autos, defense, and aerospace. According to insider reports, Shoji was anxious to show that it could lead the group as well as simply coordinate distribution, and the idea of a tie-up between two of the biggest keiretsu in the world seemed sufficiently impressive. Unfortunately, neither the Daimler-Benz people nor the other Mitsubishi companies who were rushed into the agreement seem to know exactly what it is supposed to achieve. Three years after the announcement the only visible result is that Mitsubishi Motors and Daimler-Benz are supposed to be engaged in joint R&D. For its part, the German firm was so concerned that it might appear to be forming an exclusive link with the Mitsubishi companies that it promptly signed tie-up agreements with a number of other European firms.

The failure of this one grandiose stunt should not, however, detract from Shoji's success in expanding operations overseas. For example, when the group decided to develop its global capability in the chemicals field, Shoji initiated a friendly takeover of Aristech Chemical in the United States, the first time for a Japanese trading company to do a successful cross-border acquisition on a large scale. By any estimation, Shoji is a powerhouse of a trading company. It has enough capital to start a mid-sized bank with a huge international branch network, and it is backed by the resources of the entire Mitsubishi Group.

Presidential Council. The Group's inner circle of chief executives, the *Kin'yokai* (Friday meeting), gathers on the second Friday of each month for lunch and "to listen to noted speakers" discuss subjects of national concern. Like Mitsui, there is also a *Getsuyo-kai* (Monday meeting), but this one brings together the somu bucho or managers of the general affairs departments of each Kin'yokai member. Usually it is the somu bucho who handles the day-to-day affairs of a company, making him something like a junior CEO. The parallel meetings of the presidents and the general affairs managers shows once again Mitsubishi's organizational strength.

The Kin'yokai consists of 29 companies, 23 of them flying the Mitsubishi logo, all sharing in each other's equity, and all having at least one director from another Mitsubishi company. The nucleus of the group is a trio comprised of Mitsubishi Bank, Mitsubishi Shoji, and Mitsubishi Heavy Industries. Just outside the nucleus are other key members, such as Mitsubishi Trust & Banking, Meiji Mutual Life Insurance, and Tokio Marine & Fire Insurance on the financial side, plus Mitsubishi Electric on the industrial side. Beyond the 29 core firms are other affiliates, such as the two we noted earlier, the Morimoto Group (NGK Insulators, NGK Spark Plug, Noritake, Toto, and INAX) and the Shimadzu Group (Shimadzu Seisakusho, Japan Storage Battery, and others). At the periphery are companies that have long-standing relations either with Mitsubishi Bank or with other key members of the group. This includes Nikko Securities (one of Japan's Big Four brokers) and Honda Motor Co. The Kin'yokai is also unique in that it includes the group's think tank. All the big keiretsu have private research facilities to support their operations, but the Mitsubishi Research Institute is the only one to be granted the status of a full member of the presidential council.

Summary. The Mitsubishi Group roster reads like a "Who's Who" of leading Japanese companies, and these several firms are more accustomed to working together than are those in most other giant keiretsu. Surprisingly, it is still shoring up some of its weaker parts to make the fortress even stronger. In 1990 Mitsubishi Mining and Mitsubishi Cement merged to create a more powerful new firm, Mitsubishi Materials. This increase in group strength can be a tremendous asset for business, but it also attracts a lot of attention, especially at a time when antikeiretsu sentiment is building. With the U.S. government (among others) worried about the negative influence of such groups, the group's Public Relations Committee has its work cut out for it. The Mitsubishi companies have avoided becoming involved in the scandals of recent years, partly as a result of good, conservative management. However, their very success in reforming the group into a modern version of the old Mitsubishi zaibatsu has made them an easy target for criticism both at home and abroad.

The Sumitomo Group

SNAPSHOT: The Sumitomo Group

Executive council: Hakusui-kai

Founded: April, 1951

Membership: 20 companies

Average cross-shareholding ratio: 27 percent

Number of affiliates (10 percent equity ownership): 164

Profile. In looking at the history of the zaibatsu we noted that Sumitomo began as a mining concern and was relatively slow to modernize. It spent much of its early history trying to catch up to its Tokyo-based rivals. Those days are gone. The Occupation may not have completely eliminated zaibatsu influence on the Japanese economy, but it was a great leveler: all the big groups were broken up and forced to start over again with their commercial banks at the hub. To the old Tokyo concerns that had run Japan's finance and industry for generations, this was almost too great a blow to bear, but for Sumitomo it meant a new beginning, a chance to start on a "level playing field," as it were.

While Mitsui and Mitsubishi were still in shock over the loss of their empires, the Sumitomo companies wasted no time in regrouping. Their presidential council was actually formed while the Occupation was still underway, three full years before the Mitsubishi keiretsu officially came into being. The old saying about the three groups ends with "... and for unity, Sumitomo." This is a bit of an understatement. The Sumitomo companies sometimes look more like a close-knit family than an industrial group. Most of the core firms have their headquarters within a few blocks of each other in the same part of downtown Osaka, but their management sometimes gives the impression that they are all in the same building. The group's average cross-shareholding ratio is 27 percent, second highest of the Big Six, and directors are commonly sent to other group firms. The Sumitomo Group is unique in that the top shareholder of every core firm is another Sumitomo company.

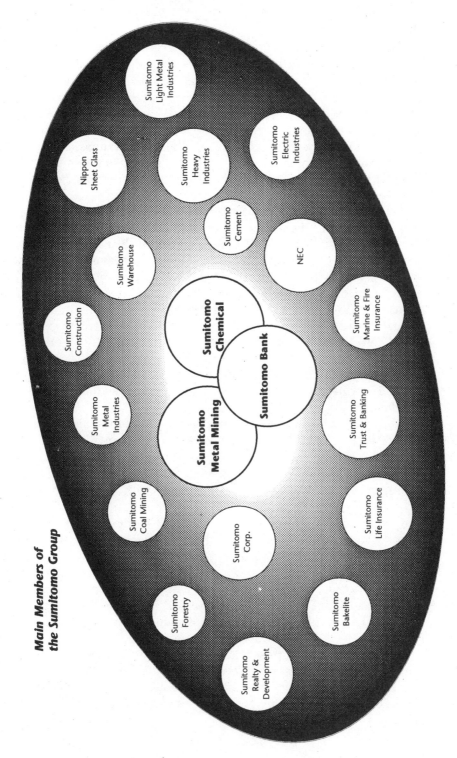

**Main Members of
the Sumitomo Group**

The Main Bank. Though ranked only third in terms of assets, Sumitomo Bank is often the most profitable of Japan's huge city banks. The explanation for this is written in stone: when you ask any banker, Japanese or foreign, about Sumitomo, they invariably reply that the bank is "aggressive." The interpretation of this is up to the listener. It is a fact that where most city banks prefer to lend only to large corporations and let their trading companies or finance affiliates handle loans to the smaller firms, Sumitomo has a reputation for eagerly scouting out loan candidates even among small- and medium-sized businesses.

Back in the go-go 1980s, Sumitomo was one of Japan's most aggressive city banks in the global merger and acquisition game. To further develop its capabilities, in 1986 it invested roughly half a billion dollars to to buy a piece of Goldman Sachs. Sumitomo may have believed it was buying 100 percent cooperation in "financial technology," the know-how that Goldman used to compete in one of the world's toughest markets, but Goldman thought otherwise. Sumitomo sank a fortune into what it thought was a partnership, one that would turn it into Japan's top international bank. Instead it got an equity position in a major New York investment bank, and little else. For a firm with Sumitomo's pride and a fierce need to keep up its "hardball" image at home, this was not the kind of publicity it needed. Heads rolled in the bank after the extent of the Goldman fiasco came to light.

The bank is universally respected, for its profitability, its street smarts, and its aggressiveness. It has played "company doctor" to more than a dozen firms in the past decade or so, and some of its turnarounds have been near miracles. That takes more than clout. Sumitomo has good managers and it knows how to run a business with an eye on the bottom line.

Sumitomo has always touted its "most profitable bank" status as proof of superior management, and there is certainly something to be said there. In 1986, it absorbed a large regional bank with enormous debts. Everyone thought that would be the end of Sumitomo's profitability for most of a decade. One year later it was back on top. There is no question that the bank is one of the outstanding players in Japanese business and the leader of a powerful group of related companies.

The Shosha. In prewar days, Sumitomo was unique among the large zaibatsu in not having its own major trading company. The group's current shosha only came into existence about six years after the war. Its direct lineage is not to a trading firm at all, but to building and real estate concerns in the Kansai area. From these rather inauspicious beginnings, the current Sumitomo Shoji or "Sumisho" (Sumitomo Corp. in English) was created.

Before this time the Sumitomo companies had used two old Osaka traders, Itochu Shoji and Marubeni (prior to 1949 the two had been one company) to support their activities. During the 1950s Sumisho was still much too small to threaten this arrangement, and Itochu and Marubeni were too busy competing with each other to notice the little upstart company. By the 1960s, however, Sumisho was growing very quickly thanks to unified support from its group companies. Sumitomo Bank gradually alienated Marubeni, pushing it further into the arms of the Fuyo Group, while Itochu gradually grew more distant from Sumitomo as the group's own trader flexed its muscles. By the 1970s Itochu and Sumitomo had effected an amicable separation and Sumisho had become the sole agent for Sumitomo Group companies.

And that is a business in itself. According to FTC figures, Sumisho buys fully one-third of the output of group companies (excluding financial firms, of course), and group firms make up more than 13 percent of its total annual sales. These are the highest in-group transaction figures for any of the Big Six shosha, proving once again that Sumitomo's ability to function as a tight-knit group can have tremendous advantages. Consider that Sumisho did not exist until about 40 years ago, while firms like Bussan and Shoji were already controlling Japanese imports and exports around the time of World War I. In that short period, Sumitomo Corp. has become the number two shosha in terms of sales, a feat perhaps no other firm could have accomplished. Predictably, the company is strongest in fields where the Sumitomo Group is strong: metals, steel, chemicals, and machinery. Just as predictably, it is one of the most profitable of the shosha.

Presidential Council. The core of the Sumitomo Group is the *Hakusui-kai* (literally White Water Club). Even most Japanese don't know why the group has this funny name, but the two characters for *haku + sui* if joined vertically become *Izumi*, the name of the copper business that began the Sumitomo fortune more than 300 years ago. The Hakusui-kai currently contains 20 members. It meets in both Tokyo and Osaka in alternate months, and its meetings are said to last only about an hour (a tribute to Sumitomo efficiency). The "unity" for which the group is famous is immediately visible from a quick glance at the list of core members: 18 of the 20 carry the Sumitomo name. Actually, it would have been 19 of 20, but after the war Sumitomo Communications Industries decided to get rid of its zaibatsu-sounding moniker and return to its old name Nippon Electric Co. Today it is known all over the world by its initials, NEC.

Like Mitsubishi, the nucleus of the Sumitomo Group is a trio, but instead of the group's main bank, shosha, and one large industrial company, Sumitomo's triumvirate consists of the main bank plus two large industrial firms, Sumitomo Metal Industries, one of the nation's top steel makers, and Sumitomo Chemical, one of the largest comprehensive chemical producers. Beyond the core companies such as NEC and Sumisho, are affiliates and "independent" firms that like to stay close to the Sumitomo umbrella. These include Asahi Breweries, Mazda Motors, and Kajima Construction.

One characteristic of the group that is at least as well known as its unity is its quest for profit. Although Sumitomo companies may not be the biggest firms in their sectors, they are often the most profitable and most of the firms boast exceptionally strong balance sheets. Cross-shareholding among the companies is relatively high, and the ratio of assigned directors is about average, but the sense of group identity is much stronger than the figures would suggest. Despite getting a "new deal" after the war, the group still seems to be trying to catch up in both size and prestige with its old rivals, and so there is added incentive for its member firms to be more competitive.

Summary. The Sumitomo name is as old as Mitsui and its group was always one of the biggest in Japan. In many ways it has held its "family" together better than Mitsui, and its bank never had to suffer the ignominy of a merger to pump up its status. Yet Sumitomo seems forever to have a chip on its shoulder.

Many of the Sumitomo companies are leaders in their fields and individually many of them are highly respected. But the group's identity ultimately emanates from the bank, and Sumitomo Bank's way of doing business has become something of a PR liability for the rest of the group. People talk about "unity" as the group's hallmark, but the truth is that unity is sometimes enforced from above. The same tactics that occasionally land the bank on the front page of the newspapers, rather than the financial page, have spread to the real estate firm and others in the group. This is not only to their own detriment but to that of the rest of the member companies as well.

Granted all this, Sumitomo Bank is still one of the strongest, most important banks in the country, and most of its group companies are among the best in the nation. Compared to the New Three keiretsu, or even rival Mitsui, the group works together like a well-oiled machine. With a change in orientation at the center, the Sumitomo Group could remain profitable, continue to expand its various market shares, and also be even more respected than it already is.

The Fuyo Group

SNAPSHOT: The Fuyo Group

Executive council: Fuyo-kai

Founded: January 1966

Membership: 29 companies (27 companies full-time)

Average cross-shareholding ratio: 15 percent

Number of affiliates (10 percent equity ownership): 223

Profile. We noted before that the Fuyo Group has at its core the center of the old "financial zaibatsu," the Yasuda group. While Yasuda Bank chose not to return to its old name after the Occupation, Yasuda Trust & Banking, Yasuda Life Insurance, and Yasuda Fire and Marine Insurance all retain the old zaibatsu name. In addition, many of its old zaibatsu subsidiaries came along for the ride: Fuyo Group member Toho Rayon came from a Yasuda zaibatsu company called Teikoku Sen'i; the current Showa Kaiun (Showa Line) is descended from the zaibatsu's old shipping line, Toyo Kisen; and both electronics maker Oki Denki and real estate developer Tokyo Tatemono were group members in the prewar days as well.

There is nothing remarkable in the fact that the nucleus of the Fuyo Group is directly descended from a famous zaibatsu. What is unusual about Fuyo is that in addition to rebuilding the core of the old Yasuda group, it somehow became a shelter for wayward zaibatsu orphans. A number of large companies from various smaller zaibatsu managed to survive the Occupation in one form or another, but had no relation to any of the Big Four. To build their businesses they needed to borrow from a bank, and Mitsui, Mitsubishi, and Sumitomo were already committed to their own firms. So what was a big steel maker like NKK (a former member of the Asano zaibatsu) to do?

The steel business grew rapidly in the later 1950s, but trying to go it alone against the quasi-government colossus Nippon Steel or the big steel firms belonging to the Old Three keiretsu would be commercial suicide. Fortunately, the old Yasuda group was strong in finance but weak in heavy industry, while the Asano zaibatsu had no main bank. This left both Fuji Bank and NKK with something valuable to offer the other, and soon enough Fuji became the steel maker's main lender and NKK slipped into the Fuyo Group.

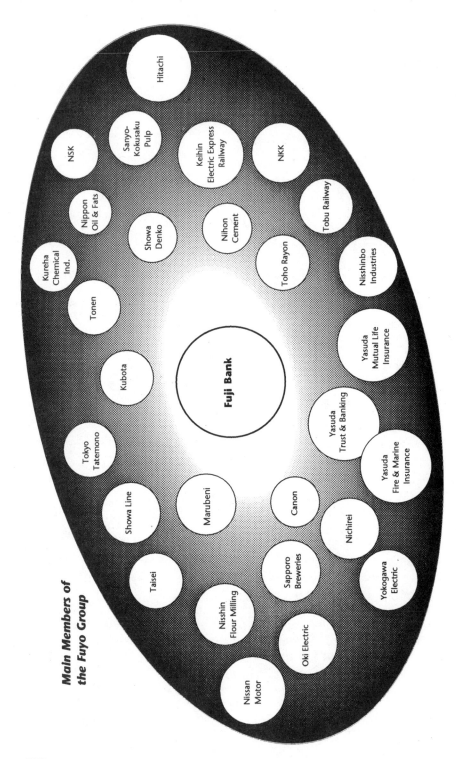

Main Members of the Fuyo Group

Fuji Bank

Hitachi
NSK
Sanyo-Kokusaku Pulp
Keihin Electric Express Railway
NKK
Nippon Oil & Fats
Showa Denko
Nihon Cement
Tobu Railway
Kureha Chemical Ind.
Tonen
Toho Rayon
Nisshinbo Industries
Kubota
Yasuda Mutual Life Insurance
Tokyo Tatemono
Yasuda Trust & Banking
Showa Line
Marubeni
Yasuda Fire & Marine Insurance
Canon
Taisei
Nichirei
Nisshin Flour Milling
Sapporo Breweries
Yokogawa Electric
Nissan Motor
Oki Electric

But Asano wasn't the only old group without a strong main bank. There was the Okura zaibatsu, the Nissan "new zaibatsu" of the 1930s, the wartime Daiken Sangyo, the Nezu zaibatsu, the Mori zaibatsu, and others. There were survivors from each group drifting about after the war, with industrial prowess to offer but desperately in need of a strong main bank. Over the next decade one company after another came under Fuji's umbrella.

Nippon Cement joined from the Asano zaibatsu. Taisei Construction came from the Okura zaibatsu. Daiken Sangyo provided the Marubeni trading house. The breakup of the Nissan group contributed Nissan Motor, food maker Nichirei, chemical maker Nippon Oil and Fats, and electronic machinery giant Hitachi (which first joined the Fuyo Group before sharing its favors with the Sanwa and DKB). From the Nezu zaibatsu came Nisshin Flour Milling, Nisshinbo Industries, NSK, and Tobu Railway, and from the Mori zaibatsu came Showa Denko. Thus, the Fuyo Group combined the financial power of the old Yasuda zaibatsu with the industrial base of a dozen others which did not survive the Occupation. This was a good marriage for both sides, and within just a few years it made Fuyo a major player in Japanese industry, something the old Yasuda group never achieved.

As the group began to grow in the 1960s (it only formalized its shacho-kai in 1966), more companies decided to get under its wing, including such major firms as Canon, Sapporo Beer, and machinery maker Kubota. This gave the Fuyo Group a collection of solid, well-established industries with their own vertical keiretsu, some of which are quite large (the Taisei Group alone consists of 80 companies, the NKK Group has 95 firms, the Canon Group about 100). The Fuyo Group's big achievement is that it doesn't look like a bunch of old industrial zaibatsu firms. In other words, Fuji Bank's postwar makeover has been successful. The group looks and feels like a big horizontal keiretsu, but it doesn't project an image of old shipbuilders, steel companies, and chemicals plants the way three of its rivals do.

The Main Bank. Fuji Bank is ranked fourth in total fund volume, and is usually right behind Sumitomo in profitability. This seems to irk the bank's management. Observers say that Fuji worries more about Sumitomo than do the other city banks, and many believe that Fuji wants to be number one. The bank emphasizes trading and appears anxious to get into the securities business legally now that the Ministry of Finance is opening the door. It is also active in international finance. Fuji purchased the Walter E. Heller group in California to add a U.S.–based financial advisory, and bought Kleinwort Benson Government Securities to obtain a primary dealership for U.S. Treasury securities. In addition, the bank has a tie-up with James Wolfensohn, the elite investment house that is now home to former Federal Reserve Board Chairman Paul Volker (who is extremely well-known in Japanese business circles).

The Shosha. Marubeni is one of Japan's top traders, ranking third in total sales behind its old rival and newcomer Sumitomo Shoji. Unlike the other firms, which tend to be overweighted in specific fields (two-thirds of Sumisho's sales are in metals and machinery), Marubeni is well balanced, with roughly a quarter of its sales coming from metals & minerals, a quarter from machinery & construction, and a quarter from energy & chemicals. Textiles still account for about 10 percent of its business. Marubeni has about 150 offices and over 300 subsidiaries and affiliates outside of Japan. It is also involved in numerous cooperative ventures with the other big shosha.

Perhaps the most interesting feature of Marubeni from our perspective is its relative lack of clout in the Fuyo Group. This is not to say the firm has no influence—quite the contrary—but where we might expect to find Fuji Bank and Marubeni together in the group's nucleus, we find only the bank. All the top shosha except Marubeni send directors to other firms in their groups—for example, almost 40 percent of all Mitsubishi Group firms have board members who originated in Mitsubishi Shoji. No directors from Marubeni are posted to any core group firms. Although the trader buys about 10 percent of the group's total output, which is a higher percentage than the shosha in either the DKB or Sanwa Groups, in-group purchases account for only 2 percent of Marubeni's sales, the lowest in the Big Six. It certainly appears to outside observers as if Marubeni is trying hard to be the Fuyo Group's trader, but the group has not been responding.

Presidential Council. There are a total of 29 companies in the official *Fuyo-kai*, the group executives' monthly luncheon meeting (*fuyo*, by the way, means hibiscus, a traditional Japanese allusion to nature, which doesn't smell at all like a nasty old zaibatsu; score one for the PR department). At the same time that the Fuyo-kai was formalized, a second-tier meeting, the *Fuji-kai*, was created. This group also meets once a month and is open to one managing director, senior managing director or vice president from each Fuyo-kai member company. There is yet another parallel meeting, this one for the managers of the planning divisions at each of the 29 companies, and it also meets once a month. There is an even bigger (67 companies) meeting, the *Fuyo Kondan-kai*, designed to introduce the members' new products and services to the rest of the group and to help managers from the different companies get to know each other (interestingly, this group was started two years before the Fuyo-kai came into being). No one can fault the group for a lack of central organization.

All the New Three keiretsu have part-time members. The biggest is Hitachi, which has seats on all three shacho-kai, but they all have at least one more. In the Fuyo Group the other "floating" member is Nissan Motor Co. Although Nissan is a full member of the Fuyo-kai, not an "observer" as Toyota likes to be called, it also has very strong ties with the Industrial Bank of Japan, which was a major lender both before and after the war. Even without Hitachi and Nissan, the group is strong in electronics and machinery. The core firms include high-tech companies such as Canon, Oki Electric, and Yokogawa Electric, (plus affiliates such as Yokogawa Medical Systems, and Japan Radio), and machinery leaders like Kubota and bearing maker NSK. Another strong suit is construction, which is led by one of the industry's largest companies, Taisei Corp., and developer Tokyo Tatemono. Affiliates include Penta-Ocean Construction, Ohki Construction, Toa Corp., Maeda Corp., Nishimatsu Construction, and to a lesser extent, Tobishima Corp. The group also has three food companies, three chemical companies, and two railroads, a pretty well-rounded keiretsu for a group that got off to a late start.

Summary. In recent years the Fuyo group has been trying to look more like a real keiretsu (i.e., like its three ex-zaibatsu rivals) instead of a loose collection of borrowers. As it begins to function more as a group, there is a greater emphasis for member companies to use each other's goods and services (Fuyo members are not as loyal to Sapporo beer as Mitsubishi employees are to Kirin or Sumitomo employees to Asahi) and also to cooperate on joint projects. The group is currently active in the Tokyo Teleport project, one of many gigantic developments in the capital's waterfront district. It also has a special group to study the business potential of China, another on information systems, and others focused on both the new Kansai and Chubu (Nagoya) airport projects.

Ultimately, because of its structure, the success of the group will depend to a great extent on the bank itself. Fuji Bank is still one of Japan's largest, and most profitable. But if it truly intends to build a cohesive group and to operate internationally, the bank must pull its group members together and give them a stronger group identity.

The Sanwa Group

Profile. While the Sumitomo Group has long been the standard-bearer of companies in the Kansai region, it is not the only Kansai-based keiretsu. A newer group centered around Sanwa Bank has provided an

---

SNAPSHOT: The Sanwa Group

Executive council: Sansui-kai

Founded: February 1967

Membership: 44 (originally 24) companies (49 companies full-time)

Average cross-shareholding ratio: 16.5 percent

Number of affiliates (10 percent equity ownership): 247

---

alternative for dozens of Kansai firms that do not bear the Sumitomo name. However, Sanwa is not exactly a "new" bank. It was formed in December of 1933 by the merger of three smaller banks, each with a long history of its own (one of them was established in 1878, only two years after Mitsui Bank). The combined power of these banks provided a stronger base to compete with Osaka financial institutions like Sumitomo Bank and the old Nomura Bank.

Osaka was still the center of Japanese commerce before the war, and Sanwa began by supporting the textile companies that made up much of the area's business. Sanwa Bank lent to firms such as Teikoku Jinzo Kenshi (later abbreviated to Teijin), formerly a subsidiary of the Kansai-based Suzuki zaibatsu. When Mitsui and Mitsubishi helped topple the Suzuki group, the subsidiaries were up for grabs. Teijin managed to avoid being swallowed by either of the big Tokyo zaibatsu, but it needed financing to stay afloat. Sanwa Bank stepped in, and a long-term relationship was born. Sixty years later, Teijin is the nation's number one maker of polyester fibers and a core member of the Sanwa Group.

After the war, as Sanwa made efforts to expand its client list, it was essential to attract heavy industries. Through a massive lending program, it seduced companies like Kobe Steel, Hitachi Zosen (shipbuilding), and Sekisui Chemical into its sphere of influence. All are important firms in their fields and now all are members of Sanwa's inner circle.

Although the Sanwa Group is noticeably looser than the Old Three groups, it is well-rounded in terms of industrial sectors and has surprising depth in a number of areas. It is known for tremendous financial resources, thanks to core member Nippon Life Insurance and family-friend Nomura Securities, both Osaka-based, and both the biggest firms in their respective fields.

The Main Bank. For many years Sanwa kept a low profile outside of industrial circles. People thought of the bank as a commercial lender, not

Main Members of the Sanwa Group

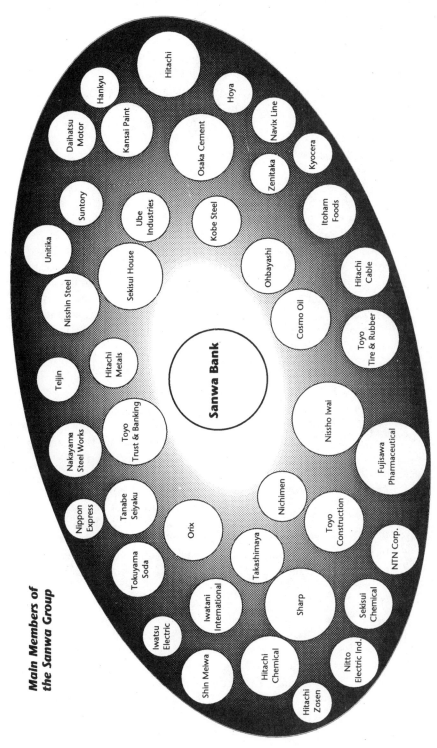

the friendly bank on the corner—especially not in Tokyo. All that has been changing recently. For one thing, the bank's main office is still in the center of Osaka, reassuring old clients that nothing has changed, but its legal headquarters is now in Otemachi, the financial center of Tokyo. This is also a clear declaration that the bank is a major player in both domestic and international markets.

In 1984, Sanwa bought Continental Illinois Leasing in the United States. Two years later the bank's California subsidiary bought Lloyd's Bank of California. In 1988 the firm did a major internal reorganization aimed at turning Sanwa into a "universal bank" along the lines of the big German banks. It has since strengthened its investment banking and M&A businesses. Recently, it has even engineered a campaign to make Sanwa a popular street corner bank in Tokyo. New Sanwa branches and scores of automated teller outlets are popping up all over the capital. Sanwa will soon have the largest total number of outlets of any bank in Japan, topping even former leader Sakura. The message is clear: Sanwa wants to be seen, and it wants to attract new business, retail as well as commercial. In addition, its profitability has soared, boosting it (at least temporarily) past rival Sumitomo.

The bank is also reported to be active in developing international business through a unique strategy. It has become a major lender to world airlines, especially national carriers (including those in France, Germany, and Switzerland). The idea is not to put Sanwa into the aviation business, but to get its universal banking scheme off the ground in a multitude of world markets. The bank hopes that, because national flag carriers have the support of their governments and are well connected with important companies in their respective countries, they will make the ideal partners to introduce new clients in each target region. Another of the bank's specific targets is Indonesia, where Sanwa has been very active. A joint venture it established there with a local bank is now the largest bank in the nation. Considering the tremendous growth in the Indonesian economy and its importance to Japan, both as a manufacturing base and as a source of energy liquefied natural gas (LNG) imports, Sanwa's gambit looks like a smart move.

The Shosha. Sanwa is somewhat like the Fuyo Group in having only a bank in its nucleus. Yet Sanwa Bank goes farther than Fuji Bank in sharing at least some organizational responsibilities with its main group trading house, Nissho Iwai. One reason the group is not more strongly influenced by its shosha is that Nissho Iwai is a part-time member—it also sits on the shacho-kai of the DKB Group. However, since DKB has one of the top shosha (Itochu) in its nucleus, Nissho Iwai's loyalty is thought to lie closer to Sanwa. But the real reason the shosha is not more influential in the group is that it is not more influential in its own sector. Big though it is, Nissho Iwai is nowhere near as strong as the five giants. Unlike rivals Itochu and Marubeni, which were once part of a single company, Nissho Iwai was created through a merger of two smaller traders.

Sanwa Bank is acutely aware that its top trader can't really stand toe-to-toe with the likes of Mitsubishi Shoji or Itochu, and it has a plan to remedy the situation. There is another big shosha in the core of the Sanwa Group, the number eight general trader, Nichimen. Nichimen is big in metals, machinery, and lumber trading. It has about 80 overseas offices and is quite strong in Eastern Europe. To the bank's way of thinking, if one were to combine Nissho Iwai, which is strong in steel, aircraft, ships, LNG, and Southeast Asian operations, with Nichimen, the result would be a real group shosha with some serious clout. Just their combined sales would rank the firm in the top three, and if the synergies from the merger were nurtured properly, the firm could rival the big boys in every category. There's only one problem. Nichimen is a proud old Osaka firm with a history dating to 1892. The company somehow managed to remain independent through all the economic turmoil, zaibatsu wars, and keiretsu competition of the past century. It is not in a hurry to throw all that away and rush into anybody's arms, including Nissho Iwai's.

Still, the bank has many ways to influence its group members. Sanwa is Nichimen's number two shareholder (group companies account for all but one of the top five stockholders) and Nichimen's vice president is originally from Sanwa Bank. The bank will be patient, but sooner or later it will probably get its way, and the result will be a plus for the entire group. If and when the merger comes about, the new firm will most likely join the bank, forming a two-part nucleus like that in the DKB Group.

Presidential Council. The Sanwa Group shacho-kai is called the *Sansui-kai* (Third Wednesday Club). The group officially came together in 1967, just one year after the Fuyo-kai. Like Fuyo, the bank's keiretsu existed long before formalizing the relationship with a shacho-kai. But unlike Fuyo it has nearly doubled in size since then. In 1967 Sanwa had only 24 members. Today there are 44 companies in the Sansui-kai, and 53 in the overlapping *Clover-kai* (a parallel meeting for group vice presidents and senior managing directors), and Sanwa is still growing. There is also a study group on telecom networking systems (Sannet) with 71 member companies, a biotech research group (Sanbio) with 42 members, a China study group (62 member companies), a Japan development study group (54 companies), and a Kansai Airport study group (113 companies).

Because Sanwa Bank's aggressive lending policies over the years have often meant financing rival firms within the same sector, the group breaks the old zaibatsu rule of "one firm per sector." We have already noted the two trading firms, but there are also four construction firms in the Sansui-kai: Ohbayashi, Toyo, Zenitaka, and Sekisui House. Textile maker Unitika, Ltd., is almost as big as sector leader Teijin, and both are core members. Tanabe Seiyaku and Fujisawa Pharmaceutical are also rivals. If we look beyond the core members to the larger Clover-kai and other affiliates, we would find many more competitors under the Sanwa umbrella.

Why would major companies put up with being crowded in with their rivals in a single keiretsu? Part of the answer is Sanwa's role as the "default keiretsu" for Kansai, that is, the only option for Osaka-based companies that are not members of the Sumitomo Group. Earlier we noted the strong regional identities of Kanto and Kansai firms and the traces of a lingering rivalry between these two areas. On the surface of it, there is no reason why an Osaka firm that wanted to be part of a big keiretsu couldn't join a loose "modern" alliance such as the Fuyo group, or even a relatively loose "old" group such as Mitsui. Both groups have a strong banking presence all over the country, not just in Tokyo. But a lot of Osaka firms prefer to do business with other Osaka companies. Thus, important Kansai firms like Suntory (liquor), Hoya (optics), and Kyocera (electronics) have chosen to become associated with Sanwa because it's the only game in town. The Sumitomo Group is built like a fortress, and no one inside remembers where they put the "Welcome" mat. Besides, Sumitomo Bank has a reputation for keeping very close tabs on its group members, not something that more "casual" keiretsu firms would appreciate. Consequently, Osaka-area companies that want easy access to Big Six bank financing and connections with a major group have little choice but to tie up with Sanwa.

The irony is that Sanwa Bank is becoming less and less an old-time Osaka institution. We noted that its headquarters is in Tokyo and that the bank is working hard to expand its branch network and its image in the Tokyo area. In addition, the Sansui-kai meets in Tokyo in odd-numbered months and in Osaka in even-numbered months. This singular combination of identities in the two commercial capitals should make Sanwa even more attractive to newer, unaffiliated companies looking for a keiretsu.

Another distinctive characteristic of the Sanwa Group is its large number of part-time members. A few of the firms that joined the group in 1967 or later on also gravitated toward DKB when it suddenly became the biggest bank in Japan (and the world), and they joined the DKB Group when it formed in 1978. So, for example, we find not only Nissho Iwai in both groups, but also Kobe Steel and Nippon Express. Then, of course, there is the keiretsu butterfly, Hitachi, which is a member of both groups as well as the Fuyo Group.

Summary. Sanwa Group is in some ways one of the most interesting among the Big Six. It straddles the Tokyo and Osaka business communities, and although it has few number one companies, it is strong in critical sectors such as finance, construction, chemicals, steel, electronics, and commerce. Sumitomo will always be the standard-bearer Kansai keiretsu, but Sanwa has proved it can stand on its own and also attract important new members. There is every reason to believe the keiretsu will continue to grow in the years to come. And if it somehow engineers a merger between Nissho Iwai and Nichimen, the group will have a powerful shosha and a stronger nucleus.

The DKB (Dai-Ichi Kangyo Bank) Group

SNAPSHOT: The DKB Group

Executive council: Sankin-kai

Founded: January 1978

Membership: 48 companies (42 companies full-time)

Average cross-shareholding ratio: 12 percent

Number of affiliates (10 percent equity ownership): 190

Profile. DKB is the newest of the New Three keiretsu banks. In a sense, it is the only really "new" keiretsu, a product of the 1970s. That is to say, it is big and loosely organized. Its members meet infrequently and tend to be quite independent. All too often observers note that this is because Dai-Ichi Kangyo Bank is extremely young—the product of a merger in 1971—and imply that it has had little time to gather its own keiretsu. While it is true that the merged bank has only been around for a little over two decades, its two component parts, Dai-Ichi Bank and Nippon Kangyo Bank, have been in business since 1873 and 1897, respectively. In fact, as we saw earlier, the Dai-Ichi Bank was founded by Eiichi Shibusawa, who used the bank to form his own zaibatsu. In the process, Dai-Ichi became Japan's second biggest bank after Mitsui.

One of Shibusawa's friends in the early days was Ichibei Furukawa,

Main Members of the DKB Group

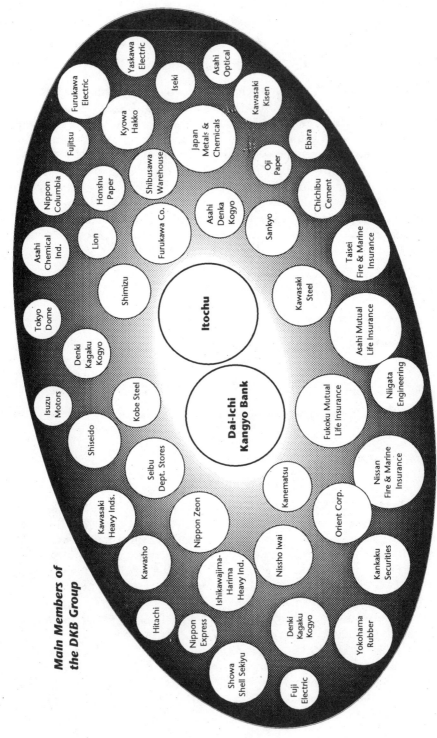

a merchant long on dreams but short on cash. Shibusawa's bank lent Furukawa a large sum to buy a copper mine, and with it he founded the Furukawa zaibatsu, leaving him forever indebted to his friend (and to his friend's bank). Shibusawa was also a patron of the Matsukata (often misnamed Kawasaki) zaibatsu. Many decades later, when Dai-Ichi Bank tied the knot with Nippon Kangyo Bank, it still had close ties with both the old Furukawa zaibatsu firms (Furukawa Electric, Fuji Electric, Nippon Light Metal, etc.) and the Matsukata firms (Kawasaki Steel, Kawasaki Heavy Industries, Kawasaki Kisen, etc.).

Though quite small compared to the Mitsubishi or Mitsui combines, the government-sponsored Nippon Kangyo Bank had its own lending keiretsu called "The 15 Companies," including firms like Honshu Paper, Denki Kagaku, and Sankyo pharmaceutical. It was also authorized by the government to manage the *takarakuji* national lottery, which is tremendously popular even today. While neither institution had the size or clout of the old Big Four zaibatsu banks, their combination created the largest bank in Japan, boasting long pedigrees, good connections with both government and industry, lots of capital, and the foundation on which to build a much larger keiretsu.

The Main Bank. Despite its venerable ancestry, the merger gave DKB a "born yesterday" image which proved very attractive to some of its clients. Like Sanwa in Osaka, Tokyo-based DKB provides a nexus for large companies with little or no zaibatsu ties who want to get some of the benefits of Big Six membership. Because of its "youth," the bank lacked a strong identity at its inception. This was no doubt one of the biggest attractions for companies that needed main-bank-style financing but preferred a minimum of group involvement with their businesses. The result is that DKB has acquired a very large clientele, many of whom have taken seats on its shacho-kai.

The bank, as large and powerful at it is, has a reputation in the industry as a follower rather than as a leader. For the first decade or so after the merger, the bank had a less than stellar reputation in the industry. Japanese mergers are always awkward (for example, instead of forming one central personnel department, they normally form three: one for company A staff, one for company B staff, and one for people who joined after the merger), and DKB was no exception. The merger created redundancy galore and had a serious impact on management efficiency. But that was years ago. Twenty-odd years into the new system there is a whole new class of DKB employees, many of whom have risen to middle-management positions. Today the bank is seen to have digested the merger and be running smoothly.

In addition to its domestic dominance, DKB has expanded overseas. In December of 1989 it bought CIT Group Holdings, Inc., a wholly owned subsidiary of Manufacturers' Hanover Trust and one of the top ten business financing companies in the United States. It also took a small but significant stake in Manny Hanny itself, showing that the bank has aspirations to expand in the United States and needs partners.

The Shosha. The nucleus of the DKB Group has a double star: the bank plus trading giant Itochu Shoji (until 1992 known as C. Itoh & Co. in English). For many years Itochu was the main shosha for the Sumitomo Group, which is still its largest shareholder (though DKB companies finish a close second), and it seems to have picked up the Sumitomo drive to always be first in its class. For the past six years Itochu has been Japan's top trading house in terms of annual sales, racking up awesome figures. However, rivals quietly point to its profit figures, which are only a little more than sixth-ranked Nissho Iwai and less than a third of Mitsubishi Shoji.

Still, with a global network spanning 90 countries (over 400 domestic subsidiaries and affiliates and more than 300 overseas), Itochu is a major force both at home and abroad. The firm is strong in traditional fields such as machinery, construction equipment, and metals, and like Marubeni, textiles still make up at least 10 percent of its business. But the Osaka trader's current strategy is shifting more toward telecommunications and entertainment. Itochu is a leader of the JCSAT satellite communications project, an investor in a private international phone service in Japan, and in 1991 took a 6 percent interest in a new subsidiary of Time Warner (together with Toshiba). Although neither a hardware nor software maker such as Sony or Matsushita, Itochu has shown a strong interest in Hollywood and has backed a number of films.

Presidential Council. The group's shacho-kai is called the *Sankin-kai* (Third Friday Club) and meets for lunch just four times a year. The group currently counts 48 companies as members, the largest of any of the Big Six. There is also a Sankin Contact Club composed of the directors and general managers from the 48 Sankin-kai members; it meets about one week before the shacho-kai. Another group for directors and general managers of the 48 members is the Sankin Information Systems Research Group, which discusses telecommunications, system networking, new technologies, etc. It also sends study teams to the United States and Europe. In addition, there are separate organizations for projects involving the DKB members and for projects connected with the new Kansai International Airport (this latter run by Itochu).

One estimate puts the total assets of the group's core members at $800 billion, total sales at $416 billion, and total capitalization at $16 billion. Thus, the DKB Group is usually described as the largest in both size and power. However, with six companies only "sitting in," and those firms among the largest in terms of sales and assets, we could argue that the total group figures are somewhat less impressive than they appear at first glance.

It is interesting to note the large overlap between the Sanwa and DKB groups. As noted before, DKB members Nissho Iwai, Hitachi, Kobe Steel, and Nippon Express also belong to the Sanwa Group, but very few belong to any other groups. The conclusion to be drawn from this is that a number of large companies who wanted easy access to bank financing in the 1960s but were not related to the Old Three or Fuyo drifted to Sanwa's corner; but when another group appeared in the 1970s with equally deep pockets, they were happy to drift that way as well. If yet another bank merger should create another giant city bank in the 1990s, some of these firms, plus several others from both Sanwa and DKB, can be expected to sign up with the new keiretsu.

Like Sanwa, the DKB Group contains a number of rival firms in the same sector. Currently, the Sankin-kai includes four trading companies, two steel companies, two heavy machinery makers, two life insurance firms and two non-life firms. Part of the reason for this is the two ex-zaibatsu subgroups, which came on board with Dai-Ichi Bank, Furukawa and Matsukata (Kawasaki), plus the circle of firms that came with the Nippon Kangyo Bank. But more than its prewar connections, the group is a result of recent lending activities, which are aimed at acquiring as many big clients as possible rather than putting together a bank-led zaibatsu like the Old Three, with one key firm in each sector.

Summary. DKB is certainly the biggest of the Big Six groups. Unlike most of the others, its membership is fairly open and a number of its firms belong to other horizontal keiretsu. Companies without specific group identities seem comfortable being Sankin-kai members. For just this reason, the DKB Group will probably continue to grow over the years. As long as the bank stays on top, it will have the funds necessary to keep its old clients and attract new ones. The Old Three banks can do the same thing, of course, but are far less likely to invite their clients to become shacho-kai members. DKB is already seen as a fairly loose association of companies, with considerable redundancy in many industrial sectors, so adding a few more firms to the core will neither surprise nor offend anyone. This is undoubtedly the group's greatest strength.

6
The Vertical
Keiretsu

We have seen how the Big Six horizontal keiretsu grew into enormous groups of corporations, each with a core of dozens of members big enough to be listed on the First Section of the TSE. These firms, whether they are huge, like Toyota and Hitachi or relatively small, like Osaka Cement in the Sanwa Group, are all members of the same club, and so their relations are "horizontal." The vertical keiretsu are a different breed. Each "pyramid" descends from a single powerful company. The size of the firm at the top indicates the size of the unseen pyramid down below. In the very largest vertical keiretsu, such as Toyota, Hitachi, and Matsushita Electric, the uppermost levels of the pyramid are visible. They are big enough to be listed themselves on the TSE. Beneath these companies there are at least a few hundred smaller, unlisted firms in each vertical keiretsu, and they are arranged hierarchically.

There are two basic types of vertical keiretsu: *production keiretsu*, in which a myriad of parts suppliers and assemblers put together products for a single end-product manufacturer, such as in the auto or electronics industries; and *distribution keiretsu*, in which a single firm, usually a manufacturer, moves products out to market through a network of wholesalers and retailers that depend on the parent firm for goods. Since most manufacturers have both types of keiretsu, we could envision the two like an hourglass: an upside-down pyramid on top supplies parts to fewer and fewer companies until in the "center" the parent firm is responsible for the end products. Those products are sent down into another pyramid where it is spread farther and farther outward into the marketplace.

Of course, production and distribution keiretsu are not limited to companies with big factories spewing out cars or video decks. They exist in almost every industry in Japan, from oil to cosmetics to advertising to broadcasting. There are some cases in which the distribution keiretsu is actually more important than the production keiretsu that creates the product. For example, Shiseido, the nation's top cosmetics firm, has about 400 wholesalers moving its products to a network of over 200,000 vendors nationwide. Manufacturing is relatively simple and cheap; the name of the game is selling. For most industries, however, it is the other way around. Selling is important, but it is the quality, speed, and cost of manufacturing that makes or breaks a business. For this reason, we will examine first the production and then the distribution systems of the representative vertical keiretsu.

The Production Keiretsu

Japan's two most representative types of production keiretsu are in its two best-known industries, automobiles and electronics. These industries in particular developed parallel production and distribution pyramids that could create entire product lines—everything from toasters to Toyotas—and bring them to market efficiently. Since these also happen to be the nation's two biggest sources of export income, and thus the two biggest columns of red ink in the annual U.S. trade deficit, an examination of their production and marketing structures should be especially interesting.

Because the Japanese auto and electronics industries developed so rapidly in the 1960s and 1970s, gulping global market share and even driving rivals out of certain areas of their businesses, it is easy to forget that both industries were well established in Japan before the war. The Japanese government was already subsidizing automobile manufacture back in the 1920s—on the condition that the vehicles produced would not be compatible with either Ford or GM imports. This reminds us that the auto business (and the electronics business, too, later on) were part of the bureaucracy's keiretsification game plan, which included emphasizing the primacy of designated large-scale manufacturers at the expense of smaller firms. The government encouraged large manufacturers in both fields to build up their groups of captive suppliers into strong, hierarchical pyramids of subcontractors.

Although neither subcontracting nor the government's antagonistic policy toward small suppliers were postwar inventions, the postwar officials (notably at MITI) redefined both. In the 1920s and 1930s the small- and medium-sized enterprises (SMEs) that made up the bulk of the Japanese economy (as they still do today) had their own cartels, just as the bigger firms did, and a variety of associations to represent their interests. Although the zaibatsu-owned industries controlled much of the economy, by most accounts the SMEs had a certain amount of freedom to negotiate with the firms with whom they were doing business. Of course, the bigger firms had the power and the financial clout, but there was still the understanding that without the resources of the SMEs, large-scale manufacturing, and even exporting was not possible.

The war changed all that. As the Army began marching into China, the government wanted to shift the economy into high gear, and that was hard to do with an economy made up of hundreds of thousands of tiny machine shops and weavers. Beginning around 1938 the military-influenced government began passing laws to reorganize the structure of the economy. Many of the SMEs were simply wiped out as a result, and most of the remainder were harnessed to the war machine. One ordinance allowed the government to force any business to convert to munitions production, and another put all munitions-related SMEs at the disposal of the larger firms they were supplying. Many small firms were amalgamated into slightly larger firms, then these were merged into medium-sized firms and they were made directly accountable to the big manufacturers (we hear a subcontractor talk about this period in Chapter 8).

The old sense of identity among the SMEs and the flexibility to negotiate with the big firms vanished completely. Simply put, the new policy was that large firms were essential to the national welfare, and small firms were expendable. It was, after all, wartime.

The war ended, the Occupation came and went, and the clock turned right back to 1938. The old Ministry of Munitions became the new MITI—a change in name only; most of the important officials stayed on. No surprise, then, that when they looked at postwar industry their response to the problem of how to build it up was not much different than before. The only goal that mattered was increasing the scale and production efficiency of heavy industries, exactly what they had been doing a decade earlier. The result was a government brake on the early attempts of the SMEs to get out from under the control of the big firms and a green light to the big companies to set up subcontracting hierarchies. The combination of government ordinances, pressure from the giant manufacturers, and the ultimate leverage of capital control provided by the main banks was all it took to build pyramids from which subcontractors did not escape. They learned loyalty and strict obedience to their individual "parent" firms, or they watched their companies go bankrupt.

These keiretsu, which were solidified in the later 1950s and throughout the 1960s, continued to operate without a major problem for 20 years thereafter. It is only in recent times that there have been ominous rumblings inside the pyramids and cracks have appeared in the walls. We will come back to this topic and the future of the system in Chapter 9.

In Japan It's Always a Little Different

There is nothing unique about having production keiretsu. Relations between manufacturers and suppliers are similar all over the world; in the best of cases they are symbiotic, but they are always hierarchical. Japan's only distinction is in creating such enormous formalized structures tying thousands of firms to a single manufacturer so rigidly. More interesting, however, is the way in which the suppliers are used in Japan. In the United States, where for example, somewhere around 30 percent of auto parts are made by subcontractors, the big makers traditionally design the parts that they want their suppliers to manufacture. The auto maker's engineering department then gives "spec sheets" and blueprints of the design to the supplier who produces the items "to spec."

In Japan it works a little differently. First of all, the in-house/sub-contracting parts ratio is the inverse of that in the United States: about 70 percent of all auto parts are made by outside subcontractors. In many cases the parent company does not design the part; it simply draws up a description and a list of desired specifications. It is up to the supplier to design a suitable part to meet those specs and the supplier's engineering department must submit its drawings and blueprints for approval by the parent.

Why the different approaches? In the United States, where the big firms are used to dealing with independent suppliers over whom they have little control, there is no incentive to give the subcontractor any more work than is necessary. Moreover, with U.S. labor laws and relatively strong unions around the country, there is no sizable cost benefit in out-sourcing a lot of work. In many ways, it is ultimately cheaper and more reliable to keep a lot of the work in house. Since suppliers have traditionally been chosen on a spot-market basis, that is, the "low bid" gets the contract, there is no guarantee that this year's supplier will be next year's supplier. Why make your company dependent on the design expertise of some firm that may wind up supplying one of your rivals next season?

In Japan the big firms have never liked dealing with independent subcontractors, precisely because they are independent. If a manufacturer effectively controls its subcontractors, the whole structure of manufacturing changes. First, a large part of design work can be farmed out, freeing up staff at the parent company for other projects. Second, the quality as well as the efficiency of production can be assured because the parent and the subcontractor exist in a long-term relationship. The parent can help its primary subcontractors invest in new technology, it can transfer technology (both know-how and equipment) from its own factories, and it can send its own engineers to help the subcontractor improve his production. All of these are excellent reasons for Japanese firms to develop extensive subcontracting systems. But they are all secondary reasons.

The key point in the growth of the Japanese system is cost: it is invariably cheaper to do the exact same work in a subcontracting plant than in the parent's main plant. Why? There are two reasons: labor costs and overhead.

Labor Costs. Big manufacturers compete with each other and with other top Japanese companies to get new management-track recruits from among the graduates of the nation's top universities. To attract them means paying competitive salaries, usually with an implicit lifetime guarantee (not only of employment but steady raises as well), plus a host of employee benefits, including housing. Even line workers at the big manufacturers are paid relatively well. All of that places a hefty burden on the parent firm's cost structure. The "flexibility" of costs in the subcontracting pyramid is what makes all this possible.

One step below the parent company, at the primary, or first-tier subcontractor level, there are very few, if any, graduates from the top schools, and both pay scales and benefits are noticeably lower than at the parent. Lifetime employment may or may not be part of the deal. Down another level or two, at the second- and third-tier subcontractors, wages drop lower still and benefits disappear. Job security is subject to economic conditions. Go down to the bottom, the fourth-tier (or even fifth-tier in some industries), and wages are minimal. Salaries are paid monthly, sometimes weekly, and sometimes not at all—companies pay for "piece work." There is never any guarantee of work the following month. All of this is built into the labor system of the vertical pyramid. Without it costs for the big manufacturers would skyrocket, lifetime employment would disappear, and the foundations of the Japanese manufacturing system would crumble.

Overhead. Many parent companies maintain plush head offices in either downtown Tokyo or Osaka. In addition, their dormitories and main factories are usually located in or near major cities. Even with land prices declining rapidly since 1990, urban real estate in Japan is still some of the most expensive in the world. If the great majority of auto parts weren't being made out in the suburbs (and sometimes out in the countryside) by subcontracting firms, a Toyota Corolla would cost more than a Rolls Royce.

Then there are manufacturing costs. We noted that a parent firm could invest in equipment for its primary subcontractors (and many do). However, it is far more common for the parent to instruct the subcontractor to invest in equipment. At the lower levels of the pyramid, there is no question of the parent buying new equipment for the subcontractors, and when it comes to ordering them to invest in new equipment, this is handled by one of the higher-level subcontractors, never the parent.

Over time, this brings the parent firm all the advantages of state-of-the-art production equipment with little or none of the cost. It also means the subcontractors develop larger and more technically advanced factories—both of which are good for the parent—but have no profits left over. More likely than not, they had to take out a loan from the parent's main bank to cover the costs of capital investment. "An important feature of the Japanese system of [parent companies] controlling purchasing is that there is never any cash on hand even though profits are made," explains Professor Shoichiro Sei of Kanto Gakuin University, who has spent years studying auto manufacturing in both the West (as part of a research team at MIT) and in Japan. "For Japanese parts companies, the idea of profit has been replaced by the idea of growth."

In addition to arranging for equipment investment by their affiliated suppliers, the parent companies can push their subcontractors to work extra hours, deliver parts at the parent's convenience (part of the famous just-in-time system), and accept payment when the parent's cash flow permits. Most important of all, unlike the United States, where suppliers submit a bid for a specific job (and in many cases cost overruns mean the supplier is actually paid more than was agreed upon), in the upside-down world of Japanese manufacturing, the parent firm tells the supplier how much he will pay for the parts. To put it another way, the buyer tells the seller what to charge for his goods.

Here's how the system works: When a Japanese auto maker gets ready to develop a new car, it sets a target retail price for the car. It also decides what parts are available and what parts must be designed and built. Each piece is assigned a target cost. The maker then presents its target costs to its main parts suppliers. These companies reply with their own estimates of what it will cost them (and their own subcontractors) to manufacture the parts. Often the supplier states unequivocally that his manufacturing cost will be double the target set by the auto maker. Negotiations between the parent and the suppliers continue for months, but all this time the suppliers are expected to start producing samples. In many cases the parent only settles on a price and signs a contract just as its new model is going into mass production. Not surprisingly, the subcontractors are expected to compromise far more than the parent in determining the final price. Even so, the final contract price is totally meaning-less.

All the parent firms deny it, and the government swears that no such thing exists in Japan, but subcontractors in both the auto and electronics fields report that not only are part prices set by the parent firms, they are adjusted—always downward—at least twice a year and usually for at least 5 to 10 percent each time. One industry observer explains that a midlevel subcontractor may expect to make a very small profit on the first year's production of a certain part. By the second year, the maker has cut the price for that part by 10 to 20 percent and, even after cutting costs to the bone, the supplier is losing money on it. By Year 3 he is losing big. If the parent firm decides to do a model change which requires a new part, it may slash the price it pays for the old parts in Year 4 by up to 90 percent of the original cost.

Although a small number of subcontractors have grown influential enough that they are not bound by these rules (some can even dictate terms to the big makers—car electronics specialist Nippondenso is the best-known example), such companies are still few and far between. However, because of their size and visibility, both the big makers and government officials point to them as evidence that the old "master and serf" keiretsu system of the 1960s is a relic of the past (the other side of the story appears in Chapter 8).

Structure of the Production
Keiretsu

At the apex of the manufacturing pyramid is the parent company, the firm that is ultimately responsible for coordinating the vast, complex system of design, development, manufacture, and assembly inside the pyramid, then advertising the finished products under its own name, and delivering them to the market. Production is essentially carried on outside the parent firm, but some steps, such as final assembly, are also performed in-house. Below the parent there are usually three fairly clearly defined levels of subcontractors, upper, middle, and lower. Each level is responsible for coordinating the activities of the firms in the level below it. The parent is in regular, direct contact with both the upper-level companies, in which it usually owns equity and to whose boards it has assigned directors, and with some of the middle-group companies, in which it may have some equity and occasionally a director on the board. The parent seldom has any contact, equity, or other direct relations with the lower-level firms.

The upper-level of the pyramid consists of the first-tier subcontractors, usually about a dozen or so companies, some of which are big enough to be listed on the TSE. These firms handle many of the final steps in the production process and also play an important role in coordinating the second- and third-tier subcontractors.

The middle-level subcontractors are generally much smaller, and few of them are publicly listed. In most manufacturing pyramids the main middle-level firms are organized by their parents into groups called *kyoryoku-kai* (cooperation associations). The subcontractors' representatives, usually senior executives, meet with representatives (usually lower- or middle-level executives) of the parent companies several times a year. Occasionally these are social events designed to promote group unity, but more often they are opportunities for the parent to explain its upcoming pricing policy for new parts and assemblies. Awards are given out at these meetings for outstanding production efficiency, fewest defects, and so on, the idea being to drum up a spirit of competition among the suppliers. The public relations department of almost any major auto firm in Japan will gladly tell visitors about the close relations between the parent and its subcontractors and the need to have regular meetings to stay in close contact with these valued suppliers. The subcontractors don't always see things quite the same way.

The Distribution Keiretsu

Both the auto and electronics industries developed huge networks of affiliated dealers during the 1950s and 1960s, and these sales keiretsu have been instrumental in promoting their products. Toyota's multilayered sales network is so strong that foreign makers are scrambling to get Toyota to put their cars into its showrooms. One by-product of this system is direct savings for the parent firms as affiliates share in marketing costs. For example, in 1989, Toyota Motor's total spending on domestic advertising was only one-third that of rival GM, number two Nissan spent only about 55 percent as much as its U.S. counterpart Ford, and number three Honda only 58 percent of Chrysler's outlay. Money saved on advertising gets plowed right back into development and production costs.

But when it comes to distribution networks, even the auto firms have to take a back seat to the consumer electronics industry. Their distribution pyramids are phenomenal: some of the smaller networks among the big makers have more than double Toyota's number of total outlets, and the bigger players such as Matsushita seem to have a shop on every street corner in Japan. It didn't happen overnight. These sales systems grew in the decade beginning in the late 1950s as demand for TVs, radios, and electric rice cookers exploded.

As competition among the keiretsu reached new heights, the makers formalized a system in which their products were carried almost exclusively by stores under their control. They did not have the capital to own the land or the buildings or even the tens of thousands of little companies that became their distributors, but they controlled them just the same. The big makers provided their directly affiliated retail stores with something more valuable than money—the right to display the company name prominently—in an era when big companies were revered even more so than they are today. The smaller the retailer, the more likely that the store name or the owner's name was displayed only half the size of the National or Toshiba sign out front. The makers would often contribute these company signs, as well as posters, display stands, and occasional newspaper ads. In short, the maker supplied the goods, the marketing tools, and most of all, the prestige, and the store owner supplied the space, the friendly smile, and the labor.

As long as the owner did his job, which meant being visible in the neighborhood, going out to customers' homes to install equipment when necessary, and staying open late hours to service what he sold, he would earn enough to make a living. If he protested in any way, the parent companies could and did take strict measures to keep him in line. The ultimate penalty was to ostracize him—the parent firm would retract the owner's right to display the company's goods and its name. Moreover, someone who was cut off from one respected maker stood little chance of selling his services (the most important being loyalty) to another firm. To be cut off by the parent meant both an end to business in the electronics field and a black mark against one's name in the neighborhood. Even today this is not something a retailer would do lightly, but in Japan 20 or 30 years ago it was all but unthinkable.

In the 1950s and 1960s most Japanese households became brand-affiliated by default. That is, they did not make a conscious decision to buy every appliance and gadget for the next 20 years from one maker, but when they did buy their first TV or automatic washing machine many bought it from a neighborhood store. There were a few department stores in the big cities, but the existence of the neighborhood *denki-ya* (electronics shop) provided something better than a maker's warranty: the denki-ya-san was right there, everybody knew him, and you knew that if anything broke you could always take it back to him. The custom of buying from a local shopowner whom everyone knows and trusts goes back centuries, and it has not disappeared even in the urban sprawl of Tokyo, much less in the countryside.

It was easy for the big electronics manufacturers to develop retail networks that meshed nicely with this traditional concept. Consumers not only became attached to a specific store, but because the store sold only one product line, to a brand name as well. Thus, the majority of Japanese households became brand-loyal. If they bought a National (Matsushita's domestic brand name) vacuum cleaner at the nearby store and they liked it, they bought a National washing machine and air conditioner and refrigerator and everything else over the years from the same store. If they happened to move to a new neighborhood, they would instinctively seek out the nearest Matsushita store. Thus, most families unwittingly became "National families" or "Toshiba families" or "Hitachi families" and so on. Those who have not spent time at home with a Japanese family would be surprised to see how many people retain this habit in spite of the proliferation of big retailers, discount stores, and mail-order services.

The system had elements of genius. The huge, sprawling electronics companies were represented in every city neighborhood, in every town, and even in the smallest village by a friendly local representative. Because each maker ran its own network of stores, it had, in effect, private display space and exclusive retailing agents for its products. Makers sometimes paid a "monopoly rebate" to dealers who guaranteed that no rival product would ever darken their shelves. This went beyond brand loyalty; it eliminated the danger that customers might accidentally "comparison shop."

The system had obvious attractions for both sides, and the distribution keiretsu grew like a house on fire. By 1982 there were 71,283 consumer electronics retailers in Japan, about two-thirds of them controlled by the top five makers (Matsushita, Toshiba, Hitachi, Sony, and Sanyo) and more than half of those by a single company: Matsushita.

Because the makers controlled their own retailing networks, they could also control prices and profit margins in a way that simple wholesaling does not allow. Since the keiretsu stores had a virtual monopoly on their goods in many areas, they could charge high prices, which translated into fat profit margins that allowed them to export the same goods at much slimmer margins (some say, negative margins) in order to capture market share abroad.

Through their distribution keiretsu, the manufacturers developed a closed market, protected from infiltration by domestic rivals and foreign competitors alike. With the number of market entrants essentially fixed, the competition among makers came to center on (1) increasing the quality and improving the features of products to steadily improve each company's public image and (2) developing ever-larger distribution networks to bring those products as close as possible to consumers' homes.

Matsushita won the latter contest hands-down, establishing over 25,000 National outlets nationwide. The fact that the firm has until very recently dwarfed its rival, Sony, has less to do with Matsushita's technology and a lot to do with its distribution muscle.

Of course, this competition resulted in tangible benefits for the consumer as well—new products were generated one after another, and product quality and features increased dramatically over the years. Service at the local stores was extremely good (most keiretsu stores will fix anything in their parent's lineup for a very nominal sum, often without charge). Within a relatively short time the Japanese consumer became spoiled, expecting extremely high product quality and total service. The makers were happy to provide both because all the costs—and more—came out of the consumer's pocket in the first place. The manufacturers essentially had a captive market: once consumers decided that they would buy from their local National or Toshiba store, they had to pay whatever prices were charged by that store. Since the manufacturers rigidly controlled prices throughout their keiretsu networks, there was no point in looking for another store in the same chain in the hope of getting a small discount. Any retailer who launched a discount program without the maker's prior approval could lose his business (a case study appears in Chapter 9). The result was that Japanese consumers paid dearly for the quality and service they took for granted.

The Vertical Keiretsu under Attack

All of this might have continued for many more years had not the United States upset the apple cart. In the first half of the 1980s, Japan was churning out exports, then as now, mostly cars and electronics. Reagan administration officials worried about the spiraling trade deficit. Not only were cheap Japanese imports pouring into the United States, but American companies were also pressuring the administration to do something to help them export to the chaste Japanese market. This led to the Plaza Accord of September 1985 in which the G-7 nations agreed in principle to let world currencies adjust to new market realities. But what they really meant was to let the dollar fall against the yen.

Almost immediately the dollar began a nosedive, ultimately dropping to roughly half its pre-Plaza value. As Professor Kenneth Courtis, the Tokyo-based global strategist for Deutsche Bank, puts it, "the idea was to throw the Japanese export machine out of gear." The dollar fell and the yen soared, which meant that the big Japanese exporters (i.e., the auto and electronics makers) were suddenly looking into the abyss. They could either double their retail prices overseas or earn only half as much yen value in return for their goods. The first option would kill their overseas sales, and the second would turn the big manufacturers into multimillion dollar charities. There was something of a panic in Japanese industry in 1986, and even the most conservative business magazines carried regular stories about the "end of Japan's golden age." All that had been gained by the postwar buildup would soon be destroyed, factories would have to be shut down and moved overseas, unemployment would skyrocket, and the economy would soon plummet to 1955 levels, they said.

These dire predictions, as well as the U.S. ploy to lower the trade deficit by forcing Japanese makers to hike prices, underestimated the resilience of the vertical keiretsu and the resourcefulness of the Japanese government.

The big manufacturers responded to their predicament with old-fashioned keiretsu logic. The whole jack-the-yen strategy hinged on the manufacturers being unable to earn enough profits overseas to cover their costs at home. The immediate answer was obvious: cut costs drastically. This is where the famous production keiretsu "shock absorber" came into play. In order to squeeze double the profit from the same unit sales, you must cut costs in half. How can a manufacturer do that? When you in effect set the prices you pay for your components, it's not very difficult. The big makers already had some experience with this kind of crisis management, having employed the shock absorber at least twice in recent memory to take the bumps out of the oil shocks in the 1970s. The early 1980s had been a little more relaxed, and a bit of air had been let back into the system, but in 1986 everyone got ready for a rough ride ahead.

True to form, the parent companies demanded bigger and bigger cuts from their subcontractors. The small companies didn't have a lot of profit margin to work with in the first place, but when the orders came to cut all costs 25 percent as of this week, and then another 20 percent a couple of months later, and then another 10 percent a month after that, there was blood in the streets. The bottom-level subcontractors are little shops with a handful of employees, most of them in their fifties. They stay in business only because they can produce some small part or perform some process that a middle-tier company needs, do it cheap, and do it fast. Their profits are problematic. Sometimes they make money on an order, sometimes they lose. When the squeeze comes from up above, everybody loses.

The results were predictable (and should have been to the U.S. government planners who came up with the idea). Thousands of small businesses simply vanished. Many old-timers threw in the towel. Above them, even many of the middle-tier companies went bust, and those that didn't were deeply in the red. Belts were tightened from the first-tier sub-contractors right on down the line, although the people up top never seemed to tighten quite as much as those one level below. And, according to a number of sources, the big manufacturers made only cosmetic attempts to cut costs. One giant automaker's announcement that it had ordered staff to use pencils down to the stubs and cut up waste paper to use for notes was seen by many a subcontractor as symbolic of the way big companies can calmly order their suppliers to fire staff, work 24-hour shifts, and sell at a loss, but wince at the thought of tightening their own belts in any meaningful way.

Another purpose of the dollar/yen revaluation was to make imports far more attractive, since the yen could now buy twice as much as it had before. Indeed, imports did increase, although not quite the way U.S. officials had planned. One thing that did happen, though, was that clever local entrepreneurs, trying to "arbitrage" the old difference between traditionally high-priced Japanese goods at home and cheaper Japanese goods overseas, began importing Japanese exports. Small operators went to Hong Kong, Singapore, even to the United States and bought name-brand Japanese cameras and electrical equipment and brought them back to Tokyo, where they could be sold cheaper than keiretsu-store prices and still turn a handsome profit for the importer.

The fact that a number of small operators were making the same kind of fat profits that the big makers had enjoyed for years did not pose the slightest threat to the manufacturers. But the idea that the word might begin to spread among Japanese consumers that something was rotten in the state of keiretsu retailing was downright terrifying. There was always the possibility that normally docile Japanese consumers might begin to say to their friends, "Why are we paying so much for 'Japanese quality' if the exact same products are selling overseas for less?" Sooner or later Japanese housewives would start to wonder why their supposedly well-to-do American counterparts were buying the same Japanese appliances for less than they were. In effect, they would realize, the Japanese consumer had been tricked into subsidizing American and European shoppers so that the big domestic makers could scoop up market share abroad.

There is a famous story of an electronics importer in Tokyo's glittering Akihabara district, the 10-block-square electronics bazaar that accounts for a sizable part of all electrical appliance sales in Japan. This enterprising fellow imported a few hundred Japanese-made cordless telephones from a dealer in California. Although the export-version phones were identical to a model currently selling in Japan with a famous brand name, they only cost about one-third as much. The street-side retailer put them on sale in Akihabara for about 50 percent of the going Tokyo price.

As if this weren't bad enough, all the Japanese telephone makers had been saying for years that American telephone equipment and Japanese telephone equipment were totally incompatible. To sell his cut-rate phones the importer had to explain to the public that the makers' information was incorrect. Yes, he said, the big companies have lied to you for years. Cheap, reliable American phones work just fine on Japanese lines, and Japanese-made phones sold in America do just as well. With a big smile and a line as old as hard cash, the importer called out to shoppers, "Why pay more?" The soundness of the argument was surpassed only by its novelty to Japanese ears.

If the maker of the phones he was selling has a crisis control center, a giant room deep inside some dark mountain with enormous screens up on the wall and dozens of uniformed officers with headsets monitoring potential incoming threats to both the manufacturing and distribution groups, it must have gone to Condition Red that morning. Alarm bells must have started ringing, lights flashing, and damage-control teams come rushing out, blue suits crisply pressed and black shoes gleaming, ready to contain the emergency. Before you could say "free market" dozens of smartly dressed young "shoppers" hit the pavement in Akihabara, too well-groomed and tailored to fit in with the crush of housewives, students, and dishevelled businessmen who normally shuffle through the district. Within hours the entire stock of cheap imported phones was gone, most purchased in large lots, and the sale was finished. The importer knew exactly what had happened and happily told everyone he met that day: "They [the manufacturer] sent a bunch of guys around here and bought up all my stock. What do I care? They paid full price for everything and they paid in cash!"

There were more or less similar stories about all the big electronics firms buying up "imported exports" in an effort to avoid revealing their low export prices. In effect, the big makers wanted to keep a good thing going as long as possible. The whole structure of their market situation was under attack—overseas through the need to raise prices and at home through the need to lower them—and just when they most needed those fat domestic margins to offset their foreign losses.

To lower costs at home, they would have to invest huge sums to rationalize their production lines. To counter the effects of the yen appreciation overseas they would need to build plants in areas with cheap labor and low overhead like Southeast Asia or build factories right inside the United States so they could avoid exporting entirely. Either way, they needed a lot of cash, and with the yen rising and the economy in a tailspin, taking on billions of dollars in new loans was not something any director of a big manufacturing firm wanted to do. It is fair to assume that when the heads of the big vertical keiretsu met for their monthly presidential council luncheons with their colleagues in the horizonal keiretsu, they had more to talk about than golf.

The primary result was just short of miraculous. The Ministry of Finance, working overtime to find a way to save Japanese industry, came up with a plan. By lowering interest rates, increasing liquidity, pumping up the stock market, and deregulating controls on certain kinds of transactions, it would be possible to channel an ocean of cash to the nation's biggest corporations. When the coming year brought low interest rates, increasing money supply, and cheap oil (Japan's biggest import), the business press started singing a different tune. The high yen could be the best import since McDonald's. Within a short time the stock market took off, and big companies found they could issue equity-linked debt to raise millions of dollars at nearly zero interest. Smaller, unlisted companies could borrow from banks at rock-bottom rates using their land as collateral, and everyone could reinvest in new production equipment at home and new factories overseas.

The secondary result was, of course, the infamous Japanese asset "bubble," a sudden climb in the value of stocks, land, and everything else that could be traded or speculated on. The economics of it all is another story, but the effects on the vertical keiretsu, in terms of both production and distribution, were enormous.

The production side felt the squeeze well beyond the end of 1986, but gradually things began to ease up. The companies that went out of business were gone for good, but those that remained found that business in the "bubble era" was booming. They also found that their parent firms were now loaded with cash and anxious to invest in new production equipment. Japanese capital investment took off (it was already higher than in the United States on a per capita basis even in the depths of 1986, and it grew rapidly). Although borrowing from up above in a vertical keiretsu is like buying at the Company Store in an old coal mining town, many of the smaller subcontractors took loans from the companies higher up in the pyramid to beef up their own production lines. When all was said and done, though, those SMEs that survived the "yen shock" were better off for a simple reason: during the bubble years they had steady work, which is all a subcontractor can reasonably hope for.

On the distribution side, the change in the distribution keiretsu resulted in part from U.S. pressure, but it was not merely the Plaza-triggered yen appreciation that brought it about. During the "bubble years" the United States inaugurated the Structural Impediments Initiative (SII) talks. One of the fruits of persistent SII negotiation was the 1990 revision of Japan's Large-Scale Retail Store Law, which had given small shop owners the power to block construction of any store over a certain size in their area. Of course, revising this law helped the big Japanese department stores (which have keiretsu of their own), but it also opened the way for enterprising discount chains to open branches in areas where they had never before ventured. In spite of the popular image of the "new rich" Japanese with two Mercedes and a house in Hawaii, the majority of consumers were left out of the wild "bubble profits." To the average consumer, the proliferation of discount stores was a very welcome event.

With the double impact of cheap imports and an increasing number of stores willing to sell at reduced prices, the market for certain goods became more competitive than ever before. For years the big manufacturers had stated, as if it were indisputable fact, that Japanese consumers are not bargain hunters—they want high quality and good service and are willing to pay for it. Since the keiretsu stores dominated retailing, and since they offered only expensive, good-quality merchandise backed by good service, there was little evidence to the contrary. But the expansion of discount stores and discount brands put that myth out to pasture very quickly. Japanese shoppers rushed to buy cheap, equally reliable imports, many from other Asian producers. Even some smaller Japanese makers took advantage of the trend, producing basic, no-frills products for considerably less than the fancy name brands that cost half a month's salary. And this was still in the years before the recession.

In the early 1990s the excesses of those years caught up with the big firms. The asset bubble disappeared like a mirage, the Nikkei stock index turned around and began digging a hole in the ground, and the banks hung permanent "Out to Lunch" signs in front of their loan departments. Companies that had financed heavily, built plants overseas, hired hundreds of excess staff, and invested large sums in depreciating equipment were once again caught in the jaws of a recession. As corporate debt levels soared, consumers abandoned the traditional keiretsu stores in droves, cutting off the steady stream of fixed-price sales on which the makers depended.

The discount shops offered a dozen famous name brands side by side, so a new generation of consumers could judge which product delivered the most for the money. This forced the manufacturers to do something unthinkable just a decade before: compete seriously on prices. Not only were the electronics companies forced to lower their retail prices on "low-tech" goods (anything that cheaper rivals could produce easily), but they had to increase sales to discount outlets and mail-order firms, the only retailers who could move inventory in a recession. Large- and small-scale discount stores everywhere looked like the floor of the stock exchange had just a few years ago—jammed with buyers elbowing each other and clamoring to get what they wanted. *Mo hito koe!* (C'mon, you can do better than that!) became the rallying cry of housewives and office workers alike as they dickered over video cameras the way they might over salmon in an open-air fish market.

The advent of real discount shops (not the old price-fixed electronics department stores in Akihabara) and the loss of a good part of the electronics makers' regular income came just as the recession was building steam. Discount auto dealers didn't pop up for obvious reasons (unlike the audio business, there was a lack of cheap Taiwanese or Hong Kong–made imports to drive around), but with the collapsing bubble, Japanese consumers suddenly lost interest in buying a new car every four years. Used car sales jumped for a while, but even that trend slowed as people decided to keep the family car going for another year or two. Sales at all the auto makers plummeted.

The result has been the worst crunch for all the biggest vertical keiretsu in recent memory. Needless to say, that means an even bigger crunch for the multitude of SMEs in their production and distribution pyramids. When the yen shock hit in 1986, it was easy enough to compress the shock absorber once again, but when the makers tried to do the same in 1992, strange things began to happen. We look at that story in our final analysis of the current state and future trends of the keiretsu in Chapter 9.

7

The Leading
Vertical Keiretsu

Almost everyone outside of Japan knows the names of many if not all of the big vertical keiretsu in the two fields we have discussed, automobiles and electronics. But very few people (including few Japanese) think of these firms as only the very top of a giant pyramid of parts subcontractors and distributors, even though that is their main function. Many of the big manufacturers are coordinators first and manufacturers second. As one medium-sized electronics subcontractor in Kanagawa Prefecture told us, "The big companies are nothing more than shosha (traders). They make very little. We subcontractors design most of the parts, test them, produce them, assemble them, and sometimes deliver finished products straight to the dealers without them ever passing through one of the parent's factories. Our parent ultimately supplies the money and the advertising. That's all."

While this description is only sometimes true in electronics, and not quite true in the auto industry, it does serve to illustrate the extent to which the best-known vertical keiretsu operate. However, to really understand the size and scope of the production and distribution pyramids, we should examine some of the biggest "parent" companies in those two key sectors and the keiretsu they control. In both fields we will (in good Japanese tradition) pay much more attention to the number one company and its group, and cover the also-rans a little more briefly.

Automobiles

The Toyota Group

> SNAPSHOT: The Toyota Group
>
> *Keiretsu ties:* Member of the Mitsui Group, but very independent
>
> *Main banks:* Sakura (Mitsui), Tokai
>
> *Top shareholders:* Sakura Bank, Tokai Bank, Sanwa Bank, Toyoda Automatic Loom Works, Nippon Life Insurance, LTCB, Mitsui Marine & Fire Insurance, Daiwa Bank, Mitsui Life
>
> *Stable shareholding:* 35.6 percent
>
> *Directors' connections:* Toyoda Automatic Loom Works

The Parent. If you asked most Americans to name one company that embodies the technical innovation, market leadership, and sales power that we have come to associate with Japanese firms, 9 out of 10 people would probably say "Sony." This reply would bring a smile to most Japanese, for at home Sony is still widely perceived as a young, relatively small, upstart firm that only yesterday managed to grow big enough to stand toe-to-toe with its much larger rival, Matsushita. To the Japanese, it is unthinkable that a firm which has never led its market and whose history as a "heavyweight" in its sector is measured in years rather than decades could ever be considered a symbol of Japanese industry. To the Japanese there is only one firm that combines a long history, awesome manufacturing muscle, tremendous financial power, a huge group of affiliates, and a market position so strong it borders on a monopoly. That firm is Toyota Motor Corp.

Toyota is not a car company—it is *the* car company against which all Japanese makers (and these days, U.S. and European makers as well) are compared. Toyota perennially tops the list not only of domestic auto makers but of all Japanese manufacturing industry in terms of sales and profits, and in good years it leads all companies period. In those rare years when it isn't on the top of the list, it's usually close enough to it. The parent firm alone generates $72 billion every year in sales, and it does so with a staff of 72,000. One million dollars in annual sales per employee is not bad for a company of that size (it's roughly six times the figure for GM). More than two-thirds of Toyota's business comes from motor vehicles, mostly passenger cars. It has completely dominated the world's second biggest (and probably most lucrative) auto market for longer than most dealers can remember. Its share of the Japanese pie usually hovers around 50 percent and never falls below 40 percent. This would not be quite so impressive if the firm were not competing with 10 other domestic vehicle makers plus a bevy of attractive imports. Yet a Toyota model has been the best-selling car in Japan for 24 consecutive years, and in the list of best-sellers for 1992 Toyotas hogged 7 of the top 10 spots. That's market clout.

The Group. How can one company, even a $72 billion company, have so much clout in the Japanese economy? The answer, of course, is that it is not Toyota Motor Corp. alone, but the keiretsu muscle it flexes. The Toyota Group is the largest industrial combine in Japan. If we exclude the Big Six and the Industrial Bank of Japan horizontal groups, Toyota is the biggest keiretsu in the nation and no other group even comes close.

Upper level: The Toyota Group includes 10 first-tier subcontractors, and all 10 are listed on the First Section of the TSE, a unique achievement in Japanese industry. Many first-tier firms at other companies are on the smaller Second Section and many more aren't even large enough to be listed. There are actually two more nonmanufacturing companies directly under Toyota, an in-house real estate firm and a research lab. Together, these 12 firms make up the upper level of the Toyota Group pyramid. In addition to these official first-tier subcontractors, the upper level includes two firms that would seem to be rival car makers. They have been swallowed by the number one company in the process of eliminating what government officials refer to as "excess competition." The fact is, Toyota grew so fast back in the sixties that it began to devour its rivals. It purchased substantial chunks of two of the other ten makers: Daihatsu Motor, which produces minicars (thus allowing Toyota to stay out of this highly competitive, low-margin field), and Hino Motors, a major truck maker that gave up producing passenger cars under its own name but still makes them with the Toyota logo on the grille.

Middle level: In the middle of the pyramid there are two groups of parts makers which include both second- and third-tier subcontractors. The larger of the two groups is the Kyoho-kai (Toyota Cooperative Assn.), which consists of 183 companies; the Eiho-kai (Toyota Prosperity Assn.) has another 65 equipment makers. These nearly 250 companies make up the visible bulk of the Toyota Group. Quite a few of them are also publicly traded. The middle level of the pyramid is fairly stable, although its membership does change slightly—for example, the Kyoho-kai grew by three firms in the past year. In contrast, the composition of the upper level of a group such as Toyota's almost never changes.

Lower level: At the bottom of the pyramid, beneath all the officially designated subcontractors, are hundreds upon hundreds of smaller companies, subcontractors to the subcontractors to the subcontractors to Toyota Motor Corp. They have no official associations and no one outside the Toyota Group knows how many there are, but the number could run well over a thousand.

If we set aside figures for the real estate firm and the research lab and focus only on the 10 core companies in the upper level of the Toyota pyramid, we find this level alone employs 90,000 workers and generates $50 billion in sales annually. Add to these totals the figures for Daihatsu and Hino, and those numbers become 110,000 employees and over $61 billion in sales. And this is only the top level of the Toyota pyramid. While the size of the individual companies is smaller in the middle level and much smaller still in the bottom level, the total manufacturing output of those thousands of firms is tremendous and the number of people employed directly or indirectly under the Toyota umbrella is enormous.

Horizontally Inclined.   One of the problems with a group as big as Toyota is that it spills over the sides of the neat definition of a vertical keiretsu. We said it was big enough to be compared with the biggest horizontal keiretsu, and in fact Toyota is growing into something between a purely vertical and a horizontal keiretsu. The group is classified as vertical because it is primarily a manufacturing group and it displays the typical manufacturing pyramid. But Toyota is more than a manufacturer. It is a major participant in three telecommunications companies; it is the principal investor in a computer system development firm (together with partners Toshiba and IBM Japan); and it holds 36 percent of the equity in Chiyoda Fire and Marine Insurance, a midranked nonlife firm which derives more than half of its premium income from auto insurance.

Toyota operates two real estate firms, Towa Real Estate and Toyota Home, as well as two financial firms, Toyota Finance and Toyota Lease. Over the years the parent firm has also been developing a very serious interest in airplanes, but it is moving slowly so as not to alarm anyone in that field. It has already invested in a small import firm and in a charter service and has been experimenting with the development of small-scale airplane engines.

Through a related group, Toyota is moving more aggressively in the United States to develop a next-generation tilt-wing passenger plane (it already owns two companies in the United States devoted to this business). Observers say that with Toyota's manufacturing muscle, technical skill, and financial reserves, it could start producing a competitive line of single- and twin-engine prop planes at any time it chooses. If the car maker wanted to use that as a first step toward a long-range goal of more serious involvement in the global aviation industry (for example, by tying up with one of the Japanese firms that already subcontract for Boeing), it would not be out of the question.

From this perspective, then, Toyota does look a lot like a fledgling horizontal keiretsu. Unlike the Big Six, however, it is manufacturer-centered rather than bank-centered. Yet Toyota is not without its own financial connections. The parent company and almost all of its subsidiaries and main affiliates are located in Aichi Prefecture. The largest financial institution in Aichi is Tokai Bank, the largest city bank outside the Big Six. Tokai is trying to build its own keiretsu and likes to think of Toyota as a member. Tokai is one of three banks sharing equal shares in Toyota's stock, but it clearly does not share equal status. As we saw in looking at the Mitsui Group, the auto maker is a full member of the Nimoku-kai. If it were a core member of the Tokai Group, it would certainly be a member of the nucleus of that group. It is not.

Furthermore, a close inspection of Tokai Bank reveals something very odd. Although it is generally viewed as Toyota's main bank, it makes no loans to the firm (to be fair, neither does any other bank—Toyota has no need to borrow). Nor does it send directors to Toyota. On the contrary, one of Tokai Bank's directors comes from Toyota. And unlike all the other city banks, Tokai's leading shareholder is not a financial institution but a manufacturer: Toyota. Conclusion: Toyota holds far more sway with Tokai Bank than vice versa. It would be an exaggeration to say that Tokai Bank is actually part of the Toyota Group, but not so very far from the truth.

Lastly, we should highlight one more aspect of this phenomenal group: its distribution channels. The parent company supports four major distribution networks: Tokyo Toyota Motor, Tokyo Toyopet, Osaka Toyopet, and Toyota Tokyo Corolla. These four firms comprise roughly 180 subcompanies with a combined staff of 87,000 employees. In addition, there are two more dealer networks devoted to Toyota, with a total of 132 subcompanies and 30,000 employees. Altogether, the Toyota Group's distribution network has under its wing over 300 companies, more than 4750 dealer outlets, and a total staff of almost 120,000 people. Add to that total 33 companies selling forklifts, 34 companies selling auto parts, and 29 companies selling houses and you have a rough idea of the Toyota Group's distribution clout.

Recently, Volkswagen terminated a sales agreement with Japan's best-known retailer of foreign cars to tie up with Toyota (this was a neat trick, since VW had a long-standing agreement with arch-rival Nissan to produce certain VW models in Japan). Now General Motors is also looking to put its cars in all those shiny Toyota showrooms from Hokkaido to Okinawa. Why are companies like GM and VW happy to tie up with a rival which boasts that it will soon capture 10 percent of the global auto market—in part by stealing share from those two firms? The principal reason is this monolithic distribution system, which Toyota could put to work selling Chevys just as easily as Corollas if it wants to. With the higher prices Japanese expect to pay for everything from overseas, the domestic market can be highly profitable. Both VW and GM expect to see the results of Toyota's marketing muscle show up on their bottom lines in the next few years.

The Nissan Group

SNAPSHOT: The Nissan Group

Keiretsu ties: Member of the Fuyo Group, but with strong ties to IBJ

Main banks: IBJ, Fuji

Top shareholders: Dai-Ichi Life, IBJ, Fuji Bank, Nippon Life, Asahi Bank, Sumitomo Bank, Yasuda Trust, Sumitomo Life, Meiji Life Insurance, Nissan Fire & Marine Insurance

Stable shareholding: 49 percent

Directors' connections: IBJ, Fuji Bank, MITI, Asahi Bank

Nissan Motor Co. is Japan's number two auto maker, an appellation the company would just as soon do without. Say instead that the firm ranks fourth in the world, just behind Ford, and it somehow sounds more significant. It is an inescapable fact that Nissan is the perennial runner-up at home, sometimes gaining on but never coming close to overtaking Toyota. Of course, with a market share hovering around 25 percent, being second isn't all that bad. With annual sales of roughly $34 billion and over 55,000 employees, the parent company alone is a solid member of the business community, but when its group pyramid is included, it becomes a major force in Japanese industry. Just adding up about three dozen of Nissan's major subcontractors yields a sales total of over $35 billion.

Predictably, its organizational structure is quite similar to Toyota's. Underneath the parent firm is a core group of about a dozen key subcontractors in which the parent holds an average 40 percent equity stake (much higher than Toyota's interest in its top 12). Under these first-tier firms is a group of second- and third-tier subcontractors which, like Toyota's, are not well differentiated. Until a few years ago the Nissan keiretsu had two distinct classes of subcontractors—those primarily loyal to Nissan and the "independents," firms that had somehow managed to keep control of their own destiny and used that precarious position to conduct business with a variety of different auto makers. In the early 1990s, however, Nissan's profits began a stomach-wrenching downward spiral that led to the firm posting its first red-ink settlement since listing in 1951. As the company began severe production cutbacks, its captive parts makers were naturally envious of the independents' freedom to turn to other makers for orders. Thus, Nissan merged its second- and third-tier suppliers, the loyalists and the independents alike, into a single organization, the Nissho-kai, which consists of almost 200 companies. The larger among these firms are publicly listed, but the majority are small and not well known. Beneath this level, of course, are the hundreds of even smaller companies who supply the middle-ranked Nissho-kai members. They are almost without exception captive makers, and the cutbacks in production ultimately hit them the hardest.

Like Toyota, Nissan has under its wing two of the other 10 vehicle companies: Nissan Diesel Motor (one of Japan's top truck makers) and Fuji Heavy Industries (maker of Subaru cars). There is an interesting historical reason for this. As we saw in our examination of the zaibatsu, the Occupation forces broke up the "Nissan" combine after the war into its several component parts, including the modern auto firm. One of the other industrial groups GHQ wanted broken up was Nakajima Aircraft, a major contributor to the war effort. Nakajima became Fuji Heavy Industries after the war. Both the Nissan conglomerate and Nakajima Aircraft were part of a real prewar keiretsu, a bank-centered industrial group revolving around the Japan Industrial Bank, which became the Industrial Bank of Japan (IBJ) after the war. Half a century later, IBJ is still a de facto main bank for Nissan and Fuji Heavy as well as the number two shareholder for both.

Like Toyota, Nissan has a second pyramid, a huge sales and distribution network. Altogether, as of 1991, the company's national sales group comprised over 200 firms (all the big ones having directors seconded from Nissan), more than 3000 new car dealerships, and roughly 75,000 employees. In addition, there are 100 percent-owned land- and sea-based transport companies and a car leasing firm, all with Nissan-assigned directors on board. Nissan Credit covers financing for the sales side. Nissan Trading sounds impressive, but actually turns less than a tenth the sales volume of its counterpart at Toyota. And there is even a tiny Nissan Real Estate Development to give the appearance of diversification. The firm is also relatively close to both Nissan Life Insurance and Nissan Fire & Marine Insurance, which are distant relatives from the old prewar conglomerate.

The Honda Group

SNAPSHOT: The Honda Group

Keiretsu ties: Officially, none, but close to Mitsubishi Bank

Main banks: Mitsubishi, Mitsubishi Trust

Top shareholders: Mitsubishi Bank, Mitsubishi Trust, Tokio Marine & Fire Insurance, Tokai Bank, BOT, Asahi Bank, Sanwa Bank, Meiji Life, Nippon Life Insurance, Yasuda Fire & Marine Insurance

Stable shareholding: 47.5 percent

Directors' connections: Mitsubishi Bank, Mitsubishi Trust, Ministry of Foreign Affairs

It is one of the great mysteries of cultural difference that Honda Motor Co. is far more popular in the United States than it is in Japan. Many Japanese are still puzzled as to why the Accord was the best-selling car in America for so long. Most Japanese beyond college age still see Honda as a Johnny-come-lately, a motorcycle company that branched out into autos, then became obsessed with winning races. Honda's domination of the F1 circuits thrilled teenagers and Honda engineers, but did little to change the firm's image as a maverick in the industry, hardly a legitimate pretender to Toyota or Nissan's thrones.

As we have seen, the Toyota and Nissan keiretsu are like two fortresses commanding roughly two-thirds of the domestic car market. Assaulting the Big Two would be idiotic, and fighting Mazda, Mitsubishi, Isuzu, and Suzuki for what remained of the market would be unrewarding. Instead, Honda turned its attention to overseas markets, particularly the United States, where its motorcycles had already established the company's reputation. Today, even with substantial local production in the United States, Canada, and the United Kingdom, Honda's export ratio remains higher than that of any Japanese auto maker.

In the process, it would be normal for Honda to have built up its own pyramid-type production keiretsu. Here again, the firm is a bit of a maverick. Although it has a circle of subsidiaries and affiliates, there are far fewer of them than for any manufacturer of similar size. Some estimates indicate there are only a few dozen parts makers that could be identified as belonging principally to the Honda organization. Just for comparison, the total Honda Group is said to have about 85,000 employees, which is less than the 10 auto-related companies in Toyota's first-tier circle. The parent firm, Honda Motor, generates annual sales of about $23.2 billion, far less than Nissan and only about a third of Toyota's figure.

Thus, we begin to see that the gaps between the auto keiretsu are huge, much more so than the simple one, two, three ranking would indicate. Honda currently holds the number three spot, but it is only slightly ahead of Mazda and Mitsubishi, both of which are determined to win the only real battle in the industry—third place. Looked at in this way, Toyota, though big enough to be one of the Big Six, has aligned itself with the Mitsui Group. Nissan is a member of the Fuyo Group. Mazda is an unofficial member of the Sumitomo Group. And Mitsubishi Motors is . . . Mitsubishi Motors. The odd man out is Honda.

Without a powerful keiretsu of its own and without a Big Six group to assure it of a certain minimum level of sales every year, the firm must do something difficult: sell entirely to the general public simply on the basis of the quality and appeal of its products. Showroom sales are nice, but they are no substitute for being able to sell whole fleets of cars to your keiretsu partners regardless of a car's merits (the famous Mitsubishi Debonair, sometimes referred to as the Japanese Edsel, did not send consumers rushing to their local Mitsubishi dealer, but sold thanks to "group purchases" by scores of Mitsubishi affiliates). Since the chances of Honda besting its bigger rivals are slim, the firm continues to emphasize overseas sales, for it is only in markets such as the United States and Europe that it can compete on an equal footing with Toyota and Nissan.

Although Honda is not a member of any of the Big Six, it shares a main bank with one of its hottest competitors. Honda's top two shareholders are Mitsubishi Bank and Mitsubishi Trust, the number three shareholder is Tokio Marine & Fire Insurance, and number eight is Meiji Life Insurance, all key Mitsubishi companies. In sum, the Mitsubishi Group owns 15.6 percent of Honda's equity and Mitsubishi Bank has a director on Honda's board. In spite of such cozy connections, Honda has always been exceptionally independent and is not considered a Mitsubishi company. Nor is it likely to become one. At the time the Mitsubishi financial firms invested in Honda it was one of Japan's fastest-growing companies and Mitsubishi Motor Corp. did not yet exist. Now that the latter has been born (following a decades-long pregnancy by Mitsubishi Heavy Industries) and is growing rapidly, the group has a duty to take care of its own. Very recently, Honda has supplemented its loans from Mitsubishi Group banks by substantially increasing its borrowings from the Export-Import Bank.

Perhaps the most outstanding feature of the Honda Group, then, is its small size. The parent prefers to deal with independent suppliers, such as Koito Mfg., a member of the Toyota Group that also does considerable business with most of the other car makers, and Kasai Kogyo and Jidosha Denki Kogyo, both members of the Nissan Group.

Of course, a company can survive without its own captive production keiretsu, but it is difficult to do business without a distribution keiretsu. Honda, just like Toyota and Nissan, has a nationwide sales group divided into different channels. Whereas Toyota has five distinct sales channels and Nissan is quickly consolidating its five into four, Honda has only three separate dealerships in Japan, totaling about 1500 sales companies and over 25,000 employees. These dealerships are only for cars—there is also a huge network of motorcycle dealers. Like its bigger rivals, the Honda Group also has a finance company, a trading company, a transportation company, and a real estate firm. But in many ways the group's most important sales arms are outside Japan.

Electronics

The Matsushita Group

SNAPSHOT: The Matsushita Group

Keiretsu ties: Officially, none, but close to Sumitomo

Main banks: Sumitomo, Asahi

Top shareholders: Sumitomo Bank, Sumitomo Life, Nippon Life, Asahi Bank, Sumitomo Trust, Sumitomo Marine & Fire, Mitsubishi Trust

Stable shareholding: 27 percent

Directors' connections: MITI, IBJ, Sumitomo Bank, Sumitomo Life, Matsushita Electric Works

---

The Parent.   There are dozens of electronics makers in Japan, many of whom have become household names overseas as well. Hitachi, Toshiba, Sony, Sharp, Sanyo, and a dozen others have stamped their names on millions of radios, TVs, video decks, and so on, and shipped them around the world. Yet by far the biggest company in this field was the one that seldom used its own name to promote its goods. Matsushita trademarks such as "Panasonic" and "Technics" became popular outside of Japan (where the company's goods are still known by the "National" brand), but the parent company's name remained all but unknown. That is no longer the case, especially after 1990 when the nucleus of the mammoth group, Matsushita Electric Industrial (MEI), dropped $6 billion on Hollywood giant MCA.

Sony's chairman Akio Morita may be well known in the United States, but in Japan his fame pales in comparison to that of Konosuke Matsushita. The founder of the Matsushita Group was not merely respected, but revered in the Japanese business world—so much so that he was often referred to as Japan's "God of Management" in print. In large part, this was testimony to his drive and skill in bringing his company up from humble beginnings to international prominence in just a few decades. Americans may wonder why his younger rival at Sony was not equally revered for achieving the same thing, but this only highlights the huge information gap between the two countries. Until recently, Sony could have passed for a large division or a subsidiary of a real giant such as Matsushita or Hitachi.

Konosuke's success was not simply in building up his company and his group, however. He developed a new method of running his empire called *jigyo bussei*. This essentially meant that the company's major divisions were split off as separate operating units, each with a certain amount of start-up capital provided by the head office, but each on its own when it came to turning a profit. This gave division managers both freedom and incentive, but the drive for profit was relentless. If a division ran out of operating funds, it was not allowed to go "outside" the group to borrow. Funds had to come from the MEI head office, usually at high interest rates.

Division managers were under tremendous pressure to mass-produce high-quality electric appliances and to keep costs down. The success that resulted is legendary. MEI is not only Japan's biggest but one of the world's biggest consumer electronics manufacturers, with about 50 production plants around the globe. The parent alone turns about $40 billion a year in sales, and its consolidated group (over 160 companies) generates another $20 billion. Just this official group near the upper end of the pyramid includes over 200,000 employees, and the bottom of its production pyramid must comprise tens of thousands more.

The firm has always been known as something of a "low tech" specialist. That is, families would pay a premium to buy a National refrigerator or washing machine, but few Japanese would rush out to buy a Panasonic computer. The company is now working hard to change that. It is developing its computer-related businesses and trying to adopt a more high-tech profile. MEI is hoping that tie-ups with Cray Research, Sun Microsystems, Tandy, Philips, and Siemens will help its image substantially.

Another bit of local color that seldom makes it across the Pacific is Matsushita's old reputation for "borrowing" successful new product designs. While the firm is universally respected for its ability to mass produce good equipment, from vacuum cleaners to high-definition TVs, it was once known in Japan not as Matsushita Denki, (Matsushita Electric) but *Maneshita* Denki (Copycat Electric). The verb *mane* ("mahnay") means to imitate, and *mane shita* means to have copied something. The play on words expresses the popular idea that Matsushita's original R&D was not always up to that of its rivals. Some Japanese felt that Matsushita used other companies, like Sony, as research labs, allowing them to develop new products, then changing them slightly and cranking them out in volume. Once Matsushita stuffed these products into its enormous distribution pipeline, it was almost guaranteed to outsell the original brand. Of course, Matsushita officials were appropriately enraged by such charges in public, but when the firm's manufacturing and marketing muscle can pull off coups such as turning the VHS video format into a world standard, they cried all the way to the bank. Today, the *maneshita* label is long since forgotten, as the Matsushita companies regularly turn out products just as good and often better than their well-known rivals.

The Group. Matsushita's strategy of spinning off and developing divisions was so successful that many became strong independent firms. Subsidiary Matsushita Electric Works is now an $8 billion company in its own right, and Matsushita Communication Industrial racks up $3.65 billion a year. Not bad for side businesses. Meanwhile, other independent firms, such as Victor Co. of Japan (known as JVC in the United States), which fell into difficulties years ago and tied up with Matsushita, are now MEI subsidiaries.

To market its products, Matsushita developed Japan's biggest chain of appliance retail outlets and service shops. It is this marketing army which boosted Matsushita to the top in the consumer electronics competition. It was also this same vertical keiretsu which brought Matsushita to the attention of U.S. negotiators during the SII talks. The chances of a foreign-brand electrical appliance sitting on the shelf next to a National product are about as good as a Sony TV being displayed in the same store with Matsushita's own. Distribution keiretsu are by their very nature exclusive or at least semiexclusive. Matsushita had a variety of ways of rewarding its distributors, but it was just as famous for its inflexibility in dealing with shop owners who did not follow the head office's commands to the letter (see Chapter 9). It is this kind of attitude which has won all the distribution keiretsu a reputation for narrow-minded regimentation that

turns off their current dealers and scares away outsiders considering opening a store.

Matsushita is considered an independent firm rather than a member
of any particular keiretsu. However, it is also a very important Kansai
business, and something would be very odd if it were not on especially
good terms with at least one of the big Osaka banks. Indeed, Matsushita is
usually considered "close" to the Sumitomo Group. Most writers are careful to point out, however, that MEI does not have membership in the
Hakusui-kai, has no historical Sumitomo affiliation, and that its relations
with Sumitomo Bank are not exclusive.

This determination to prove that an "independent" firm is truly independent is always interesting. Not only is Sumitomo Bank the number one
shareholder in MEI, but both the bank and Sumitomo Life have directors
on Matsushita's board. Sumitomo companies make up four of its top eight
shareholders, giving the group a total of 12.7 percent of the parent's equity.
Viewed as a whole, Sumitomo Group companies make up the second
largest shareholder (after MEI) of eight of the nine Matsushita subsidiaries
listed on the TSE First Section. To say that Matsushita is close to Sumitomo
is a bit of an understatement.

The Hitachi Group

SNAPSHOT: The Hitachi Group

Keiretsu ties: Member of Fuyo, Sanwa, and DKB Groups, but with a
strongly independent stance

Main banks: IBJ, Sanwa, DKB, Fuji

Top shareholders: Nippon Life, Dai-Ichi Life, Mitsubishi Trust, IBJ,
Sanwa Bank, Meiji Life, Sumitomo Trust, DKB

Stable shareholding: 36 percent

Directors' connections: NTT, Bank of Japan, MITI

The Parent. Hitachi is another firm like Toyota that is considered
representative of Japanese industry as a whole. It is huge, it is old, it has a
mammoth keiretsu, and it has tremendous clout in the business community. In the annual rankings of corporations by declared income,
Hitachi placed fourth among all nonfinancial industries in fiscal 1991 (up

from fifth the year before), behind Matsushita, telephone giant NTT, and perennial number one Toyota.

Unlike consumer electronics specialists such as Matsushita and Sony, Hitachi and its main rival, Toshiba, are comprehensive electric machinery makers. That is, if power flows through it, they make it. Hitachi's mainstay is the computer business, where it makes everything from disk drives to mainframes, and it is also a major global producer of semiconductors. It dabbles in consumer electronics (but wishes it didn't) and traffic control systems, but the parent's real strength is in heavy electrical equipment—nuclear power generators, railroad equipment, and so on. It has tie-ups with Texas Instruments (semiconductors), TRW (aerospace), General Electric (nuclear power), and others. The parent's annual sales hover around $32 billion, but consolidated sales are almost double that figure.

The firm shares ancestry with Nissan Motors and its related firms. Yet unlike Nissan, Hitachi stands out among modern industries for its independence from the keiretsu, or perhaps its "in it but not of it" stance. Hitachi seems to get all the benefits of keiretsu membership while appearing to remain aloof from the system. It is the only company that is a member of three shacho-kai—Fuyo, Sanwa, and DKB—and it continues to borrow roughly equal amounts from all three main banks. Like Nissan, though, Hitachi also has strong historical ties with IBJ and continues to borrow more each year from that bank than from any of the Big Six. If we were forced to pick one institution to label as the firm's "main" main bank, it would have to be IBJ.

The Group. The Hitachi Group is enormous. It includes 29 listed companies and about 370,000 people in 742 consolidated subsidiaries. The reason for this large number of official subsidiaries goes back to the 1950s when Hitachi began spinning off strong divisions into separate companies. The firm became famous for this policy and a model for other large Japanese companies to follow. The effectiveness of Hitachi's approach can be seen from a quick look at its income record. Consolidated sales in the fiscal year ending in March 1992 were 1.98 times the parent's sales figures. In other words, Hitachi's subsidiaries contribute roughly as much to group sales as does the parent. Just for comparison, at the number two firm, Toshiba, the figure was 1.48, at number three Mitsubishi Electric, it was only 1.28, and at number four NEC, only 1.23.

Lately, there are signs that Hitachi may have overexpanded, decentralizing its operations too far and creating too many subsidiaries. Industry observers have been saying for some time that the firm is suffering from "big company disease" and that its vast group actually inhibits efficient operations. Some say that Hitachi is too bureaucratic, out of step with the times, and point to the fact that it trails rivals Toshiba and NEC in a number of key areas, especially semiconductors, personal computers, and word processors. Hitachi's response has been to totally revamp its organization, including the elimination of its old factory profit center structure. For years Hitachi made each of its plants almost an autonomous company (somewhat similar to the Matsushita system), responsible for its own product planning and design as well as generating its own profits. This approach, which was appropriate for a much earlier stage in the growth of Japanese industry, is no longer effective, and the company has belatedly admitted as much.

On the distribution side, Hitachi has approximately 10,000 affiliated stores nationwide. Their primary function is to market the firm's home appliances and audio/video gear, which is becoming more difficult all the time. Although it makes TVs, video recorders, camcorders, and stereo systems, Hitachi has never held the top share in any segment of the consumer electronics market. Moreover, the old image of Hitachi home appliances— sturdy and reliable, but usually big and clunky—sounds more like a description of the high-speed "bullet trains" the firm proudly manufactures, not exactly the kind of cute thing the average Japanese housewife wants in her kitchen or closet. The company is working to change that image, but it will take time. While figures for changes in the number of Hitachi keiretsu stores are not available, it seems more than likely that the firm's distribution side is already contracting.

The Toshiba Group

SNAPSHOT: The Toshiba Group

Keiretsu ties: Member of Mitsui Group, but with a strongly independent stance

Main bank: Sakura (Mitsui)

Top shareholders: Dai-Ichi Life Insurance, Sakura Bank, Nippon Life Insurance, Mitsui Life Insurance, Mitsui Trust, Mitsubishi Trust, Sumitomo Trust, Nippon Fire & Marine Insurance, LTCB, Tokai Bank

Stable shareholding: 37 percent

Directors' connections: NTT; Min. of Posts & Telecommunications; MITI; Ishikawajima-Harima Heavy Industries (IHI)

The Parent. Hitachi has a problem, and it's called Toshiba. Every year, as Hitachi ranks in the top four or five nonfinancial businesses in the country, Toshiba is right behind it, snapping at its heels. The two have been number one and number two in their field for decades and will probably stay that way for some time. But unlike the car industry, no one doubts that number two has plans to move up sooner or later. On a parent basis, the firms look pretty well matched: both are comprehensive electric machinery makers, involved in almost identical product lines. In the fiscal year ended March 1992, Toshiba's sales were about $25 billion versus about $31 billion for Hitachi. Toshiba had about 74,000 employees to Hitachi's 82,000. However, the difference in scale becomes apparent when we look at the firms as the heads of vertical keiretsu. Toshiba had only 186 consolidated subsidiaries in its group compared to Hitachi's 742. When we compare the two groups' consolidated sales for that year, the difference is a whopping $24 billion. While the two firms may look the same up close, their two pyramids are very different. Number two still has a long way to go.

Like Hitachi, Toshiba is a leader in semiconductor production (it actually passed Hitachi years ago), one of the leading producers of nuclear generators in a nation politically committed to nuclear power, and active in computers and information equipment. Yet few Japanese think of Toshiba in terms of heavy industry. The company is best known at home for its popular word processors and its tremendously successful line of laptop computers. The irony is that Toshiba failed miserably to establish itself as an important maker of large-scale computers, while watching rivals Hitachi and NEC steal headlines every month with competing claims for their supercomputers. Instead, Toshiba went after the bottom end of the computer market, selling to average consumers rather than research institutes, and was as dramatically successful there as it had been unsuccessful with the bigger machines.

Toshiba is a member of the Mitsui Group, but like fellow member Toyota, has a very independent image. Although about 20 percent of its total borrowings come from Mitsui Group banks, it spreads the remainder out among all the Big Six groups (particularly Fuyo and Sumitomo) and another dozen banks. Like Hitachi, it has directors from NTT (the telephone company, also a major client) and MITI, but also one from the Ministry of Posts and Telecommunications, which regulates expansion of the telecom field. It should thus come as no surprise to discover that Toshiba is a big player in the communication satellite business. It also has a board member on loan from IHI (Ishikawajima-Harima Heavy Industries), with which it maintains strong ties. Internationally, Toshiba is closely allied with GE in nuclear power, Motorola and AT&T in telecom, Siemens in semiconductors, and Olivetti in computers. In recent years the firm has announced additional tie-ups with IBM and Apple Computer, showing management's strategy to survive the coming techno-wars through broad-based international cooperation.

The Group. The numbers quoted above for the size of the Toshiba Group are only those for consolidated accounting purposes, and do not reflect the group's real size. One source lists no fewer than 509 subsidiaries in the group, plus 161 affiliates, and obviously these are only the upper- and middle-level firms. There are four main subsidiaries listed on the First Section of the TSE, and all four have presidents and senior directors seconded from Toshiba. Several years ago one of the four was involved in illicit sales of defense-related equipment to the former Soviet Union. That incident seems to have faded in memory along with the end of the Cold War, but the televised drama of U.S. Congressmen smashing Toshiba equipment in front of the Capitol building will not soon be forgotten by Toshiba management. The firm's president was forced to step down from his post, and Toshiba's various businesses in the United States suffered as a result. As we might expect, the Mitsui keiretsu pulled together to support Toshiba during that difficult period.

Toshiba's distribution network is actually larger than Hitachi's, with 12,000 retail outlets nationwide. Its home products have a better reputation as well. In addition to a large distribution network, the group includes a credit company, an insurance company, a leasing firm, a building company, and a travel agency.

The Sony Group

SNAPSHOT: The Sony Group

Keiretsu ties: Officially, none, but still friendly with Mitsui

Main bank: None. Close to Sakura (Mitsui), BOT, Mitsubishi, Fuji, IBJ, etc.

Top shareholders: Mitsui Trust, Sakura Bank, Mitsubishi Trust, Sumitomo Trust, Toyo Trust, Yasuda Trust

Stable shareholding: 28.5 percent

Directors' connections: NTT; Min. of Posts & Telecommunications; Export-Import Bank; Sakura Bank; MITI, IHI

The Parent. Probably no Japanese brand name is as familiar around the world as Sony. It is linked inextricably with the image of Japanese consumer electronics, just as its flamboyant chairman, Akio Morita, is linked with discussions of Japanese trade and industrial policy overseas. The parent, Sony Corp., turns roughly $16 billion in annual sales in Japan, with consolidated earnings roughly double that figure. Like Honda (another postwar growth phenomenon), Sony wanted to be independent. Of course, it needed huge amounts of capital to grow, and in its early years it borrowed heavily from Mitsui Bank, although it made increasingly strong efforts to remain outside the formal perimeter of the Mitsui Group. Like Honda, however, the firm knew that becoming a major player on a field occupied by older, larger, and better-connected companies would be next to impossible without powerful keiretsu affiliations. The only option for turbocharging growth was to shift to foreign markets, which was exactly what both small companies did.

Today Sony is one of Japan's most representative multinational firms, with production bases around the world and listings on 20 global stock exchanges. It still sells more in the United States than it does at home, and the parent's export ratio is 65 percent. With the yen strong against the dollar and weak consumer spending at home to prop up the other side of the business, that spells trouble. In March of 1992 Sony registered its first operating loss since going public.

During the equity financing mania of the late 1980s, Sony was able to raise several billion dollars without going near a bank, and both the parent and its major subsidiaries still show an aversion to bank borrowing. One of the reasons Sony needed to raise so much cash at that time was a policy of strategic acquisitions: in 1988 it bought CBS Records (now Sony Music Entertainment, Inc.); then in 1989 it picked up Columbia Pictures Entertainment (now Sony Pictures Entertainment, Inc.). Having already become a key player in the audiovisual hardware business with its Trinitron TVs, 8mm video cameras, and two different formats of compact disks, the firm decided to move into the even more lucrative software side, producing and distributing the music and films that are played on its equipment. The combination gives Sony enormous clout in the development of new products and standards in the multimedia race that is just now beginning. Sony is also developing its telecom and information businesses and has its own computer workstation. It also produced one of the popular Apple laptop computers and has become a major subcontractor for Apple.

Mitsui Trust and Sakura Bank are Sony's top keiretsu shareholders, and the composition of the company's board of directors indicates its desire to cover all bases: MITI, the Ministry of Posts and Telecommunications, NTT, the Export-Import Bank of Japan, Sakura Bank, and the Bank of Tokyo.

The Group. Being something of an arriviste in the big leagues, Sony again resembles newcomer Honda in not having a big, powerful keiretsu at its command. It does have a few large, listed subsidiaries, such as Aiwa and Sony Chemicals, but that is about the extent of the upper-level firms in its production pyramid.

On the distribution side, Sony has a wholesaling subsidiary, Sony Network Hanbai, set up in 1988 to handle high-volume sales, and Sony Consumer Marketing, formed in 1991 from the amalgamation of 18 regional distribution companies to move its products to general consumers. This latter function is handled by a nationwide network of 3000 keiretsu stores and another 20,000 stores licensed to represent the firm's product line. For the past several years the parent has been trying to get its retailers to get rid of the corner appliance shop image and convert their stores into trendy, fashionable places for young shoppers to check out the newest technology. If anyone can make a go of this, Sony can, but with the prolonged downturn in audiovisual sales and even the tendency among young shoppers' to keep their money in their pockets, Sony is in for a rough few years.

8

Voices from Inside the Pyramid

A number of researchers, both Japanese and foreign, have attempted to peer inside the manufacturing groups. To do so, they have visited the companies at the top of the pyramids and talked at length about the Japanese system of subcontracting. Not surprisingly, their research resulted in the conclusion that the manufacturers treat their subcontractors rather well; in many ways they nurture the little companies in their groups and help them to grow; the big manufacturers and their subcontractors exist in a mutually beneficial relationship, each helping the other, each respecting the other for its relative strengths. The MITI office responsible for monitoring small businesses has given basically this same response throughout the years.

While we believe that this is true to some extent, our knowledge of Japanese business, especially the SMEs, made it difficult to accept that this was the whole story. Thus, we decided to pursue another approach—talking directly to subcontractors inside production pyramids. We spoke with dozens of managers from companies in the Kanto (Greater Tokyo) region. Their firms ran the gamut from very small electrical machinery shops to first-tier subcontractors for giant auto manufacturers. The comments of these subcontractors are revealing.

One of the conditions for obtaining these interviews was our guarantee of strict anonymity for the participants. In accordance with their wishes, we have assigned fictitious names to all the speakers here, but their comments appear with a minimum of editing.

The first section is a discussion among four managers, all friends, from three firms in Tokyo's Ota ward, a center of small-scale manufacturing. All are involved in making parts for the electronics industry. The second section contains comments from various managers of subcontracting firms in the electronics industry, and the third group is from the auto industry.

Round Table

Four men agreed to meet with us one evening to talk about the keiretsu they see every day. The participants were Takaharu Yoshida, 70-ish, the president of a small manufacturing company in Ota-ku, Tokyo, Masamitsu Hara, 59, the foreman of Yoshida's firm, Hiroshi Takita, 47, and Tetsuo Kudo, 63, both presidents of small machinery shops located within a half a mile of the Yoshida factory.

YOSHIDA: I don't know what happens in other countries, so I can't say. Perhaps our subcontracting system is not so different from other places. But I know that before the war we subcontractors were not so tightly controlled as we are now. The control began during the war.

In 1938 the government passed a law which basically allowed them to do whatever they wanted to with industry. The aim of the law was to unite all strategic businesses and industries. Everyone was talking about *shin taisei*, making the country a single new body. People thought that we couldn't fight a war with every little firm going its own way, thinking only of its own profits, so the laws were designed to pull all the companies together for the national good.

Up until that time, when we thought of big industry we thought of textiles. You know, the big spinning companies were the most important firms. But then heavy industry and steel and ships became strong. Shin taisei required this shift. Most of the companies in Japan used to be little shops like my father's. He had just six employees, but he liked his work. The war changed all that. In 1943 the government passed another law, ordering even more corporate integration, and they basically scrapped all the small factories. They combined all the little firms into bigger units to help fight the war. My father's factory was merged with a bigger factory down the road, one with about a hundred workers. The new plant was designated as a supplier to the Mitsubishi zaibatsu, and it had to make parts for weapons.

A lot of companies like that sprang up, not really small, but not big enough to be important. They were all just subcontractors in the arms business. But a lot of those companies were made up of little firms that weren't really good manufacturers to begin with. They weren't competent to produce some of the things they were asked to turn out, so a lot of the weapons were defective. When I look back on those days and the kind of manufacturing people were doing, it's no wonder we lost the war.

The war also changed the labor unions. Before the war our labor unions used to be like those in America, set up by occupation not by company. But back in the thirties the government ordered the unions to unite with management to fight the war. After the defeat, the Americans wouldn't stand for that, so they separated management and labor once again, but the idea of the company labor union somehow remained. Now we've got separate unions for each company, so none of the unions will ever grow very strong.

You know, I think back on the war a lot, and those laws and how everything changed. In a lot of ways it never changed back again. During the war the government had legal control over production at every firm. From that time on industry became completely production-centered and highly government-controlled. I believe that after the war things didn't change much. I've been running a machine shop since the war ended, and my impression is that the same basic principles were kept in force. Industry remained production-centered, but the focus was shifted from military demand to consumer demand. I remember how during the war the big banks all took care of the firms in their zaibatsu. All the banks did the same thing. To me that was the beginning of what we call the *kinyu keiretsu* today. It all stemmed from the shin taisei of the war period.

Another thing . . . the relationship between the automobile industry and the machinery industry and their subcontractors also developed during the war and has continued ever since. A good friend of mine became a subcontractor for Toyota during the war, and today he's still a member of the Toyota supply organization. Things like that don't change much. When you look at it strictly from the point of view of the subcontractor, things were much better during the war than they are now. A lot of big companies did well as a result of the huge demand from the military for all kinds of equipment, and the subcontractors under them prospered. All this stuff about the parent companies squeezing down prices and double-checking every stage of production, all of that came later.

HARA: Nobody knows what the real figures are, but we often hear that the in-house production ratio at most of the big companies is about 20 to 30 percent. In the auto industry, for example, we hear that it's roughly 30 percent in-house and 70 percent subcontracted. Everybody takes that for granted. In electronics, no one knows for sure, but I'm willing to bet the subcontract ratio is a lot higher.

For instance, a company goes to build a personal computer. The heart of the computer is a microprocessor and some memory chips that sit on a very complex printed circuit board. Now, the big companies make those microprocessors and those memory chips themselves, but just about everything else in the entire computer is subcontracted. The circuit board, the disk drive, the power supply, the keyboard, the case—everything. The big companies aren't going to make any of that stuff because there's no profit in it. They tell one of the little electric firms in their keiretsu to make the power supply, and a little cable maker produces the cable and the plug, and a metal-working firm stamps out the cases, and a board maker does the pc boards, and so on. Those are all places where the parent company can squeeze down the costs anytime they want to.

The big firms spend their money on R&D, usually developing new chips and designing plans for new computers. Of course, they also do some assembling of the finished products, but even there the ratio is usually very low. Final assembly is often left to one of the bigger subcontractors. The big companies also spend money on advertising and sales, and management expenses, which of course includes the cost of managing the subcontractors.

Why use so many subcontractors in the first place? That's obvious: to save money. The biggest merit for big firms is that they don't have to make huge investments in capital equipment, at least not anywhere near what they would have to if they produced everything in-house. Equipment is expensive, and maintaining it is expensive, and replacing it is expensive. By putting that burden on the subcontractors, the big firms limit their investment to just the equipment they really want, like very high-tech lines to produce ICs.

You know where the majority of the equipment used to produce the big company's products is? It's in the subcontractors' factories. Think of how much the big companies have to borrow to run their business. Now, multiply that by 20 or 30 times and you've got some idea of how much they'd have to borrow if they produced all their own goods. Then think of the risk involved in manufacturing anything these days. Suppose some new product comes along that looks like it might sell, but nobody really knows. Is a big company going to invest a lot of money in setting up production lines for that product? Not likely. They'll do the absolute minimum they can in-house and let their subcontractors invest in whatever equipment is necessary for the rest. Then, if the product dies on the market, for whatever reason, the subcontractor is stuck with a lot of useless equipment, not the parent. Using subcontractors gives them a tremendous amount of flexibility, both in terms of freeing up capital and keeping the risky side of production outside of their company.

But there's a problem with subcontracting everything, a problem the big firms never see until it's too late. Their own technology suffers from having so much done outside. You know, everybody's always talking about innovation, but they forget that innovation is not like a thunderbolt from the blue. It's something that comes from manufacturing day after day, accumulating experience year after year and then suddenly realizing how to make improvements. That's why so much of the real innovation in manufacturing comes at the subcontractor level.

Sometimes the R&D labs at one of the big companies come up with something truly innovative. They design a new product or a new way of employing technology, and it looks exciting. Do the big companies jump right in and apply that research? No way. That would be too risky. Usually they'll send the plans to one of their trusted subcontractors to start trial production. If they like the results, maybe they'll continue production. If the product is going to become a big hit and they have reason to bring it in-house, they may switch to full-scale mass production in one of the parent company's main plants.

There is no question that the big companies have some really top-notch researchers from the best universities, some real brains who can design tremendous things. But the applied technology is not in the companies they work for. It's here, at the subcontractor level.

When new workers join a big firm, like a big electronics maker, they are shown all the different steps in the production process. It comes as a surprise to many of them to discover that the giant company they've joined doesn't have a molding division, a pressing division, a painting division, or a dozen other normal functions of the manufacturing business. When the time comes for them to see how all of these various steps are done, they are taken around to some of the firm's major subcontractors. We see these kids come wandering through our factories, looking like college tour groups, careful not to get their new blue suits dirty. Their supervisors tell them everything they need to know about the plants they're visiting, so there's no chance they'll talk to any of us and find out what's really going on in these factories. I'm not even sure they'd believe us if we told them.

TAKITA: Another reason why big firms have used subcontractors in the past is that they needed to maintain the lifetime employment system. Even if the economy turns sour and sales drop to nothing, the big companies can't just lay off employees.

When times get tough, they cut orders to their subcontractors. Then they tell the ones who're still getting a few orders to slash their prices. You know the result: the big companies cut their costs dramatically and the subcontractors get squeezed. Some go out of business. Others get by, but only by firing a lot of their workers. The funny thing is that through all of this the big companies go right on talking about the "lifetime employment" system as if it was the basic right of every Japanese worker.

Sure, things are changing now—the recession has even the big firms scared. They're urging people to take early retirement and that kind of thing. But nobody's getting fired yet. Companies like Hitachi made news a while ago with their "layoffs," but when you read all the details, it turns out that all they did was tell a bunch of employees not to come in on Saturdays. Their salaries are guaranteed, just take a holiday. Other big firms shift their excess personnel to their subsidiaries or other related businesses, but they still pay their full salaries. Believe me, those aren't layoffs. If you work for a small company, you know what layoffs are all about.

But everyone cooperates to maintain the big myth. Like now, when there's a recession, the newspapers all do surveys of industry and report in big headlines, "Recession Squeezes Industry But No One Laid Off." Of course, as long as they only talk to companies listed on the stock exchange, that's true. The other 99.9 percent of Japanese companies are ignored. The vast majority of Japanese workers have never had any kind of job security and they never will.

The whole song and dance stops as soon as you look below the big companies' first-tier factories. At the first-tier subcontractors, things may not be too bad, but as you go down to the second and third and fourth tiers, people are being fired left and right.

So, by using subcontractors, the big firms can insulate themselves from all but the worst recessions. They can pay their people good wages and guarantee them indefinitely, so the companies maintain their reputations for job security. By having a lot of subcontractors in their keiretsu, they increase the flexibility of their organization. The people on top of the pile are protected, but the people down below can be fired or laid off for as long as necessary or have their salaries cut in half, and of course they're paid a lot less to begin with.

Things are starting to change these days, but I would say most small-company employees do not have yearly contracts. Most are paid by the month, and some are paid only by the day. What kind of life is that? But the subcontractor knows he cannot promise any more. If his main client suddenly stops placing orders for whatever reason, business grinds to a halt. These little firms have no fat profit margins and no retained earnings to fall back on. So to protect themselves against sudden changes in the market—or to put it another way, to protect themselves against their clients—the subcontractors must keep employee commitments to a minimum. Workers at the subcontractor level know that any paycheck could be their last.

HARA: There are many different types of subcontractors. In a real vertical keiretsu, thousands of small makers supply parts for a single big company which ultimately controls all the firms beneath it. Subcontractors in these pyramids are absolutely forbidden to take orders from other firms. This structure was practically universal from the middle 1950s to the late seventies. As the economy grew, the big companies grew, too, and they wanted to be sure of steady sources of supply for all their necessary parts. That meant they didn't want their subcontractors working for anyone else. The system was absolutely closed.

Subcontractors were brought together in "cooperative groups" to foster a feeling of unity, like "we're all in this together." Once a month we'd all eat together, the heads of the various companies would play golf together, maybe take an overnight trip somewhere, and when times were really good a bunch of them would get to go to Hong Kong or Hawaii together. It was that kind of thing. If you worked in the Toshiba keiretsu, everything was Toshiba, Toshiba, Toshiba. If you were inside Hitachi, it was Hitachi this and Hitachi that. The idea was to keep everyone together, not to let them circulate or know what was going on in anybody else's keiretsu. What they really couldn't stand was the idea that quality subcontractors might try to work as free agents.

Even today the big firms still want all their subcontractors to be completely loyal. But the markets are much tougher than a decade ago. Now when the big companies get squeezed by competition, they say to their subcontractors, "Hey, don't count on us for everything. We can't carry you like in the old days. You've got to watch out for yourselves." Like they felt obliged to look after us before but now the rules have changed. Who are they kidding? When times are good, the big companies feed their subcontractors plenty of orders. Everybody has lots of work. But when times get bad, they just close down the order pipeline and tell the subcontractors to get by as best they can. One thing doesn't change, though: the very best subcontractors, the ones with really talented engineers and good equipment, are told to stay loyal no matter what, just like in the past. The big companies all talk about the new "freedom" to tie up with whomever you want, but none of them wants its key subcontractors drifting to another keiretsu.

TAKITA: Just look back to the two oil shocks in the seventies, and the high yen shock in the eighties. The big exporters were hurting. So what did they do? Slash prices on all their exports? Hell, no. Instead, they rationalized like never before. I love that word, "rationalization." It has a nice, clean, academic sound to it, doesn't it? But that wasn't what life was like in '86 and '87. The big firms crunched down like never before. They ordered us to drop prices overnight, and at the same time cut orders by 50 or 60 percent, and then told us to restructure our factories. Where two guys were doing some job, they said "Let one guy do it." Where a bunch of people where doing a job, they said "Install robots and put them on-line full-time, round the clock."

Sure, it was rationalization, all right. Thousands of small companies got "rationalized" right out of existence. Companies went bust, people were told not to come to work any more. But did a single big firm go under as a result of the yen appreciation? Not that I heard of. Afterwards, all the papers and the TV people said, "Japan has survived the yen shock! The Japanese economy has triumphed!" Sure, a couple of hundred big companies all survived, but a lot of little companies nobody's ever heard of got sacrificed.

I look around at the men who run factories in my area, and they're tired. Tired of "rationalizing," tired of being told to cut costs again and again, tired of being told how much they can charge for their work, and so on. These guys are the foundation of modern Japanese industry, but they get treated like lazy servants. Why do they put up with it? There's no money in it, that's for sure. A lot of them go under, and the ones who survive know that they may be next.

Why do they keep going? I'll tell you, because I feel exactly the same way: Pride. We are proud of what we do. We love manufacturing. We love it because we know the big companies could never replace us. We are the only companies in Japan, maybe in the world, that can make what they want, when they want it, and at the lowest prices. And we must be the only people on earth who would work day and night for a week straight to make some little valve or switch just right, knowing all the time that we're going to lose money on it and probably get not the slightest word of thanks from our parent. We do it because we love to make things, and because we know the big companies couldn't do it even if they tried.

HARA: These days we hear a lot about *jitan* (shorter working hours). The government tells us that in other countries the average employee works only about 1800 hours annually, while the average Japanese worker puts in around 2300 hours. I don't know where they get those numbers, and I don't know whether they're right or not. What I do know is that they only apply to big companies. No small company I know could stay in business very long unless everyone was working a lot more than that.

Now the government is saying that to avoid friction with other countries we should work less. Of course, all the salaried employees at the big firms think this is a great idea—they get paid the same whether they work a six-day week or a five-day week. So now everyone is talking about *jitan*. Like I say, this is wonderful if you happen to work for a big company.

If you're a subcontractor like me, it's a joke. We already work longer hours than any big manufacturer; when those guys start cutting back on their work time, who do you think is going to have to make up the difference?

Our jobs don't run from nine to five. Our customers come at any hour, any day, and tell us what they want and how soon they want it. Most of the time they wanted it yesterday. Sometimes a guy from our main client will show up with no advance notice. He'll have some very complicated piece of machinery in his hand. "We need three of these right away," he'll say. "Two days, max. Can you do it?" Well, one look tells me we probably can't do it. If we stop everything else and put everybody in the plant on the project, I know we could do it in a week. "Two days. Yes or no?" he says. What can we do? If I say no, he'll just take it to another plant and give them the work, even if they do a sloppy job. And the next time they need something, maybe something we can do easily, will they come around here? No, of course not. They'll go to the guy down the street first, and if he says no, they'll go somewhere else. In that sense, we've got no choice, we have to take it. So I say yes. And then we all work like crazy, all day and all night for two days. And somehow we just barely finish the things.

My staff are so tired they can't stand up; I'm exhausted and dizzy. I have to have someone drive me over to the company's office with the finished job, but I smile when I hand it over to their representative. "We did it," I say and just from my voice he can tell how proud I am. Of course, I don't expect anything from him, that's not their way. But even so it's tough when he just says "Right" and nods towards the door. Sometimes I'm angry and sometimes I'm frustrated, but there's nothing I can say or do. That's the way big companies are. We're nothing to them, and what we did is nothing more than they expect. If a firm like ours is worth anything, we should be able to fill their order and deliver it on time. That's the way they think. If we do what we're supposed to, and they're satisfied, they'll give us more work.

KUDO: Japan has been exporting steel and cars and semiconductors, and now we've got "trade friction" with the rest of the world. We turn on our TVs and what do we see? American auto workers who've been laid off smashing up Japanese cars and radios. Do they really think that Japanese companies are so strong just because American workers are being laid off? That seems very strange to me.

Look closer at Japan and you see that tens of thousands of Japanese workers are being laid off, too. The only difference is that big American firms actually fire their own employees, while Japanese firms force their subcontractors to do the firing instead. The end result is the same, except that the big American companies look battered and have all sorts of labor troubles as a result, while big Japanese companies look strong and keep smiling. I think people who say that Japanese industries are strong don't really understand how our system works.

After the war, the big manufacturing companies became intoxicated with the idea of efficiency. The parent company would specify which tools we'd need for a certain job, how many minutes should be allotted for Process A, how many seconds for Process B, how many minutes a man should rest, how many seconds he should spend looking at the spec sheets, and then what the total time should be to produce a set number of units of a given product in one day. All this was given to us by the big firm's Production Manager, which is amusing because our parent doesn't actually produce very much. The Production Manager's job is to watch over all the subcontractors who do the real work. You can bet all this efficiency management stuff was never applied to their own head offices. If they started running a stopwatch on their own staff and telling them how to be more productive, I think they'd have serious trouble on their hands.

The fact is, our parent company [One of Japan's best-known electronics makers] doesn't understand the joy of making things because all they do is mass production. They only care about how many units we can make in the shortest period of time. Every few years they come up with a new variation on the old production efficiency theme. We've lived through management theories called ZD and IE, VE and VA, and I'm sure they'll have some new system next year. But it all boils down to what they think of as efficiency. They want us to make more units, make them cheaper, and deliver them on time. They don't care at all about the kind of technical skills that allow a really experienced operator to work to within a micron of accuracy on some piece of work. The parent company reps don't know anything about real manufacturing. They just keep giving orders: Faster! Cheaper! More units per day! And we do it. We manage to speed up the work a little more than before, we somehow squeeze our costs a little lower, and we do it all without lowering quality in any way.

There isn't a subcontractor alive who doesn't feel, "We've done extraordinary work. We should charge more for this." But no one says a word. The parent company reps tell us, "Lower your prices, and we'll increase our orders." If we say no, give us a fair price for our work, they simply take their orders to another subcontractor. With things the way they are, you can bet there are dozens of shops that are dying for work, and they'll jump at the offer. What can we do? If we have some unique process or some special equipment that no other subcontractor has, maybe we have a little leverage, but most of us don't have that edge. The big firms might as well own us outright.

YOSHIDA: In the Keihin area [from Tokyo's southern wards of Ota and Shinagawa down towards Yokohama and Kawasaki City] there are thousands of little factories, all subcontractors for somebody. And their level of skill is unbelievable. I would go so far as to say that there's nothing mechanical in the world that couldn't be made in that area. Anything a company would ever want could be made at one of these little companies. If one of them doesn't have the right equipment, the word goes around pretty fast, and when some other firm has what is necessary, the job gets done. Because manufacturers in this area are so good, all sorts of orders come our way.

For example, a while ago my firm got a tiny order from our parent company. It was just for two pieces of a small precision part, so we knew right away it was a money-loser. But the part was crucial for something that was going into the space shuttle. The Americans had asked one of the big Japanese electronics firms to make something for their space program. The big company was delighted to take the order—I bet they've got a gold plaque or something from NASA up in the lobby of their headquarters— but they knew they couldn't do it. So they passed the job down to our factory. Of course we could see that costwise it was a total waste of time and energy for us to work on it. But we took the order gladly. And we did a beautiful job on it, too—not to impress the Americans, because they'll never in a million years know who made those parts, but just because we were so damn proud to do it. I bet no other plant in Japan could have done it.

Just getting that order from our parent firm was the same as them saying to us, "We know you're the best. Can you do it and make us look good?" We did it, and we enjoyed it. Everybody in my shop pitched in one way or another. Nobody said a word about it, but I knew they were just as proud as I was. I wish we had a few more jobs like that, because that's the kind of thing that keeps us going.

HARA: An old guy I know is a top engineer for a subcontractor to one of the giant firms, a very famous company in the consumer electronics business. Years ago this big company asked him to come up with a new way to cut magnetic film for making audio and video tapes. You probably know that magnetic film is made in wide sheets and then little blades slice it into very narrow strips of exactly the same width so that it can be wound onto audio or video cassettes. The problem is that these tapes are covered with various kinds of metal oxides. You run a metal-covered film across a razor-sharp cutting head for a day or two and that cutting head is going to lose its edge in no time. But if the heads aren't extremely sharp they don't cut properly, so the big company was always replacing the cutters in its film plant. That meant stopping production all the time, which meant low efficiency, which meant the managers were tearing their hair out. You get the picture.

So my friend worked and worked, and finally came up with a radical new design for a cutting head. His own factory produced it and the big electronics maker tested it. Nobody could believe the results. His cutter was every bit as precise as the old ones, but ran much, much longer without any need for replacement. They told him productivity in the film plant went up not just a little, but maybe a hundred times. All of that increased efficiency went right to this big company's bottom line. Since they didn't drop their tape prices for quite a while, it's hard to guess how much they made, but we're talking about a whole division of a company suddenly swimming in unexpected profit. How do you think they rewarded the subcontractor who made all this possible? They paid him for the materials he used in development, and they paid him for his actual manufacturing costs. That's it.

Now, in America, I guess a guy like that would have filed a patent application. If my friend had done so, he could have licensed his tape-production technology to half a dozen makers in Japan and retired the next day with fifty million dollars in the bank. But this is Japan, and subcontractors aren't allowed to do such things. If you design something that your parent company ordered, you are supposed to feel grateful to the parent. It's an unwritten rule, but it might as well be law. Of course the parent firm did take out a patent on that technology, but my friend could not. As a result, his little company is struggling along just as it was before.

A little while ago I heard that his son told him he doesn't want to go into his father's business, and I guess I can understand his feelings. When that old engineer dies, his factory will close and they'll probably build a 7 Eleven or something on the spot. That's what it's all about. I could give you dozens of examples just like that.

TAKITA: I'll tell you one. My cousin was a very skilled engineer. He had his own little company in Kamata [a part of Ota ward in Tokyo] and did really superb work for one of the big firms. Needless to say, he was proud of his shop. One day he came up with a way to literally double his production capacity on a key item. I was amazed. I honestly thought the guy was a genius. But he was so proud of his discovery he got carried away and mentioned it to the parent company rep, and that was the end of it. They told him that beginning the next day they would only pay him 50 percent of the previous price for his work. They didn't want to negotiate, they just gave him an order: cut your prices in half starting tomorrow. He was furious.

He quit his little company and refused to have anything to do with that firm again. Today he lives on his pension, which is hardly enough to get by. His parent company took the technology he developed and put it to good use in a few dozen other firms. What did he achieve?

YOSHIDA: We often hear in Japan how famous American companies like Apple Computer started in someone's garage. In Japan we don't have so many garages, but we do have a lot of small, creative companies. Our subcontracting factories are Japan's "garage" industry, and also its garage R&D plants as well.

In Japan, big companies make nearly impossible demands on the firms they control. They might tell a company to make a difficult order in very little time, for half what it should cost, with no defects, and deliver it to the parent's plant on a certain day. In one sense, it's absolutely ridiculous. But it does no good to complain, so why bother? Instead, we look at it positively. It is these impossible demands that force us to grow as manufacturers. We have to push ourselves to the limits, we have to be creative, or we'll never figure out a new process to shave days off our production schedule. We're always under pressure, and pressure can be very good for creativity. Life as a small company in a big keiretsu is tough, believe me. But you also learn to survive, and you only survive by being good. Right here in Ota-ku there are about 8000 subcontractors. There used to be over 9000, but business has not been good recently. The ones who survive are tough and skillful. Whoever is left, you can bet they're the best in the business.

When I look out at Japan's electronics business, its automobile business, its machinery business, and so on, all I see is small companies. Hundreds of thousands of small companies. The real power of Japanese industry, the real foundation on which all of these businesses were built, is thousands upon thousands of small companies, companies no one has ever heard of. Probably many of those little firms don't even exist today; many others are still working. They built Japanese industry. I mean literally. They built the things that made this economy strong.

KUDO: Have you ever heard of VA or VE? They stand for "value analysis" and "value engineering." They are ways of looking at a manufacturer's operations to determine how it could make something cheaper, better, and faster. Our parent firms make us submit VA and VE reports every month. You have to list up several items in each report telling the parent company how you could improve operating efficiency. If there aren't enough suggestions on your list one month, they'll give it back to you and say "Do it again."

Let me give you an example. Suppose you're making parts for some big electronics company. The VA/VE manager comes around and tells you to reexamine your entire system top to bottom. Look at raw materials costs, processing costs, operating costs, and so on. Isn't there some way to squeeze these expenses by even a few percent? Then look at the shape of materials being used, their weight, their size, the production volume, the way they're transported from one station to another inside your factory. Isn't there some way to improve your system and crunch down costs a tiny fraction? What about personnel costs, packaging costs, shipping costs, utility costs, maintenance costs, insurance costs, anything at all? Where can you cut corners, squeeze two into one, shave a few seconds or a few yen off what you're doing now?

Does this sound progressive to you? C'mon! This is what every factory in the world does already. And, believe me, we've been thinking and doing this kind of thing for years or we wouldn't be around today. But now it's a system, and we have to fill out all sorts of stupid forms and write down our possible areas for cost control, then submit these "suggestions" to our parent company. And do you think for one minute they believe us? No way. The big companies send people around to all the little factories. A guy comes in with a stopwatch and times everything, looks at everything, writes down everything. How long does it take to solder a wire or turn a screw or paint a casing? They know our companies inside out. And then they say to each firm, "You've still got room to improve. Tighten your belt."

YOSHIDA: In the old days big companies did a lot of production in-house, so they understood a lot of the problems with manufacturing. They knew how long it takes to make something. But now they do less and less of their own production, so they understand less and less about the real world of manufacturing.

The production supervisor from the big parent firm comes around with his stopwatch and clocks one operation at 30 seconds. "You can do it in 10," he says. What makes him think so? Maybe we've been working for a year to get it down to 30 seconds, and even that is tough. He doesn't understand how difficult the process is. If his own firm tried to do the same operation, they'd never get anywhere near 30 seconds, but he doesn't know that and he doesn't care. He sits at a desk in the big company and says to himself, "Well, if they can do it in 30 they ought to be able to do it in 20; and if they can do it in 20, why not do it in 10?" He just wants to write up in his efficiency report that he pushed the subcontractors real hard.

HARA: Let's say you start making some new device. You can produce it for 95 yen and you sell it to your parent for 100 yen. Then you have to fill out VA and VE reports. You have to find ways to cut production time and most of all, cut costs. So you figure out how to get your costs down to maybe 92 yen, and if you're smart you report on your VA/VE sheets that you can do it for 95.

The company doesn't give you a hard time at first. They know you're still making a profit, but they pay the 95 yen. A little while later they begin to put the pressure on. "Where are your VA/VE reports? We expect to see that product at 90 yen this month." What they mean is they're only going to pay 90 yen per unit, so you'd better show that you can produce for 90 yen. You squeeze your system again. Maybe you can actually get it to 90 yen, maybe not. In either case, you have to report that you can and the price drops to 90 yen. After a few months it automatically goes down to 85. Then to 80. There's no way you can turn a profit no matter how hard you squeeze. The irony of the system is that by forcing us to produce these VA/VE sheets, the big companies make us give them suggestions about how to cut our own throats. And what's more, everybody does it.

This is normal and we've all come to accept it. The worst thing in the business is when some other subcontractor finds a way to lower his costs a fraction, and instead of keeping his mouth shut about it and making what profits he can for a few months, reports it to the parent. The big company rep is down there in a flash, demanding that this company lower their costs immediately. Then he comes around to all the other firms in the same general line and says, "X Company is doing this for 88 yen. Submit reports about how you will lower your prices to 88 yen."

Sometimes everything is going fine. The parent knows you can make 10 units of something in a fixed period of time. Maybe you could make 11 if you went all out for a few days, but you're already pushing hard and not getting paid for it. Then some jerk at another company hands in his VE sheet and says he can do 13 pieces in the same period of time. The big companies love this. They write up a nice Certificate of Achievement and present it to this guy's little factory. The president hangs it on the wall for all his employees to see. Then the big company tells him to start cranking out 13 units per set time period with no letup. Even that doesn't bother me. But then they come around to all the other little plants and tell us that so-and-so is doing 13, so starting tomorrow you've got to do 13. Go along with it or kiss your order book good-bye.

TAKITA: I can't understand what kind of subcontractor willingly hands in VA/VE sheets. You're tightening the noose around your own neck. You're already cutting your profits to the bone, then the parent comes and tightens a little more.

Many of the medium-sized subcontractors have to show their books to their parent companies. I mean everything. The parent doesn't just know how long it takes you to produce some piece of equipment; they find out everything about your payroll, your insurance costs, welfare payments, rent, shipping costs, office supplies, I mean everything! Once you open your books to the parent company, your life is over. They know exactly how far they can squeeze you without putting you out of business, and that's exactly the kind of information a big firm likes to have on its keiretsu subcontractors.

YOSHIDA: Does it sound like all we subcontractors ever do is complain? I hope you don't get that impression, because it's not true. When we talk among ourselves we almost never complain. We've been living like this for decades. Nothing will change. We know that. There are good times and bad times, but never different times. So what's the use of complaining? We're in the fix we're in because we chose this life. We like to make things. Little wires and pc boards and disk drives and auto bumpers and everything you can think of. We love to make things. We just wish it wasn't such a hard life and so many good people didn't get stepped on the way they do.

Years ago Japanese industry was much more open. There weren't the kind of strict vertical keiretsu we have today. In those days a small company had a chance to grow, to accumulate a little profit, start up new production and become bigger. Lots of big companies today grew out of the ranks of smaller companies right after the war. But those days are gone forever. Today a subcontractor will always be a subcontractor. You're trapped. You'll never have any money, you'll never turn any substantial profit, you'll never get out of the system. All you can do is enjoy your work and make the best of it. We don't sit around complaining like this. Most of the time we're thinking about ways to get along better, to cope with the situation as it is. That's just common sense.

KUDO: Big companies need subcontractors and subcontractors need orders from big companies. It's a two-way street. If the big firms freely hired the subcontractors, and used them fairly, without squeezing them, we would all be happy. We don't hate big companies. We need them, and they need us. All in all, I think the system is pretty good as it is. It's just that we get squeezed so badly that a lot of little companies go bust. It shouldn't be that way.

I love to make things, and I suppose I could keep working for several more years. But I won't. I'm going to close my factory soon. I have two sons. I was hoping years ago that at least one of them would want to follow in my footsteps, but this has not been the case. I think they saw what this life is like, but what they couldn't see is my pleasure in working. All they knew was that I put in long hours, sometimes staying at the factory day and night for a week, and there was never an increase in pay. Because I'm the boss, they think I'm in better shape than the workers, and yet we're always broke. My sons decided that this wasn't the life they wanted. One became a teacher and the other is an engineer, but at a very large company, not a subcontractor. In a few years I'll turn this place into a small apartment building and try to live off the rent.

The Electronics Industry

AKIO KAKINUMA *runs a medium-sized machine shop near Kawasaki making parts for one of Japan's best-known electronics firms.*

A few years ago the buzzword in the car business was *design-in*. This means that even at the earliest development stages the small- and medium-sized subcontractors in a keiretsu are asked to participate. In fact, this system has existed in other fields, especially electronics, for some time. Our firm has had a lot of experience with design-in because we have special technology. Smaller firms than ours, and those without some unique technology are not going to be involved in design-in. Small firms are practically slaves for the big companies, even if they do have proprietary technology.

How does it happen? Simple. It usually goes like this: your firm starts getting a lot of orders from a single big company. They pay you in cash within 20 days of your invoice [unheard-of in normal Japanese business], so you're happy to do business with them. Then one day they tell you to cut your prices by 10 percent. You can't say no—they've become your biggest customer. To soften the blow they give you an even bigger order. You figure you can cover the 10 percent easily with the increased volume. So in effect you turn over more of your production to that client, but for less profit. Then a few months later they tell you to cut prices another 10 percent. Now you're really stuck, because if they take away their orders you're in big trouble. Gradually their payments get slower and slower, but now there's nothing you can do about it. You've become part of that big firm's keiretsu, and they own you, even without having a single share in your company. Maybe you even sell them a license to your special technology or sell them the patent outright to raise cash. Then you've got nothing. They can drop you any time or squeeze you for any amount. I see this happen all the time.

My own firm was never taken over that way, but we almost went bankrupt several years ago as a result of the same kind of thing. When we started we were independent. We had two big clients, so we weren't in anyone's keiretsu. Our orders were about 50-50 between the two firms. Then one of the companies started flooding us with orders. Our ratio went to 60-40, then 70-30, then 80-20 . . . We could see what was happening, of course, but I thought it was all right because we were making good money. A single big company was relying on us for a large amount of work. They were placing orders for a single part to the tune of around $8 million a month. We weren't about to complain.

I made it a point to get to know the people in charge of dealing with subcontractors at this big firm. We became friendly. I took them out to nice restaurants, hired geisha for them, played golf with them (and was careful to let them win). I bought a new car for the purchasing manager. When he said he wanted women, I arranged to get him women; when he moved to a new house, all our staff went over and helped his family to move. Our company even bought furniture for his new place, paid to have the house wallpapered, we even gave his family a dog for a moving-in present.

Then, one day, I had to ask a favor from this purchasing manager. Instead of ordering huge quantities of just one item (which was turning us into a mass-production factory instead of a high-quality manufacturing plant), couldn't his firm order smaller quantities of maybe three or four different parts? Then we would have more opportunities to improve our work and apply our skills. I asked very politely, and I explained our reasons for asking.

He was not happy. He called me all sorts of names and he insulted our company.

Two months later all orders from that firm stopped. I mean stopped. They didn't cut back by half or two-thirds, they cut us off cold. Nothing. One month we were making a billion yen per order, the next month zero. Looking back now, I can't complain. We learned a lot from that company. We came very close to going under. It was extremely tough for a while, but we were rescued. Another big firm that knew of our reputation heard about what had happened and they started sending us orders. Without them we would have gone out of business for sure.

Fortunately, we had invested in a lot of new technology back when things were going well, and that saved our skins, too. But from that day on I began expanding our product lines and looking for other clients. As soon as we got back on our feet we set a rule that no firm can ever account for more than 20 percent of our income.

I can't stand it when subcontractors complain about big companies. I've had my share of bad experiences, but I've learned as a result. In particular, I've learned how important it is to have proprietary technology. I don't want to gripe about the big companies behind their backs. They know how I feel. I've said things to their faces, and they understand. But please don't give any clue as to what kind of products we're making or what kind of technology we have in your book. People would find out right away who we are, and I'd rather not have that happen.

JUN HASEGAWA, *48, makes parts for a major electronic machinery maker. He is the foreman of a small factory near Kamata:*

There are lots of firms just like mine in this area. When the presidents of different subcontracting companies get together and go out drinking, they always start griping about their clients. It's natural. Sooner or later somebody always says that the way big companies deal with us is cold, nasty, even brutal. When business is good for the big firms, they shove orders at us like crazy. A guy comes around on Friday evening, drops a bunch of specs on your desk and says, "Make these up by Monday morning and bring them to our office." He's out playing golf or sleeping in a nice warm bed all the time your factory is cranking out that order. Next week they'll do it again. All we want is some regular orders, a steady flow of business to keep us going. But it never happens that way. We think, maybe if we had two or three different clients we could balance out the work load, but that's impossible. As long as the orders are coming, the company is saying, "Don't you dare take an order from anyone but us."

Then, when business turns bad, Bam! They're gone. No orders. Nothing. If we ask when things might get better, they snap, "Why do you come around here looking for work? We're a business, not a charity!"

This is normal. We all know it. And I don't blame the guys at the big companies. Sure, I've met some real bad characters. I've hated a few. But most of them are decent guys. What can they do? They work for giant firms where they have no real power. Policies are set way above their heads. If the company says cost reduction is priority one, then they have to squeeze all the subcontractors a little more this month. That's their job.

And even if some guy in one department wants to help us, we know he won't be around very long. Big firms are always rotating their staff inside the company. That's one of the weaknesses of their system—nobody ever becomes really familiar with any one job. I've become close to a few people at big firms, but they're always transferred somewhere else.

When we lose orders and we have to lay off employees that we've had for 30 years, of course we get angry and we feel that the big companies are cold and inhuman. But they're not. They're just bureaucratic. I'm sure it's the same in America and Europe.

Actually, things have improved a little. In the old days the guys who ran the subcontractors at the big companies were really tough. I mean, these guys were hated and feared. They were arrogant, they were nasty, they treated subcontractors like dirt. I remember a few that I felt like hitting, but I never did. [Smiling] There was one guy, though, the subcontracting supervisor for a big company. He was a real bastard and everybody knew it. If he had a few drinks, you wanted to be somewhere else and fast. All the subcontractors used to say, "That guy's gonna get it someday." And one day he did. The foreman of a little manufacturer in our area, a nice, even-tempered fellow named Tsuda, had to go to the parent company to hand in some reports. And this supervisor starts chewing him out something awful. I don't know the details—I'm sure he was squeezing Tsuda's company pretty badly—but Tsuda-san just got madder and madder while this guy berated him for being an imbecile and told him that his miserable little firm was an embarrassment to the industry. All of a sudden Tsuda hauls off and socks the guy. Right there in the parent's office in front of maybe 20 people. I think everybody in Kamata heard the story before Tsuda got back to his factory. He was an instant hero. If the subcontractors ever had a union, he would have been elected president unanimously.

You know how that story ended? Tsuda went off and started his own company. And the nasty supervisor at the big company? They let him go. Getting your lights punched out in front of your staff is not the way to impress management with how well you've got the subcontractors under control. Anyway, he left the big company, and where do you think he wound up a couple of years later? Old Tsuda-san hired him. I asked Tsuda about it later. "I did something shameful," he said. "I lost my temper and hit him. I was wrong. Now I feel sorry for him." You won't find many subcontractors who are that forgiving.

I'll tell you a more recent story. A certain company I know, we'll call it K. Co., is a first-tier subcontractor for a major electronics firm, and it's no small operation. K. makes entire finished products for the parent company, and it was turning well over \$3 million per month in sales at the time this happened.

K. had been rationalizing for years, squeezing its operations tighter and tighter, making its production incredibly efficient, and of course, its margins paper thin. Well, another fairly large subcontractor in the same group saw the volume of business the parent was sending to K., and they got to thinking that this was just the kind of work they'd like to be doing: large-volume assembly with a very close relationship to the parent. So the second company—I'll call them J.—went to the parent's production supervisor and said they could do the same work for 10 percent less. Parent companies love this. A little competition among subcontractors means they all get nervous and everybody tightens the screws at their own shop one more notch without any pressure from the parent. Who wins? You know the answer to that one already. So the parent transfers about half the production to J. Company right away to stir things up.

But there's a problem. K. had tightened its operation down to the last yen. In comes J. and they're good, too, but they haven't been working on this particular product the way K. has. So after only a couple of months they're deep in the red. They figure even if they could get the parent to forget about the 10 percent discount and pay them the same as K. they'll still lose money. Now they're in a bind.

So the president of J. goes to visit the president of K. He asks him if perhaps K. would like to take back the production it had lost. The president of K. was not the kind of guy you fool around with. "We didn't lose anything," he said. "You stole those orders from us. You wanted it so bad, now you've got it. I hope the purchasing department is happy with your service."

Now J. was really in a fix. The president went to the parent company, almost in tears. He begged them to take the order back. "If you don't, we'll be completely bankrupt in a few months. I asked K. to take it back but they refused. Can't you do something?"

As it happened, the supervisor was fairly close to people at K. Co. He went to K. personally and asked them to take back the production that had been transferred to J. What do you think the president of K. said? "Sure, we could think about that. But if you want us to take back production that you gave to one of our rivals, you'll have to raise the unit price. Otherwise, we couldn't even consider it." When I heard that I almost fainted. That guy must have balls of steel! They could put him out of business tomorrow if they wanted to. But you know what? The parent agreed.

I guess the point is, if you're big enough and good enough and have earned some respect at the parent company, you can get away with that kind of thing once in a while. I know K. Co. didn't get a big raise, just a little something to make life easier. But the parent may make up for it by squeezing them on some future order. Still, just to hear a story like that makes any subcontractor smile. I bet there aren't a dozen firms in ten thousand that could pull that off.

KENICHI OKADA's *electronic parts firm is across the street from Hasegawa, although his "parent" is a different consumer electronics company.*

How many companies are inside a pyramid? Well, as you know, there are first-tier subcontractors, second-tier, third-tier and so on. The farther down you go, the greater the number of companies involved. In the group I'm in, there are maybe 35 or 36 first-tier subcontractors. Below them are close to 400 second-tier companies. Below them are maybe 2000-3000 third-tier companies, and I really have no idea how many below that.

My firm is a second-tier subcontractor making parts for video decks and color TVs. My brother works for a pressing plant that does work on the same TVs we're making parts for. I would guess that production for something like a TV must go down at least as far as fourth-tier subcontractors.

All these different levels of subcontractors didn't always exist. Most of it was formalized back in the late-fifties and early sixties. For example, my father ran a factory before the war. After the war, he, my brother, and I started up our family plant again. Gradually we picked up some business, and by the late fifties we were at a critical point where we needed to expand. Television was getting to be a big thing, and we wanted to get into it. At that time our main client began a complete inventory of its subcontractors. This was going on all over Japan. Our client company checked out our plant, our equipment, our capital, our work force, everything. A little later they announced that from then on we would be a second-tier subcontractor. Until then we had assumed we were one of this firm's most important suppliers. All we needed was a little help and we would be making state-of-the-art stuff. What happened?

Well, as you can guess, the parent company picked another firm to be one of their first-tier companies. They invested heavily in that firm, installed new equipment, and even transferred some technology from their main plant. The result is that this other company now sends us orders to fill. We do simple processing for them, which they then refine and finish. This is the way things are done. They control our order flow as well as orders to dozens of other firms. This makes subcontractor management easy for the big companies. They don't have to keep an eye on four or five thousand little companies, just a few dozen. Then those few dozen are responsible for managing the work flow at the lower levels. The whole process is extremely rational and extremely beneficial for the people on top.

The thing that really burns me about the subcontracting system today is that the big companies stick their noses into everything. They tell me how much I should pay for my equipment and how much I should pay the people who operate it. They look at each operation and tell us how fast it should go, how many people should do it, and how much they should be paid. They look at a machine and say, "This handle should go up and down in X seconds; this tray should slide forward and back every Y seconds, this arm should rotate every Z seconds." Then they say how many of this unit we should be able to make in a certain number of minutes, how many in a certain number of hours. Then, based on their calculations, they set new prices for everything.

On top of it all, they go over our books with a microscope. They know my depreciation expenses better than my own accountants do. I don't mean just on the building or our heavy equipment. If I buy a word processor, if I replace a fax or a copy machine, I have to file a written report to the parent company. They want to know everything. They strip us naked. They control our orders, our income, and our profits. To the parent company, my firm is like an old car they still want to drive but don't want to spend money on. They'll give us the bare minimum of upkeep necessary to keep us from breaking down. Working in this kind of situation is a lousy feeling.

Oh, one more thing. The big companies also butt into your private life as well. They'll say to an executive at a small firm, "We heard you bought a new car recently. We don't think that kind of display is wise. Perhaps you should reconsider the purchase." Or to another guy, "It appears that you have purchased a membership in such and such Country Club. This is no time to be thinking about golf! Sell that thing and get your mind back to your business!"

I don't know how they find out everything that goes on, but they do. They know my company inside out, and that makes me sick. But what can I do? You say, "Hey, don't show them your books. They'll just use that information to squeeze you further," and I couldn't agree more. But what am I supposed to do? If I say no I'm finished. They'll throw me out of the group "cooperative" and cut off my orders before the day is done. I'll go out of business. I'm scared.

Things didn't used to be like this in the old days. We used to have very good relations with the parent. The big companies were not all that powerful; they needed the small companies, and it showed. So the relationship was much more equal. The parent would ask for our cooperation, not demand it. They'd send their best engineers to our plant for a month or two at a time to teach us all about some new technology, then they'd lend us money to buy new equipment. They helped us to grow. For example, suppose a small subcontractor was producing parts but had a defect ratio around 10 percent. The subcontracting supervisor from the big firm would come around to visit together with one of their engineers. They'd spend a lot of time with us and try to figure out why the defect ratio was so high. They'd make suggestions and help us to improve our production. We'd implement those suggestions and send them better quality work. I guess it was pretty close to an ideal relationship.

But that was when they were still relatively small. Pretty soon things changed. The big firms grew much bigger very fast, competition escalated, and then everything became "cost down" analysis. If a company sent 100 parts and 10 were defective, the whole order was returned. It was up to each individual company to become competitive. The few that did, survived. A lot who couldn't make the necessary investments or hire the most capable staff were just cut off. You might say that's business, but in the old days, it wouldn't have happened that way. They would have given us more time and helped us to adjust. Instead, one day they just said "100 percent quality or no more orders." And delivery! Same thing. Every part, on time, every time. Exactly when they want it. Not sooner, not later. You hear a lot about just-in-time production in the automobile sector, but in the electronics sector it's been around for years.

The Auto Industry

TOMOHIKO UCHIDA *knows all about the JIT system. At 54, he is vice president of a metal-working firm in Shizuoka Prefecture, not far from Tokyo, and a member of one of the large auto keiretsu:*

The big firms have slogans they've put up in all their factories: "No Inventory" and "Inventory is Bad Business." What they mean is that inventory costs money, it doesn't generate profits. No one who runs a business wants excess inventory on hand. It's a liability. By implementing the JIT system, the big manufacturers streamlined their operations and eliminated all sorts of costs and headaches. But doesn't something seem a little strange with this system? All their inventory didn't just evaporate. Where did it go?

We've got it. Right here, at all the hundreds of subcontractors these big firms employ. Now, instead of sharing the burden of keeping inventory with the parent company, we're stuck with the whole thing. What "No Inventory" really means is: Shove it onto the subcontractor. Make it his problem.

The big auto makers think that if they apply JIT properly, all their costs will drop and production will flow seamlessly, each part arriving just where it's supposed to be just when it is supposed to be there. It all sounds wonderful, but let me tell you it never works like that. In theory, JIT assumes that every related business, from thousands of parts manufacturers to hundreds of intermediary manufacturers up to the final assemblers are moving in a masterfully coordinated ballet, interacting perfectly down to the last second, with every step in the process perfectly executed. Unfortunately, manufacturing doesn't work like that. There's always a snag somewhere in production, quality control checking, delivery, somewhere. Multiply that by a few thousand companies. What you've got is some abstract, ideal system that can never be realized in real-world manufacturing.

The big companies are accustomed to placing orders and demanding immediate delivery. We only have a few days on some big orders. We stay up all night working, but you know what happens. A piece of equipment breaks down, one of the workers gets sick, some of the materials aren't right for this order, some are in the wrong boxes, we don't have enough of this or that. All of these things could be sorted out easily in a day or two, but we don't have a day or two. Sometimes there's a tiny mistake in the specs they've given us, but at 4 a.m. after not sleeping the night before, you don't notice it. We'll work for hours before we discover that what we're making cannot possibly be made from the specs they've given us. Everything has to be redone. These kinds of problems crop up every week in manufacturing, and when you're working 20 hours a day with a single shift, they happen a lot more often, believe me.

Then there's delivery. Our parent company says they want 500 pieces of part X, and they want it at their factory on Monday morning at exactly 10 a.m. So not only do we stay up every night trying to make the things and make them right, but we have to load them on our truck and deliver them to a plant two hours down the Tomei [a major highway famous for its traffic jams]. They don't want the shipment at 9:30; they want it at 10. Which means if you leave early and the traffic is OK, you have to kill a couple of hours before making the delivery. If the traffic is bad and you show up at 10:30, you have to pay a fine. If you show up at 11 or 12, they post your company's name on the wall at the Subcontractor Control Section. That's bad. If your truck rolls in sometime in the afternoon, you might as well kiss your job good-bye. They'll cut you off cold. That's "just in time."

I know of one company that tried to deliver parts to its parent firm's factory three hours before the appointed delivery time. I guess the guy thought he'd make the delivery, show that he was eager to do business, and get back to his plant early. But the receiving manager at the factory refused the shipment: "Too early," he said. So the guy parked his truck next to the factory, pulled out a magazine, and got ready to wait for three hours. Then a guard tapped on the window: "Can't park here. The foreman's a JIT nut. You'd better get this truck out of sight fast." So the guy had to drive a mile or two down the road and stay out of sight. Some of the factory foremen go crazy with JIT and start insisting that deliveries be made right on the dot, not before or after. They have this image of a line of trucks pulling in exactly at the appointed times, unloading in exactly the right number of minutes, and pulling out again, like a parade. If they see trucks loitering around the factory area waiting to unload, they go nuts. It sounds like a joke, but it's true. Some firms will even lock their gates in the morning before deliveries are due. You'll see half a dozen trucks from different suppliers driving up and down the road, burning up gas, just killing time. This is what the big firms call efficiency.

The only way to avoid this mess is for the subcontractor to make up the order even sooner than the factory demands it, and keep it in-house until the optimum delivery time. That means cutting our real working time down even farther and holding the finished goods—that's right, inventory—until it's time to ship. It sounds crazy, but that's what we have to do. Every big subcontractor I know does the same thing. If your parent company wants something in three days, you've got to make it in two and a half. If you try your own version of just-in-time production and delivery, you'll put yourself out of a job.

One company I know well is about a four- or five-hour drive from their parent's factory. When the roads get crowded, their trucks can easily be a couple of hours late, and that's the same as being a year late. So this subcontractor rented a small warehouse about 15 minutes up the road from the parent's factory and stationed one of their staff there full-time.

Now they move the goods to their warehouse the day before a shipment is due. Then the guy at the warehouse has to make absolutely sure that it gets to the parent's factory on time. All of this is great for the parent. They love it. But the subcontractor has to pay for this warehouse out of his own pocket—the parent won't cover that. He also has to pay one of his employees to sit in the warehouse day after day, reading the newspaper until a shipment comes along. That's real efficient, isn't it? Then the company has to do all its orders a day, sometimes two days in advance. And they get paid the same amount as all the other subcontractors, which means I know they're losing money on all this. But they're terrified of losing the big company's orders.

That's "just in time." The parent firm succeeds in eliminating inventory, but the subcontractor winds up with double inventory. First the parent crunches down its production costs by squeezing the subcontractor's margins to nothing. Then the subcontractor has to pick up the tab for an extra warehouse and personnel, none of which is billable to the client. It's a great system.

RYOICHI OTA, *58, is one of the few people near the top of a vertical keiretsu whom we had a chance to interview. His company is a top-level subcontractor for a major Japanese auto maker.*

There's a lot of talk these days about the keiretsu. People say they're all going to change, they'll be restructured. Others say they no longer serve a useful function. Some say they may fall apart. I don't know what's going to happen, but whatever it is, I hope it happens soon. We can't keep going like this forever.

I read in the paper where a big company was asked about its dealings with the hundreds of subcontractors under its wing. The firm's spokesman was asked if they ever insist on price cuts from their subcontractors, and of course he denied it. Those kinds of things don't happen any more, he said.

Well, I have news for you, they happen all the time. Especially right now, while the recession is biting and some of the big firms are showing red ink for the first time ever. In both the electronics and auto industries prices are knocked down twice a year, every year. This is called *periodic price reduction*. The big makers' reps come around and say all your prices have to come down. It's not a request. Normally, it's 5 percent in the spring and 5 percent in the fall, although it can be more when things get tight. That means the price we get paid for almost everything we make drops by a minimum of 10 percent every year, even in good years. Now it's worse. We've already had a 15 percent cut this year, and we're getting ready for the next round.

We're lucky to be a first-tier subcontractor. That's usually a good position to be in, but it has its ugly side, too. After Plaza [the 1985 agreement which caused the yen to soar in value] we had to go around to all of our suppliers—the second-tier companies we use regularly—and beg for their help. We urged them to automate wherever they hadn't already. We asked them to review their operations, from materials procurement to processing, assembly, labor costs, everything. We pleaded for their cooperation. And we did the same thing in our plant. We tightened our production system until it bled. I laid off a lot of people—I'd rather not remember how many. I froze salaries across the board for a couple of years and cut bonuses for all managers. I went to our main bank and took out loan after loan, and still we were in the red. We stayed in the red for a long time, too. We all suffered tremendously.

Every subcontractor I know was in the same position. It was agonizing, but ultimately we survived. And in the process we and our second-tier suppliers became a lot more efficient. Our parent company found they could turn out a brand new model in record time, and they could build in a level of quality they never had before. Their market shares overseas began to grow at the same time they were learning how to turn a profit at the new exchange levels. All of that was great, but we never saw any of the profits. Orders kept on coming, of course, and we were able to rehire people and ease up on our production a bit in the late eighties, but then this "bubble economy" blew up in everyone's face. Now things are worse than ever. We're back in the red again, and the noose is tightening. We can all feel it.

One thing that never changes between the big keiretsu companies and their subcontractors is the difference in quality of life. The big companies all pay good salaries, and of course, those jobs are for life. The unmarried men get to live in brand-new dormitories; the married ones get to buy a new apartment with a low-interest loan from the company's main bank. They get regular vacations, which they can spend at the company's mountain lodge or beach resort if they choose. They can go skiing or stay in a hot spring, all for next to nothing thanks to the company's connections.

Things are a little different for the subcontractors. Here at the first-tier level our salaries average about 70 percent of what our parent company pays, from entry level up to management. We don't have any company resorts. We don't have any nice dorms for our employees, and we sure can't get cheap loans from our main bank. But we're lucky. The second-tier firms' salaries are roughly 60 percent of the parent's, and the third-tier firms are only about half. Their employees have zero benefits. They're lucky to be working all year round. I don't mean to sound callous, but I don't think they know what a vacation is. It's not easy down there.

Look at it this way: two guys are both doing auto manufacturing. One works on a line attaching bumpers to car chassis at a big maker's assembly plant, the other works in a little third-tier subcontractor making the connectors that fasten those bumpers. I guarantee that the second guy is a much better manufacturer and his work is a lot more taxing. But the first guy lives a good life, his family will never worry about going hungry, and once or twice a year they'll pack the kids in the car and go away for a nice vacation. The second guy could be laid off tomorrow, his paycheck is always a gamble, and when his kids are home during school vacations, they wonder why they don't see their dad for a week at a time. You know, I'm not a socialist or anything, but tell me, is that fair? This is supposed to be a classless society.

My younger brother has a son, and the kid is just crazy about cars. While he was studying engineering in university he said he was dying to go to work for any company in the auto business. One weekend when he was at home, his father asked me to come over and talk to the boy. I said OK, and dropped by to visit. I brought along a catalog about our company that shows some of our parts on a famous maker's sedans. I already knew that the boy was bright, and I felt kind of proud to offer him a job. I told him we'd treat him well, that he'd have lots of opportunities to do real design work, and in time he would probably rise to senior management level.

What do you think my nephew said? "Thanks but no thanks. How could I tell my girlfriend I was going to work for some dirty little factory that nobody's ever heard of? Do I want to be a samurai with my head held high or a merchant always groveling in the dirt when his clients speak? I'm going to work for Nissan or Toyota. Then everyone will know who I am. I'll make a name for myself as an engineer at a firm like that, and some day I'll become a director. You'll see."

My eyes burned when I heard these words, but I said nothing. Later on, I had to admit that I understood how he feels. He thinks a big, famous company is a better company. And he thinks his life will be better at the big company. Maybe he's right. He'll make a better salary, that's for sure. But what about his job? At a big firm he'll be told what to do and how to do it. Is that engineering? He might as well be back in school. True, if he worked at a small plant, he would have to bow low every time anyone came around from the parent firm. Even if he's a senior engineer and some flunky office boy from the parent company shows up, he'd have to bow and show respect. I do the same thing myself. But that's business. It doesn't mean anything. Young people today don't understand that.

Never underestimate the value of keiretsu connections. I personally know of a case where there was a highway accident that was directly attributable to a defective car. The auto maker sent a representative to the scene immediately, and he did everything possible to persuade the police that the fault was not with the car, but with the driver, who happened to be a teenager. He strongly implied that the kid was a bad driver, was never in control of the car, might have been drinking or taking amphetamines.

Then the company rep found out who the kid's father was—an upper-level bureaucrat at one of the important ministries. If the ministry should hear about problems with defective cars, it could lead to all sorts of problems. Anyway, the company rep reported back to his superiors right away. What happened? You've never seen a company do an about-face so fast. They had one of their execs down at the ministry in no time flat, bowing and apologizing for any inconvenience to the bureaucrat or his family.

The next day, one of the company's senior directors appeared at the ministry. It turns out that this director used to be a very important guy at the same ministry before he "retired" into the private sector. So the bureaucrat whose son was in the accident was this retired bureaucrat's *kohai* [junior]. He has to be respectful to the old man no matter what. The company director took the bureaucrat into a private room and they had a talk. He must have said something like: "There's no reason to make a big deal out of this. I'm sure your son can be compensated, and the whole matter with the police can be cleared up right away. And other than that, there's really no problem, is there? Let's forget the whole thing ever happened."

Of course, the bureaucrat wasn't happy, but what could he do? He can't be rude to his *sempai* [senior] who's got all sorts of clout in both the ministry and the auto industry. That bureaucrat will want to retire himself someday, and he'll need introductions from people in key industries to land a cushy job with a nice salary. So he swallowed his pride a little, his son got a new car, and the whole thing got swept under the rug.

That's why companies are so happy to have directors from the big banks and the important government ministries on their boards. In that sense, you might say the ministry that supervises an industry is also part of its keiretsu.

At our company, we also have a number of directors seconded from our parent firm and one from our main bank. The parent and the bank both own chunks of our stock. How much? I'd better not say. If I did, it would be too easy to figure out which firm gave this interview and my phone would ring the next day. We're not supposed to talk about this kind of thing. Be sure you keep any reference to what we make or where our plant is located out of your book.

Frankly, I think our parent firm wants more of our stock. And they won't have much trouble getting it. They'll just order us to invest in some major new equipment. To do that we'd need a bank loan, but we won't get it. They'll suggest that we issue new shares, which sooner or later we probably will. When that time comes, the parent will pick them up easily. Or its main bank will buy some or the keiretsu insurance company or maybe both. At this point it doesn't matter. We'd be happy to have the cash input, and they're going to own us sooner or later anyway. There's no way to stop them. That's the way a keiretsu works. The more a parent firm owns of a subcontractor's stock, the less freedom the smaller firm has.

Once you need their business so badly that you do whatever they tell you to, they've already taken over in everything but name. Later on, if they want to, they can buy as much of your stock as they want. Little companies with owner-presidents fall into that trap all the time. They start off independent, but pretty soon they've got one major client and they next thing you know that client is sending one of its own men to be president. I could show you dozens of companies where the old president has had to step aside so someone from the parent company could take over.

This doesn't apply just to the car industry. As far as I can tell it's the same in all the manufacturing sectors. First the parent gives you lots of orders, then offers to invest in your business, which you can't refuse. Then the main bank wants a little piece of equity. Next thing you know, they're telling you what equipment to buy and from which company you should buy it and how much you're going to pay for it. Then it's "Could you find room for some of our excess personnel? They're being transferred to your firm next week." You can't say no. So you go along with whatever you're told to do. By then you're up to your ears in debt, and the bank says the same thing: "You wouldn't mind putting our Mr. Suzuki on your board, would you? He won't be chairman or president, just an ordinary director, and he's only there temporarily." The next thing you know, these "temporary" directors are getting settled in till retirement. In the end, either the parent company or the bank or both of them control your equity, your debt, and eventually your management. I think that's pretty much standard throughout industry, isn't it?

FUMIO SHIBATA *is the executive managing director of a leading subcontractor for one of the top three passenger car makers.*

There is nothing more important to the parent firm or your main bank than personnel placement. Sometimes the parent firm will say to you, "Your director, Mr. Y. is retiring next March. We would like to recommend a replacement." The next thing you know, the former general manager of subcontractor relations at the parent has a seat on your board.

If you gripe just a little about this move, your work flow drops right away, guaranteed. It's like a valve was closed, and your cash flow dries up. Ask anyone. They'll all tell you the same thing. The parent maintains a "cooperative organization" [*kyoryoku-kaishakai*, a forum for all the companies at one level who are working under a single parent] for its subcontractors. If there is even a little criticism of the parent at one of these meetings, order flow to the offending firms is cut the next month. The result is there is almost no overt criticism of the parent, even when it tells a bunch of subcontractors that new directors are about to be placed on their boards.

What does it mean to have such directors in your firm? At least in my experience, it means that every single thing discussed in your board room is relayed to your parent company and probably a lot of it to their main bank. The directors assigned from up above are responsible for reporting back on your operations, and they do. Subcontractors take this for granted. In our firm we haven't yet had a case where a director's report has led to meddling in our executives' private affairs, but friends in other companies tell me that it happens to them all the time.

The big companies and the banks like to keep tabs on everything, including the personal lives of small company execs. Suppose the president of a subcontracting firm has his house remodeled or makes a down payment on a summer home for his family. A few weeks later he might be invited to play golf with one of the general managers from the parent company. As he's teeing up an easy shot, the manager will say, "Well, Tanaka. I hear you've become a big-time real estate mogul." The president will try to laugh it off, say he's only fixing up his house or buying a little cottage on a two-generation mortgage, but it doesn't matter to the manager. "Don't you think that's a little inappropriate for someone in your position? Why don't you think it over and give us a call next week. Tell me what you think you should do about it." How do you think the big company knew what the president of the small company was doing with his own money on his own time? The "temporary" director on the subcontractor's board heard about it around the office and reported right back to the parent. That's one way that big companies keep their keiretsu firms in line.

The only companies that manage to maintain their independence are those who have founder-owners who are determined to keep full control of their firms, or companies with real technical prowess. Even then, if a company has its own technology but doesn't have a patent for it, it means nothing. Whatever you have belongs to your parent. In my opinion, if you can design and develop a very high level of technology but don't expect to get a patent for it, you're actually better off not to develop it in the first place. After you invest all that time and money in creating something, someone in your group will take it away from you and pay you nothing. This happens so often you'd think people would learn, but I still hear stories. I have to be careful what I say here, so let's take a hypothetical case.

Subcontractor Co. A invents something, a new part for an auto engine, let's say. It shows the part to its parent company's purchasing department and says, "This is a revolutionary. It'll double gas mileage. And we can produce it for only ¥10,000 per unit." The section chief at the parent says, "We can't say yes or no on that right away. We'll have to check with Engineering. Leave three samples. If it's as good as you say, we'll talk." You know what happens next. The big company's engineers take it into the lab, tear it apart and find out what makes it tick. Maybe they don't even bother; maybe they send it over to Subcontractor B for analysis. Co. B's people tell them it's hot, everything Co. A said in the first place. They want to know who makes it. The parent's rep says, "Maybe you if you're good enough. Co. A says they can do it for ¥9,000." Company B's engineers look the thing over again, consult with their production people, and come back with a quote: "¥8,700."

"No way," says the parent company. "Our engineers tell us it's only worth ¥6,000 a unit. Maybe we're talking to the wrong company."

More consultations.

"OK, maybe we can do it for ¥8,000, but not a yen less."

"Right. We'll get back to you."

Then they go back to Company A.

"It's good, just like you said it was. But you know, you're not the first to develop it. In fact, another company in our group came to us with a very similar device. But they can make theirs for only ¥7,000. Our engineers tell us that's a realistic price. What do you say?" That's if they're being nice. Some firms would just lay it on the line: "We asked Company B to copy it and they said, 'Sure. ¥7,500 per.' Can you match that or do we go back to B. and give 'em the green light?"

Of course, Company A's original price was higher. They invested a lot of time and money to develop the thing in the first place. Co. B is looking at a finished product and thinking how cheaply they can duplicate it. Maybe Co. A can manufacture it for under ¥8,000, but in the long run they'll lose their shirts because they didn't recoup their development costs. Then again, if they don't make it, they'll get nothing for all their work and they'll watch another company produce what they designed.

This is why I say that without a patent, you're better off not creating anything. And little companies don't get patents easily, I can assure you. Even if you do, the patent is no guarantee of anything.

Recently I heard of an independent subcontractor in the electronics business. He developed some key part for these new lightweight transceivers the kids are all taking to the ski slopes. It was less than half the size of the current parts and totally impervious to extremes of heat and cold. First, the company got a patent on the design—which only an independent would ever do—then they took it around to half a dozen of the big electric companies looking to either license the rights or produce the thing under contract. At every shop the head of the engineering division said the same thing: "Leave a sample and we'll look it over." The little company felt safe because they held the patent.

Well, you know the end of that story. Every one of these companies has well-funded research labs, with state-of-the-art scanning equipment and some of the top engineers in Japan. In probably less than a day they had all produced complete design printouts of the structure accurate down to the micron level, and their labs were doing analytical tests on any special materials used. The little company never got to sell its patent rights, and they never received a single order for production. But several of the big electronics makers applied for patents on technology only marginally different from the original, and they all put that technology to work in their own transceivers within a few months. In the electronics industry stories like this don't even raise an eyebrow.

There is a general feeling among the big firms that subcontractors should not have profits to spend. And when they do have profits, they should not increase salaries or bonuses for any of their staff more than the tiniest fraction. Even in very good years, when the parent company was rolling in cash and we subcontractors were allowed to do well compared to normal years, we still had to look to the parent firm for guidelines on our spending. If the parent raised salaries 5 percent, we could not even consider going above 5 percent—even though our pay scales are much lower—and less than that amount would be better. The result is that the salary gap between big companies and smaller companies will never close. Gradually, it may widen. You can see the advantages that presents for the big companies.

The one thing that really makes me mad is the superior attitude of people at the parent firm. The guys in charge of dealing with subcontractors must go to some special school for training, because they all have their noses in the air when they talk to us. I think it must be part of their job to make subcontractors feel like garbage. These guys literally swagger when they come into our factories. When we have to go to their plants, they invariably keep us waiting for anywhere from 30 minutes to a couple of hours just to let us know how little our visit means to them. Then they talk down to us as if we were house servants unfit to wipe their shoes. It's a rare day when I leave a meeting at our parent's office and my stomach isn't tied in knots. There are days I think, "If he says one more word about how lazy and unreliable we are, I'm going to kill the S.O.B. right here in his office. I swear it. I'll strangle him with my own two hands and I'll do it slowly."

Let me tell you a story from many years back. We had a new, young sales guy back then, a fellow named Sato. I had a feeling he was going to go far in our company. He was solidly built (I think he played rugby in college), and could hold his liquor. He had a good temper and a quick mind. I liked him, and I gave him a small entertainment budget to help promote our work. One of his jobs was to take people from our parent company out drinking, to try to build some good communication with them and become as friendly as possible. This has always been my philosophy of business. If we've got to work together for years to come, we might as well get along.

So Sato invites one of the managers in the parent firm's purchasing department out for a drink. I guess this company rep must have been in his late twenties or so, but in his mind he was already president of the firm. Like many of the young men in that company, he'd graduated from one of the good universities, but not one of the best. Still, he thought he was miles above the scum who worked for subcontractors, and he told them so at every opportunity. He thought his company was the pride of Japanese industry, and he always bragged about it. I never saw him wear a jacket without the company lapel pin, no matter what the hour or where he happened to be. I think everyone should be proud of their company and proud of their work, but that also means you should allow other people to feel the same. Not this guy. Big company life had taught him that working for a "name" company made him one of the select few, and his bosses seemed to have done nothing to disabuse him of that opinion. He once said to another subcontractor friend of mine, a man almost twice his age, "You know, people like us have the power of life and death over people like you."

So one night Sato takes this puffed-up manager out drinking not far from our plant. As it turns out, two of our other employees are there, so they all sit together. And sure enough, the company rep starts in on how great his firm is, how they're eating up market share around the world, and how the lazy subcontractors are holding them back from even greater success. I guess he was pretty drunk at this point. Anyway, like I say, our guy Sato is normally pretty coolheaded, but I guess this was more than he could take, and he walloped the guy. I mean, I wasn't there, but from what I heard later he knocked this foul-mouthed little punk across the room. Then he apologized to the owner for the mess, paid the bill, and left.

At around 7:00 the next morning I heard the story. I couldn't believe my ears. One of our people hitting somebody from the parent firm? If it was true, we could all kiss our jobs good-bye. I called in one of the other employees who had been present.

"Tell me straight and don't give me any crap. Did Sato hit the company rep?"

"Yes, sir. Hit him pretty good, too."

"Idiot! How could he do such a stupid thing? How could you let him!" I was really steamed, and I guess I was shouting. I had visions of my phone ringing any minute, being ordered up to the parent's head office, bowing till my forehead scraped the floor, and begging for forgiveness from their general manager. They'd make me fire Sato the same day, then they'd probably cancel a few orders, and God knows what else. We'd be lucky to stay in business.

"Sir," the employee said. "You've met that rep. You know what a jerk he is. Last night he was drunk and he was really over the top. He kept on and on, about how our work was such poor quality that their firm could barely tolerate using our parts together with well-made stuff from other companies, how our production is always late and our people don't try very hard. I think he was trying to get Sato's goat, but Sato didn't say a word. Then Tabuchi—he was there, too—started to defend our company, and the rep interrupted and told him to shut up. Then he looked at the three of us real slowly and said, 'You still don't get it, do you? One word from me and your jobs are history! Don't ever forget that.' That's when Sato grabbed his necktie, stood him up straight, and sent him flying over the next table. Please don't fire Sato, sir. He wasn't trying to cause trouble." I said nothing and sent the fellow away. I think there was something stuck in my throat.

I kept meaning to call Sato in to yell at him, but I never got around to it. There was nothing I could say. The funny thing was that my phone never rang. I guess the young rep was too embarrassed to tell anyone in his office what had happened. A few months later he was rotated to another department and we didn't see him again. Our order flow continued as before. We were very, very lucky.

By the way, as the years went by I promoted Sato. He's one of our managers now. And the guy he hit, he got promoted, too. He's now a division manager at the parent firm.

At fixed intervals the parent conducts inspections of all the important firms in its keiretsu. People from the Quality Control section come around and inspect your factory from top to bottom. Our people are terrified of these visits because they can use any excuse to shut you down. Usually some middle-level guy from the parent firm takes a walk around your factory while all your directors, the president, and the plant foreman all trail along behind him answering questions about your operations. If it weren't your future that's at stake the whole thing would look pretty comical. Some firms call this the *Daimyo's parade* [referring to the feudal lords of old whose casual journeys entailed huge retinues and roads lined with peasants, all bowing as the daimyo passed].

Then the QC manager passes judgment: this is OK, this could still be improved, and so on. The sharp young ones check all the machinery, ask questions of our engineers, measure production speed, check the cleanliness of every corner of the factory, that sort of thing. If one of these young guys says "Not good enough. Clean it up," we have to clean. If he thinks our uniforms are too dirty or our production time is one second too slow, we'll hear about it. That's just the way they are. They have to criticize something.

It's not all bad, of course. Sometimes they praise us for our efforts. They get all the subcontractor presidents together for occasional parties and they hand out big, nicely framed awards for Best QC or Best Production Improvement or Most Cost Reductions or some such thing. We've won a stack of those. They look nice on the wall and our younger staff are really impressed by them.

But that's all we get—awards. The money that we save the parent through QC or VA goes to their bottom line, not ours. For all our cost savings we get nothing. If we save a hundred yen per unit on some production, we will not see one yen of profit for it. In fact, the money we invested to realize that saving is usually our loss. It costs us money to save money, but we never get anything back. The unwritten rule is: profits are for the parent, plaques and awards are for the subcontractors.

Back around '86–'87 almost 20,000 small companies went bankrupt. In our company we had to fire 15 people outright and cut the remaining staff's salaries in half. You never hear about things like that on TV. Big companies have unions. If there were ever layoffs, you would hear the union screaming, and you can bet the TV cameras would be all over the place. But subcontractors don't have those kind of unions. Our people are expendable. As the yen shock settled in, the guy in the subcontractor management section of our parent firm sent down a directive: "Do some thinning among your third-tier suppliers."

We have a lot of third-tier companies under us. By "thinning" he meant get rid of a quarter of them right away. Just let them go, like they were weights on a hot-air balloon. Release the dead weight and the balloon will rise, that's how his company thinks. They never think of these companies as people, as families, as men with 30 years of experience at grinding something or polishing something suddenly being told, "No work this year. Maybe next year." Why should the big firms care? Do some thinning.

What really hurts is that the people who control us are themselves members of unions. The guy who came around to tell me to fire those 15 people was a member of his company's union, and the guy who told me to get rid of a quarter of all our suppliers was actually the leader of his union. When he's at the office he fights against rationalization. He protests loud and long when his company talks about tightening its belt. But when the Subcontractor Cost-Reduction Committee meets on Monday morning, his first response is to rationalize the hundreds of firms under his control. His job is to force these small companies to squeeze costs, to lay off staff, and to cut off some of their suppliers to help preserve his own company's profits. This is normal. The same guy who would go to court if his firm ever laid off one of his staff comes around and tells you what sacrifices you're going to make in order to improve his company's cost structure. That's the reality of life inside a keiretsu.

SHIGEO MOCHIZUKI, *53, is vice president of an electronics-related firm working within the pyramid of one of the smaller auto makers.*

There is something called the Subcontracting Law in Japan. It's just a piece of paper and it has no meaning, but it makes interesting reading. One of the things it specifically states is that no parent firm can order goods from a subcontractor and then refuse delivery. I don't have to tell you, this happens all the time. Of course, if the goods are truly defective, that's another story, but with quality control what it is today, that's almost unheard of. Many companies order something, and then, before the order is completed or delivered, they decide they don't really need it any more. Tough luck, they say. What are you going to do? Sue the company that pays your salaries?

Sometimes our client says they can accept only part of an order. "We don't have any place to store it," they'll say. "Take the rest back and hang onto it. When we need it, we'll call." Maybe a few weeks later a call will come and they'll say, "We need the rest of that order right now. Get it over here fast!" and one of our people will have to load up a truck and hustle over to their plant. Our younger workers never fail to make some wisecrack about "This is real 'just-in-time,' huh?"

The second thing the law strictly forbids is delaying payment to a subcontractor. I wonder if anyone at a big company has ever read this one. Probably not. You'd think that the one thing the big companies do have is money. After all, we never see the results of all our rationalization and cost-cutting programs, they do. So you would think that at least they'd be able to pay us for our work. Wrong.

When we deliver an order to the parent, we also hand an invoice to the purchasing supervisor in person. Does he send it around to their Accounting Department? Never. Usually he just shoves it in his desk drawer. Three months later I'll call the company, I'll plead, I'll beg for that money. Finally, I have to go around to talk to him in person. He'll pull out the invoice from a pile of dog-eared papers in his desk and pretend to look at it. "Our budget is very tight right now. Can't you be a little more patient?" he'll say as if we're trying to rob them at gunpoint. Then he'll shove it back in the drawer, pick up the phone and start talking to someone as if I wasn't there. He'll wave his hand at me to mean, "Your time is up. I listened to what you had to say. Now get back to work."

This is so common I can't tell you. It happens to every small company I know. You get paid when they feel like paying you. What can you do about it? Nothing. Every small-company president I know does exactly what I do: you bow low as you leave the supervisor's desk, you say, "Please do what you can. Thank you" in your politest voice, and then you leave quietly.

It used to be that we were paid within about 60 days of delivery. Usually they would pay us about 30 percent in cash and the rest with a draft on their main bank. Recently, we don't get paid for at least four months after delivery, and then it's all in cash. Why do you think they pay in cash? Because the more they pay us by draft, the more they have to pay in tax stamps. By paying us in cash the parent firm saves [a few hundred dollars] in tax stamps. That's fine. I'm happier that they save money that way than by trying to squeeze it out of us. But smaller companies like ours run on incredibly tight budgets—our parents see to that. So when they don't pay us for a few months, we run short of operating capital pretty fast. They know that, too.

Eventually the subcontractor pleads with someone at the parent firm that his company can't stay afloat without some cash flow. Does the parent pay up? No, he offers to help by introducing you to someone important at their main bank. "If you're short of funds, borrow from X Bank. We use them all the time. I'm sure you'll be satisfied with their service." Who's he kidding? But you don't have a choice. Of course, if you don't like dealing with a bank, they've also got a keiretsu finance company to help you out. One way or another you have to borrow the funds you need and that means you borrow from the group.

Another thing that the law forbids parent companies to do is to ask their subcontractors to reduce prices. We won't even discuss that one. Not only do they tell the first-tier subcontractors to reduce prices, they order them to do the same to the second and third-tier companies beneath them.

Parent firms are also not allowed to return delivered goods. This is different from refusing delivery. It means that after the merchandise has been delivered they can't change their minds and say, "We don't really need these after all." Product life cycles are getting shorter all the time, especially in the electronics industry. By the time your parts delivery is made, the parent may already be thinking about discontinuing a certain product and starting production of a different line. Of course, if the parts are defective, that's different, but as I say, that is seldom the case. Often someone at the parent just changes his mind. This also happens all the time. They don't want the goods they ordered, don't want to pay, and don't even want to find space for the order in their factories or warehouses, so they tell us to take it back and not bill them for it.

Another thing that is outlawed is what we call *kaitataki*. For example, your firm buys some materials to use in production. Your parent agrees to pay for the cost of materials plus the finished goods. But maybe two months go by before you use those materials and in the interim the price drops. Then the parent says they'll only pay the current market price, not your actual cost. That's kaitataki. It mostly occurs with small, low-tech firms that have no power at all. We've never had it happen to us and we've never done it to our suppliers, but I know it goes on. Needless to say, if the market price rises in the interim, the subcontractor is not allowed to make any profit. He has to charge the parent his original purchase price. Subcontractors want to keep the work flowing. They're always afraid of being cut off. So they never complain even when their clients switch prices to suit themselves. They'll also store materials for months, and run up interest and storage costs, but charge their parents nothing.

All our people love cars. They'd love to work for Toyota or Nissan or Honda, but they don't. They work here, making parts for cars. Some of our engineers dream of making better cars. They'll work for days on end, they'll forget to eat, forget to sleep, put up with all sorts of garbage from the parent company. Why? Because they enjoy the idea of making cars better. But over the years everything has changed. All the car companies became much bigger. Oil shocks hit the industry. The high yen shock followed. Now the "bubble" recession. The result is that the parent company stopped talking about making better cars and put the pressure on just to make cheaper parts.

Sure the technology is better than ever before, but the joy of manufacturing is gone. No one cares about quality except as a yardstick to measure subcontractors' performance. I don't hear the engineers at big companies talking about making great cars anymore. They're under the same pressures we are. The companies want cars made to budget, and they want them made to fit a design schedule. The result for us is constant demands to cut costs, and that is strangling us. We've cut costs again and again. I don't think we can keep going much longer. If the big companies keep squeezing, a lot of their best subcontractors are going to go belly-up. Or a lot of good people are simply going to quit.

It's all work and no reward these days. In the past, when the car companies were much smaller and we were much smaller, everyone got along pretty well. Their engineers came around and taught us how to make better parts. Looking back now we realize how poor our products were back then. Honestly speaking, without help from the parent we would never have become a world-class manufacturer. But those days are gone. They don't want to teach, they want us to teach them. They don't want to invent, they want us to do it. And they don't want to share profits or benefits of any kind. It's like we're at war, the small companies and the big companies, and that makes you wonder.

What is the purpose of a keiretsu anyway? If all it makes us do is hate the people we work for and pushes us towards bankruptcy, retirement, or an early grave, what's the point? All the big Japanese companies are competing with each other to save ¥10 on a ¥4,000,000 product. It just can't go on. We're dying. And companies like us make up 95 percent of this keiretsu, so that means the keiretsu itself is dying. There's a cancer in industry today, and if something isn't done, I fear for the future. What do I know? I'm only a subcontractor.

9

Conclusions: The Past, the Present, and the Future

The Original Purpose of the Horizontal Keiretsu

The first of the Big Six groups to officially organize a presidents' council, and thus declare itself a keiretsu, was Sumitomo back in 1951. The last was DKB in 1978. In the intervening quarter of a century the Japanese economy turned upside down. It flipped from a capital-starved importer whose major businesses were textiles and other light industries to a capital-rich exporter replete with some of the world's most prominent heavy and high-tech industries. As we know, the turnaround was anything but accidental. The very fact that the Old Three groups were re-formed during the 1950s highlights the Japanese government's desire during that period to concentrate scarce capital in selected areas—exactly what the zaibatsu had done before the war and precisely what the American Occupation forces sought to prohibit.

But the bureaucrats who controlled the economy were pragmatists. They had no intention of waiting several decades to see how Japan's "natural" economic growth might proceed. They were afraid that in a much shorter time well-financed foreign companies would take advantage of Japan's weakened circumstances to buy up its few promising industries.

To the government's way of thinking, Japan had the briefest respite in which to "rearm" the country, not militarily but economically, against the coming onslaught of foreign competition. The officials came to the same conclusion that their predecessors had almost a century before when Japan was first opened to a rich and powerful West: the best defense is a good offense. Pick your key industries, feed them steroids, and protect them from serious competition until they put on some weight. If others complain that the playing field seems to slope too steeply in the home team's favor, let them complain.

As we have seen, the bureaucrats wanted a step-by-step "keiretsification" of industry to provide the thrust for the rebuilt Japanese economy. But they made it clear that only certain businesses would be among the chosen; the rest were on their own. Since the fuel for this growth would flow through the banking system, those firms that were not born with a Mitsui, Mitsubishi, or Sumitomo pedigree, and especially those that were not on the government's short list of designated industries, clustered even closer around the unreconstructed financial centers, particularly the old Yasuda (renamed Fuji), Sanwa, and Dai-Ichi banks.

Within each major industry, smaller companies were pressured to fall into line behind the leading firms, and over the years these thousands of little companies were easily organized into subcontracting hierarchies, each loyal to a single parent, each parent part of a single bank's lending group. In short, both the horizontal and vertical keiretsu came together through a confluence of government encouragement, government protection, and private design. The industrial engine that resulted was intended to power Japan out of its Third World status in the immediate postwar era and back to economic independence. In the process it was also designed to shield key industries from foreign takeover.

Was Keiretsification Successful?

Unquestionably, yes. Keiretsification and the industrial policy that grew along with it were tremendously successful. In less than two decades from the first shacho-kai meeting, Japanese industry had transformed the nation, not only by turning it into a global leader in manufactured exports, but by raising the national standard of living from poverty levels to among the highest in the world. The scale of this achievement has probably never been equaled throughout world history. And much of the credit for this phenomenal growth goes to the government planners who promoted the keiretsu system. (Less visible, of course, are the tremendous sacrifices made by the Japanese people and a myriad of smaller businesses which made the success of "Japan, Inc." possible.)

And what did the nation give up to foreign firms in order to build this economic engine? Almost nothing. Foreign technology (licensed and otherwise) was imported wholesale like some essential raw material, whereas the foreign companies that developed those technologies were kept knocking at the door until the 1970s. A few big U.S. firms were allowed to take stakes in Japanese companies, but they and all who followed discovered the "difficulties" of competing in the Japanese market. By this time the various horizontal keiretsu had grown so large and so influential that member companies couldn't make a move without their main banks knowing about it (and many had to ask the bank's permission first). Cross-shareholdings were commonplace, directors were networked throughout key group firms, and a web of intragroup financing and trading relations spelled trouble for any outsider—Japanese or foreign—who wanted to muscle in. The hundreds of distribution keiretsu made operating in the Japanese market a labyrinthine nightmare.

Those foreign firms that had distinctive products, patient management, deep pockets, and an unstoppable drive to succeed were ultimately rewarded. They discovered that the rewards of the Japanese system for "insiders" with keiretsu clout were high retail prices and an affluent, docile consumer ready to pay them. The pot of gold at the end of the Japanese rainbow was a level of profitability that could not be achieved in other, more "open" markets. Companies such as Coca-Cola became successful in Japan beyond their wildest dreams, in part because they formed their own very powerful distribution keiretsu. Today Coca-Cola, one of the most all-American names in business, generates more profits in Japan than it does in the United States. Dozens of other famous American brands are not far behind.

In sum, the keiretsu did exactly they were designed to do, and probably better than anyone had anticipated. And many a foreign company paid them the ultimate compliment either by joining them or by copying their approach to doing business in Japan.

Why Do the Horizontal Keiretsu Still Exist?

Over the years the horizontal keiretsu tended to emphasize the positive aspects of their union and ignored or put up with the negative aspects because of the need to preserve the group itself. Clearly, in the 1950s and 1960s that need was strong. In a very real way, preserving the group ensured self-preservation for each of the member companies. Yet in the 1990s the group members are all strong, well-established companies. The majority are publicly listed (although their shares are safely held), have relations with more than one major bank, and could to all outward appearances function quite independently of any industrial group. Why, then, do they continue to stick together as they do?

Perhaps the simplest answer is that the benefits still outweigh the inconveniences. Group members find little that is onerous in membership, and suddenly bolting from a well-known group and the thousands of contacts built up there over decades is completely alien to the Japanese way of doing business. Still, if this were the only factor holding the Big Six together, they would be little more than six elite clubs in which roughly 200 of Japan's top CEOs get a chance to have lunch regularly and compare notes about how best to putt in a strong crosswind. If keiretsu membership were an anachronism, if it truly served no important function other than to solidify ties with a main bank, no large company would want to become a member.

And yet, we see examples of very large, independent firms (e.g., Suntory, Kyocera, Hoya), that have decided to ally themselves with the Big Six. We see Toyota, which by all rights should be pulling farther away from the Mitsui Group, holding a full member's seat on the Nimoku-kai. If keiretsu membership for the Old Three were basically a matter of post-zaibatsu family unity, and for the New Three were little more than opening a pipeline to a big bank, the whole system would seem to have little relevance in the 1990s. Why, then, would a senior executive of a fiercely independent, family-controlled company like Suntory comment, "We must be in a keiretsu to compete effectively"?

Before offering evidence from studies that investigated how the keiretsu do make a positive contribution to their members' businesses, we think it more sensible to appeal to common sense. After all, Japanese corporations are essentially rational entities. They may employ different strategies than Western firms, and they may place inordinate value on characteristics not common in other countries, but ultimately every company is in business for the same purpose and is striving to do what it thinks best to attain that end.

Thus, if membership in a keiretsu were not economically rational, the keiretsu themselves would gradually disappear. If membership once had great meaning and substantial benefits but now has none, the old groups might stay together simply to honor tradition, but certainly no new companies would join any of the groups. Arguably, the DKB group would never have formed in the first place.

If, however, we find both the old and the new keiretsu still intact and outside companies anxious to become members, we must conclude that there are some substantial benefits, tangible or intangible, in belonging to a large, diversified industrial group. And these benefits cannot be limited to improved borrowing from a single bank, for the trend to multiple sources of funding is nearly universal.

Conclusion: Membership in the horizontal keiretsu offers very real benefits.

Interestingly, the major benefit is not profit. Tempting though it might be for some to think that the Big Six monopolize all the important businesses in Japan and, while pretending to compete with each other, divide the profits among themselves, this is not the case. A famous study (Caves and Uekusa) compared the profitability of keiretsu and independent firms during the heady growth decade from 1961 to 1970. The results indicated that keiretsu affiliation does not lead to higher profitability for member firms.

One of the leading contemporary Japanese researchers in the field, Iwao Nakatani, did a separate study for the following decade (1971–1982) and came to the same general conclusion. That is, members of the big horizontal keiretsu are slower to grow and slower to increase profits than independent firms. In place of keiretsu profitability, however, his data uncovered an interesting pattern: "both the rate of profits and growth rate of [group] firms are less variable over time than those of [independent] firms." In simple English, keiretsu membership may provide only acceptable levels of profitability, but it offers very high levels of security.

Nakatani noted that the major benefit of membership in a horizontal keiretsu is a kind of large-scale insurance policy: "It is frequently suggested that member firms of groupings help one another in times of serious business hardship. When a financial difficulty arises, for example, the member banks usually render assistance, financial or sometimes managerial, to the firm in trouble, sometimes at a far greater cost and risk than normal business reciprocity requires. Likewise, in a buyer-seller relationship, the buyer will often accept a somewhat higher price if the seller is in the same group and is facing business difficulties. Of course, in the reverse case, when the buyer is in difficulty, the seller is willing to sell at a lower price, or take other measures. . . . This sort of business reciprocity may be taken to imply an implicit mutual insurance scheme, in which member firms are insurers and insured at the same time."

This research also confirmed that despite lower overall profits, group firms pay their employees significantly higher wages than non-keiretsu firms. This not only supports the popular image of the keiretsu firms as leaders of industry, but it also does wonders for recruiting.

In other words, the primary purpose of the horizontal keiretsu is to stabilize corporate performance. In addition, groups may share risks and profits, especially when embarking on expensive new ventures (the Mitsubishi Group's investment in satellite telecommunications is a good example). Group membership also means easy access to funds, not only from the group's main bank, but from all its financial institutions. Membership in the group is like a signed audit by the main bank, a guarantee that the firm's credit is good. Studies have confirmed that the risk of bankruptcy for group firms is lower than that for independents, despite the keiretsu firms' higher debt/equity ratios. Some have suggested that the high debt/equity ratio itself is a kind of guarantee because it implies the concerned involvement of the group's main bank in the company's business. Not only is the bank watching over the firm's management, but should there be any trouble, there is no doubt that the bank will come to the rescue.

Thus, the answer to why the keiretsu still exist is that they provide security in the broadest sense. The big groups guarantee that (1) member firms have a much larger voice in the business community than they would if they were independent; (2) members have access to greater political leverage when necessary; (3) members will not be taken over by a hostile raider; (4) members will have easy access to credit; (5) members have a small but significant safety net for their sales figures—whether the merchandise is beer, autos, or securities; and (6) in a worst case scenario, no member firm will ever fail. That kind of security alone is enough to keep the keiretsu in business and keep nonmembers on the waiting list.

If we add to all the above benefits the tremendous flow of information—political, commercial, technical, etc.—that comes through the group, the exponential growth of group power through "old boy" networks formed between group firms, the low-risk investment in new technologies through group projects, plus the opportunity to get advice about how best to putt in a stiff crosswind, membership seems well worth the price of admission.

Conclusion: The horizontal keiretsu are here to stay. Where those groups are relatively close-knit, the growth of their members is directly related to the growth of the group's power and influence, as the members are capable of functioning more as a group when they want to. The New Three will grow on paper but, because their identity as "groups" is less firm, the keiretsu will not necessarily gain in strength or influence as a result. Also, as Japan's trading relations with the international community become more complex and more politically influenced, the role of the keiretsu as policy coordinators will grow even more important.

How Are the Vertical Production Keiretsu Changing?

In just the past few years tremendous changes have appeared in the vertical keiretsu. The deepening of the recession in Japan has put unexpected strains on companies that had expected to weather the storm in just a year or two. In the short time since this book was begun, the unthinkable has happened: auto giant Nissan announced the permanent closing of one of its flagship plants and the elimination of thousands of jobs (through attrition, not firing). Other big firms, including telephone colossus NTT and steelmaker NKK, announced drastic cutback programs of their own, and over ε percent of Japanese firms replied to a survey that they were in a period of "restructuring." The immediate source of trouble in the manufacturing sector is the chilling business environment. However, a much less visible problem is the lack of flexibility inside their production pyramids. The parent companies have finally pushed their suppliers to the wall and are finding out—many for the first time—that there is a limit to how far they can be squeezed.

As the recession loomed larger in 1991, many big makers turned to the old tried-and-true shock absorber system to see them through the rough spots. Had the economy rebounded quickly, the strategy might have succeeded. But as the months went by, many manufacturers discovered that the shock absorber was compressed as far as it could go. The suppliers had no more leeway to cut costs, and some were even starting to rebel.

The announcement that some of Japan's top auto makers would lengthen the time it took to develop new car models was taken worldwide as a positive sign that Japan was willing to make concessions in the interests of harmonizing global trade. While the auto makers were no doubt delighted to be perceived as making this move willingly and with such noble intentions, subcontractors told us that the big makers had no other choice: their suppliers could no longer stand the pressure in the production pyramids. Cranking out new cars at such a pace squeezed the smaller firms too far, and they finally reached a point where they could no longer run seven-day shifts and push their people to do more work for less pay. The shock waves bumped back up through the pyramid, and the larger suppliers had to report that they could not meet delivery schedules. In the end, the car companies had to ease up or risk a serious breakdown in the supply system.

An even more dramatic situation developed in the electronics industry. Consumer spending dropped off early in the decade, and the whole consumer electronics sector was hit very hard. But the real giants in the electric business—Hitachi, Toshiba, NEC, Mitsubishi—are only minor players in the consumer electronics arena. Some of the big makers were able to accept the losses in their consumer divisions more easily because of contributions from other sectors, especially those where they held major market positions. To take one striking example, NEC was resigned to its home electronics subsidiary being awash in red ink. It took solace from the fact that the parent firm completely dominated the Japanese personal computer market; that is, until the end of 1992 when assault troops from the Intel 486 Division, established beachheads in Tokyo. U.S. firms such as Compaq and Dell, with their customary lack of respect for market seniority and the hard work that goes into building a monopoly, offered Japanese-language machines for roughly half of the cost of domestic competitors, and the price war was on.

What can a company like NEC do when its most secure markets are suddenly under attack? The automatic reaction is to compress the shock absorber once again. Just before Christmas the company gathered its main subcontractors for a secret meeting in rural Gumma Prefecture north of Tokyo and gave them the good news and the bad news. The bad news was really bad: 50 percent cuts across the board, all parts, all assemblies, everything. The good news was they had a whole three weeks to figure out how to do it.

The foolishness of this approach is obvious. The parent companies lean on their subcontractors year after year, cutting prices and squeezing their margins, keeping a majority of suppliers close to or just under the break-even point. Order them in effect to cut their revenues by another 50 percent, and you are asking small firms to commit wholesale suicide for the parent's benefit. Even if a supplier is willing to go deeply into debt just to keep his company in business, the only way to cut costs by that much would be to fire so many people that production would come to a halt. The big makers should already know this, but decades of using the old system have taught them that subcontracting companies are infinitely flexible.

When the parent puts pressure on its upper-level suppliers, it knows that the pressure ultimately gets passed down to the bottom of the pyramid, but the result has always been that the job gets done and the parent's demands are met. True, a bunch of small firms may go out of business in the process, but there are always other firms to replace them.

Now the old system doesn't work like it used to. In what some of the suppliers are calling a "movement" but to parent companies seems just short of a revolution, subcontractors are beginning to 'just say No.' In this case the subcontractors made it clear that if prices were cut 50 percent across the board the whole pyramid would crumble. Key middle-level suppliers could go belly-up, and with them would go the parent's production ability.

The result was a rare compromise—the parent would agree to cut 10 percent of the cost from its distribution keiretsu, and another 10 percent from its head office operations (unthinkable), leaving the suppliers with only a modest 30 percent across-the-board cut to make in their production costs.

The amazing thing to foreign observers is that the suppliers more or less agreed to this. "What can we do?" the head of one parts firm told us early in 1993. "They know that if we pare down our staff and take a big loss on our business for a while we will just barely manage to stay afloat." He explained that older employees who were near retirement had already been asked to leave before the Christmas meeting in preparation for what was coming. New hiring was cancelled. Finally, as the compromise developed, mainline employees had to be let go. As of this writing, his firm was operating with a skeleton staff, and losing money daily, but expected to be able to deliver its quota of parts on time.

The parent companies are wrong about one thing: it isn't a revolution. At least not yet. It is one of those "inevitable" developments, like the tearing down of the Berlin Wall, that didn't look at all inevitable to people on the inside, and then suddenly occurred. Few if any of the subcontractors expected such radical changes within this century, but now many are starting to say "the keiretsu [meaning the vertical keiretsu] are coming apart." A number of people we talked to said something to the effect that the walls between the different groups were crumbling. The parent companies that once supported them in good times or bad can no longer afford to do that.

The social contract has been broken, and the result is that small firms with good technology, modern equipment, and skilled employees are increasingly looking around for new clients. The simple principle of shopping one's skills around the marketplace, something taken for granted in the United States, is becoming more common in Japan. In the auto industry the bigger suppliers have been doing this for years. Some of the largest firms in the Toyota Group, such as Koito Mfg. (the company Boone Pickens portrayed as a Toyota puppet) and Nippondenso, do business with almost every auto maker in Japan and some overseas. A number of much smaller firms are beginning to do the same, even though Toyota or Nissan may hold 10 to 20 percent of their equity. If the parent firm can no longer give them enough work, the market principle will take over. It goes without saying, however, that the supplier will remain loyal to its main customer and major shareholder, but loyalty no longer means it can't solicit business wherever it can find it.

The bottom line is that the production keiretsu are in trouble. The parents are closing factories and are only one step short of actually firing staff. If that happens, it will send shock waves through society, and the whole manufacturing business (which already plays third fiddle to the bureaucracy and the financial sector in recruiting the nation's best and brightest college grads) will sink even farther in the public eye. Despite the mess in the banking and securities industries, at least those firms transfer employees to their affiliates rather than fire them. A few real layoffs among large, listed manufacturers will mean serious trouble.

Japanese manufacturing survived the two oil shocks of the 1970s and the yen shock of the middle 1980s through a combination of rationalizing parent company operations and forcing price cuts onto subsidiaries and subcontractors, but much more of the latter. By the time the 1990s rolled around and it was time for a new round of recession roulette, the subcontractors were pretty well rationalized. Trying to squeeze them for more cost savings is what the Japanese call "wringing out a towel that is already dry."

If the upper-tier firms squeeze too hard, the lower-tier's options are limited. The smallest subcontractors have almost no assets, perhaps their building and the small plot of land on which it sits. Most will simply fold their business, let their employees go, and build an apartment house or a convenience store—both of which will bring in revenue—on the site of the old plant. Medium-sized firms have a bigger stake in keeping their operations going, so they will be less willing to give up. Unable to find work or profits with their parent firm, and being pressed to the point where they may well go bankrupt anyway, they have no choice but to break ranks and look for business anywhere they can, including from outside their keiretsu. And the other keiretsu, which used to uphold the law that defectors can't be trusted, now welcome quality suppliers from other groups.

Conclusion: More companies will cross keiretsu lines to stay in business, and the parent firms will learn to put up with it. The vertical keiretsu will still exist, but they will become less rigid, more dynamic. The U.S.–style spot-market approach to subcontracting will never catch on because everyone sees the advantages of long-term contracting, but an increasing number of subcontractors will be able to develop long-term relations with a number of firms. The losers will be the smallest firms at the bottom of the pyramid which will be only slightly affected by the dramatic changes taking place up above.

How Are the Vertical Distribution Keiretsu Changing?

Over the past few years the rise of discount stores and the influx of cheap imports has put a tremendous strain on the distribution keiretsu. Not only can consumers now shop for the lowest price on the products they want, but they no longer expect to shop only at the local keiretsu shop. More and more consumers are turning away from their local stores, flocking instead to six-story discount department stores that are springing up in every urban center. Where a typical Japanese mother in 1970 knew that the local electronics shop was the most reliable place to buy anything, her daughter today knows that the local shop is the most expensive place for everything. The store owners know it, too. "When you add up all the costs of operating a keiretsu store, they come to three times more than mass distribution outlets," comments Isamu Nakagawa, president of Sanyo Life Electronics. Indeed, the tens of thousands of little neighborhood stores have suddenly become unfashionable, unattractive, and uneconomical. MITI figures show that the total number of such stores has fallen by the thousands in the past several years. Today keiretsu stores account for fewer than half of all the small local retail outlets, and their numbers are still dropping as more and more shop owners bail out of a losing proposition.

Perhaps the most famous case of a crossover pioneer is Yoshio Terada, who began as a keiretsu store owner, fought the group's pricing policies, and launched his own independent business in the same field. Most remarkable, he did it all more than a decade ago. Terada ran a small Matsushita electrical appliance shop in an eastern Tokyo suburb. He worked as hard as he could to follow the famed "Matsushita way" of retailing, but it didn't seem to bring in customers. In 1979, he committed heresy: he offered the company's National-brand flashlight batteries at a 20 percent discount. Unfortunately, Terada's radical marketing ploy did not send customers rushing to his door. Instead, it proved much more successful in attracting the wrath of the Matsushita organization. Regional sales managers were dispatched to reason with the young entrepreneur. But Terada wouldn't budge. All he'd done was to knock a few yen off some batteries, he said. It wasn't the end of the world, and as far as he could see it was hardly a threat to the multibillion dollar Matsushita empire.

The managers advised him to think carefully about what he was doing: when you think about it, running a National-brand shop can be a pretty comfortable living, son . . . don't blow it all over some alkaline D-cells. Terada knew what they were getting at. If he lost the Matsushita connection he was finished. He couldn't simply turn to Toshiba and say

"Sign me up," because they wouldn't take him, and if he went independent and opened a shop of his own, none of the big keiretsu wholesalers would touch him. That is part of the glue that keeps the system together. But Terada clearly had a stubborn streak where his common sense should have been, and he refused to let a bunch of desk-jockey managers tell him how to run a shop in his own neighborhood. He told the men in the dark suits to take a hike. Matsushita was not amused. Terada was unceremoniously kicked out of the organization, and the company sent a truck around to take down the big "National" sign over his door. To Terada, "Matsushita was essentially saying, 'We're forcing you out of business.' "

Terada turned his former full-service appliance shop into a very un-Japanese no-service discount shop. In no time at all the place was packed. In 1980, his first year in business, he grossed about $2 million in sales, four times his best take as a Matsushita dealer. Ten years later he was raking in well over $100 million, and his little shop, renamed STEP, had become one of the nation's fastest-growing retailers. His biggest problem today is keeping up with customer demand.

There are plenty of firms eager to emulate Terada's success. Their numbers are still insignificant compared to the armies of keiretsu wholesalers and retailers, but there is no mistaking the beginnings of a major trend. Old shop owners are unlikely to make the radical jump that Terada did, but many will simply close their stores or turn them into other businesses. Either way, the keiretsu lose another outlet. Younger people thinking about retailing already see that shoppers are voting with their feet in the competition between friendly local shops with high prices and impersonal discount stores with low prices. In other words, the discount stores are more attractive to management as well as consumers.

This leaves the big electronics manufacturers in a fix. With problems in the manufacturing pyramids as severe as they are right now, it is foolish to pump money into advertising and promotion at the local level. Yet the withdrawal of the makers' support for local retailers' advertising and other promotional activities is just one more reason for keiretsu affiliates to throw in the towel. Many of the makers are no doubt secretly hoping that their sales networks will continue to contract by some tolerable percentage to help lower their costs. At the same time they need a national distribution network to push their products when the recession ends and consumers come back to the stores.

The auto dealerships are in a somewhat similar fix, although prospects are better for the future. Having put off buying a car for a few years, many people will return to the dealerships soon enough. Moreover, local businesses, public agencies, and partners in the horizontal keiretsu still buy fleets of vehicles which helps support demand. While there may be serious problems in the auto makers' production pyramids, the distribution side is in relatively good shape. Hence the moves by GM, VW, and others to get their own products into the big keiretsu pipelines.

In other areas, such as clothing, cameras, and cosmetics, the same basic principles are at work. The parent firms are hard pressed to come up with the cash to support their distributors in the way that they traditionally have. Between declining backup from the maker and declining sales, the local stores are forced to consider other options. The simplest and most attractive is to give up exclusive or semiexclusive representation of one company's product line, introduce competing products, and do some discounting to attract new business. This may seem obvious to the Western retailer, but in Japan it means bigger and bigger cracks in the keiretsu walls.

Conclusion: Some of the distribution keiretsu are in trouble, particularly those selling mass consumer goods. Keiretsu stores will continue to close at a steady pace. Many of those that remain will cross keiretsu lines to carry rival products and will ignore the maker's pricing instructions. The makers will also turn away from their reliance on their own sales networks and move more products through discounters, mail-order firms, and mass-retail outlets. By the end of this decade only a small fraction of today's number of keiretsu stores will remain and the retail market for most goods will become much more open.

The "Keiretsu Problem"

While this book is not intended to resolve the ongoing keiretsu debate now in the United States, we would be remiss not to make a few basic observations.

The very first comment that needs to be made about the "keiretsu problem" is that the name we have given to the "problem" is telling. Most of the rhetoric about keiretsu refers to the horizontal groups, which are in no way unique to Japan. The idea of a financial/industrial combine is common throughout Europe and much of Asia—in fact, it is the United States that is the odd man out. The Germans provide the best example, with groups such as that headed by Deutsche Bank, which owns more than a quarter of the equity in some of that country's leading auto, machinery, and retailing operations. Dresdner Bank and Allianz provide similar examples. The same structure exists in one form or another in Sweden, France, and Italy, among others.

James Abegglen, chairman of Gemini Consulting (Japan) and author of *Kaisha*, is right on target when he says: "The question then becomes: Why is keiretsu an issue, and why is it only an issue vis à vis Japan? Why do we get hot under the collar about Japanese banks' industrial groups but ignore the Germans? Are we implying that the German banks are just being efficient, while the Japanese banks are doing something evil? For that matter, why do we use the word keiretsu? We have a phenomenon that is common all over the world and was even common in the United States long ago, but when we make an issue of it we tag it with a Japanese word. What's the message? Is this thing dangerous because it's foreign or because it's Japanese or what? What are we saying?"

The answer, of course, has a great deal to do with our expanding trade deficit with Japan and our growing fear of that nation's seemingly powerful industries—especially as it relates to what we perceive as a decline in our own economic prowess. In other words, we are less afraid of what the Japanese keiretsu are than of what they might do (or do to us) in the future. Even assuming that this is the case, and assuming that our concerns lead us to attack Japan rather than Germany, Sweden, or Hong Kong, what is our goal? To "level the playing field" of global commerce? Clearly not. For if we were truly concerned with the international situation, we would not be singling out one country. Is our goal instead to somehow weaken the industrial giants that we fear will grow larger and hungrier in the coming years? Effective or not, that at least would be a strategic approach.

But what would the first step be? Would we order (or threaten) Japan to change the structure of its major industries? Why should it? And if the Japanese government were to give in to such pressure, why should the keiretsu companies pay any more attention to requests from their government than they do now, especially when it is only acting as a proxy for the United States? Would we instead go after the Japanese government itself, forcing it to discontinue protection for a variety of industries? This seems to be the most workable short-term goal, but Japan has already opened up and deregulated its markets considerably (albeit under steady pressure from abroad). While there is still room for improvement, the resulting gains will be less and less dramatic. Would we bar the operation of the keiretsu in the United States? That is an interesting idea, but totally impractical. Remember how strongly American firms rallied to support sanctions against Toshiba a few years ago because of that company's links to American interests? Multiply that times 189.

In the end, it is extremely difficult to do anything effective to limit the power of the keiretsu through either legislation or arm-twisting. And if somehow it were successful, would leashing the keiretsu help to "clean up" the dirty world of Japanese business? Not much. The biggest problems foreign firms find in Japan are not the domination of a single business by the keiretsu companies, but rather control by industrial cartels, often condoned and sometimes supported by the government. Just as one example, the ongoing U.S.–Japan debate over *dango* (the private arrangement by which Japanese construction firms decide which companies will compete and which will "win" bids for new public contracts) is not a problem of keiretsu-controlled dealing. Cartels cut across keiretsu lines: the oil companies, the construction companies, the drug companies, the food companies, the retailing companies, and dozens more are allied to preserve the structure and profitability of their own markets. These are the groups directly responsible for determining which products and services enter those markets, not the giant keiretsu to which each of the individual cartel members belongs. If the keiretsu were to disappear tomorrow, these intra-industry groups would still meet regularly to allot contracts, set prices, and debate how best to admit foreign competition.

If foreign pressure is to be applied, industry-specific targets would seem to rate much higher on the list of immediate priorities than the much larger, more diffuse keiretsu. What would happen, for example, if Japan's Fair Trade Commission were to be unleashed, unmuzzled, and set free—in the spotlight of international scrutiny—to fulfill its original mission? A "mad watchdog" with real power running amok in the heretofore "safe" backyard of industrial cartels and government-sanctioned corruption would be a welcome sight.

What about American Keiretsu?

When we began researching this book, the term *keiretsu* was seldom heard in the U.S. business community. Today it is not only familiar to almost every executive, but it appears regularly in the media. The term is no longer being used to attack Japanese business practices. We find that today many American managers are discussing a more radical course: imitating the keiretsu. Back in January of 1992, *Business Week* ran a cover story called "Learning from Japan," subtitled "American Keiretsu." Since then the idea of creating localized versions of the Japanese industrial groups—both horizontal and vertical—has gained momentum. Obviously, this is a large and complex issue and certainly deserves more space than we can devote to it here. However, we would like to make a few general observations about three of the biggest questions now under discussion.

Question 1: Will U.S. companies willingly sacrifice some of their independence to form large-scale cooperative groups, and will these look like the Japanese horizontal keiretsu?

The answer to this two-pronged question is Yes and No. American companies have already formed strategic alliances (another buzzword which has sprung from the keiretsu debate), but they are far from being Japanese-style horizontal keiretsu. Especially in the high-tech field, many firms have seen the wisdom of microlevel cooperation within a macrocompetitive environment. Almost overnight previously unthinkable alliances have become the new status quo (consider the linkup between arch-rivals Apple and IBM). Hundreds of American firms, big and small, have begun to cooperate with each other to maximize their performance in changing markets. Research consortia such as Sematech, Microelectronics and Computer Technology Corp., and others have shown that U.S. companies are willing to participate in (though not always fully cooperate with) their rivals in what is termed "precompetitive" research.

Again, this is interesting and progressive, but it is far from looking like a horizontal keiretsu. In the Japanese context, the nucleus of every group is a financial institution. While manufacturers may also participate in the nucleus (e.g., Mitsubishi Heavy or Sumitomo Metal), no keiretsu is run by a manufacturer. Is this situation conceivable in the United States? The answer is no. For one thing, the United States has a very mature economy which provides easy access to nonbank financing, so the banks' primary role would be less as lender than as group coordinator. The idea of making banks the coordinators of American industry would not go down well with the manufacturing sector. For another thing, there are anti-trust laws designed to keep the banks from returning to their old zaibatsu-like roles as holding companies for U.S. industry. In 1991, the Bush Administration backed a proposal to reform some of the laws governing U.S. banks, a package that would have taken a big step toward allowing a return to bank-centered industrial combines, but the legislation foundered in Congress. Yet even without the antitrust laws, U.S. firms are not likely to welcome a return to the days of J.P. Morgan.

American companies, particularly manufacturers, are not as friendly with their bankers as are their Japanese counterparts, nor would they want the kind of intrusion in their corporate affairs that Japanese firms take for granted. No American corporate manager wants his banker to have complete access to his books, his personnel files, and his boardroom (arguably, no Japanese executive does either, but that's the way the system works). In short, the idea of large, financially centered horizontal keiretsu seems fanciful.

On the other hand, the largest U.S. manufacturers are not so very different from banks themselves. In recent years, companies such as GM and Ford have been the nation's top corporate lenders, their annual loan volume surpassing that of even the biggest banks. One might well argue that if something like horizontal keiretsu do develop in the U.S., they would be manufacturer-centered rather than bank-centered. However, such groups would undoubtedly be connected to a manufacturer's primary business. That is, a single giant car maker or computer maker, for instance, could conceivably surround itself with a group of autonomous but closely related firms, but the majority of them would likely be suppliers and distributors for the manufacturer's products. This is much closer to a vertical than a horizontal keiretsu.

In other words, we tend to use the term "keiretsu" too casually. Talking about an IBM-Apple venture is not talking about keiretsu. If, for example, Ford, General Electric, Digital Equipment, Metropolitan Life, Morgan Guarantee, Goodyear, DuPont, 3M, Kimberly Clark, Merck, Reynolds Metals, Mobil, and TRW were to tie up, exchange small percentages of their stock with other group members, exchange directors, agree to buy from each other whenever feasible, exchange information about their respective markets, cooperate on new ventures that have little direct impact on most of their businesses, cooperate to support political candidates, and lobby for legislation that would further the group's policy goals, that would be an American keiretsu.

Is this kind of large-scale link-up likely? In a word, No.

Question 2: Will Japanese-style vertical keiretsu grow in the United States?

Again, the answer is no. U.S. companies do not have the same tradition of subcontractors being controlled by their clients. In the United States, small, high-quality suppliers demand a certain amount of respect from the big manufacturers. In Japan it is just the opposite; the parent firm demands loyalty from the supplier. American companies simply would not tolerate the kind of tactics that are commonly used in Japan, nor would U.S. authorities turn a blind eye to flagrant violations of commercial and labor laws just to help big firms turn a profit.

What we will see is companies developing much closer working relations with their suppliers. Design-in technology will increase. Long-term contracting, what is now called "relational contracting," will increase. This certainly resembles the Japanese model. Manufacturers will take equity stakes in formerly independent suppliers, sometimes supplying loans or helping their suppliers to invest in new technologies. In return, they will demand high-quality, long-term supply of critical parts. Suppliers will thus become less independent and more responsive to the needs of their "parents." In some cases, this may even approach the Japanese concept of a vertical keiretsu. For example, Excel Industries, Inc., which supplies auto windows to Ford, not only gave its main client an equity stake, but literally opens its books for Ford's people to inspect. Few American companies will go this far, but the trend towards greater cooperation and mutual dependence will undoubtedly spread.

Question 3: Where should U.S. industry consider emulating the keiretsu? The area just mentioned—long-term relationships between suppliers and manufacturers—is the most outstanding. Many in U.S. industry already see the advantages of this approach. For many companies the question now is more one of how best to adopt the system than whether or not to consider it in the first place. A second key area where U.S. firms are beginning to operate on a more Japanese-like model is in downsizing their core companies by spinning off divisions as independent firms. This creates in effect a quasi-horizontal "group" of firms, such as Hitachi or Matsushita have used for decades. A third area where American firms stand to gain a great deal is in cooperative research. Consultant Abegglen notes, "The Japanese semiconductor firms worked together for a time, developed some patentable technology, and then set about competing with each other. It's a good strategy, and it could work in the United States. The problem is we're much more paranoid about cooperation than the Japanese are." Here again, the first steps have already been taken, but American firms must first learn how to cooperate. Companies still feel that if they open their doors wide to their research partners, they'll be robbed blind, but if they share too little they kill the partnership just as effectively. Grounds for trust and real cooperation must be established, both because the costs of R&D are skyrocketing, and because the markets are growing more competitive every day.

These are three important areas where American firms can profit from adapting keiretsu strategies: supplier relations, spinning off noncore businesses into affiliated subsidiaries, and learning to cooperate in R&D ventures. None of these should present a threat to our outlook on business, and all of them would be a big plus for the United States.

Afterword

We do not presume to make the final and definitive statement about the keiretsu. The subject is not only enormous and confoundingly complex, but is also changing rapidly. Ultimately, we do not believe that the keiretsu are intrinsically either good or bad. Both the horizontal and vertical groupings are natural outgrowths of the Japanese way of doing business, and as such both will continue into the foreseeable future regardless of external pressures. On the contrary, it is internal pressures that threaten the keiretsu.

The horizontal groups will continue more or less as they are because there is no major force working to weaken them. As noted above, the members' lack of dependence on the groups for their survival does not outweigh the multiple merits of group membership. The biggest apparent change is the members' freedom to do business with whomever they want whenever they want, which ultimately strengthens rather than weakens the group.

The vertical keiretsu are another story. They are already being forced to change due to pressures from within their pyramids. Manufacturers in production keiretsu are finding it harder to maintain loyalty among their suppliers, which weakens their grip on their subsidiaries. And some of the distribution keiretsu, most notably in areas such as consumer electronics, are weakening through attrition of their members. The remaining store owners are less inclined to sell only one brand and to sell it the way the parent firms decree.

As for the current "keiretsu debate" in America, we feel that it will have little impact on the keiretsu themselves. Regardless of what policy decisions are made in either Washington or Tokyo over the next few years, one fact is certain: the keiretsu will not disappear. They will certainly continue to change; in some respects they may change quite significantly, but the elements that make them keiretsu will not change. The best long-term approach that Western firms can take is to turn the tables. Not to set up copies of the Japanese keiretsu, but to do exactly what the keiretsu have been doing with regard to American and European business for a century: learn about their operations, understand their strengths and weaknesses, and find ways to profit from that knowledge.

Notes

Chapter 2

Information on the growth and dissolution of the zaibatsu on pp. 21 to 42 was drawn from many sources, both Japanese and Western. The main source for the history of the zaibatsu was Professor Hidemasa Morikawa's excellent and detailed history entitled *Zaibatsu* (University of Tokyo Press, Tokyo, 1992). The best background on the Occupation's attitudes and actions is contained in Eleanor M. Hadley's *Anti-Trust in Japan* (Princeton University Press, Princeton, N.J., 1970). Both books are superb and recommended to readers who wish to know more about these critical periods in Japanese history.

The quote from MacArthur's Basic Directive on p. 31 is from Hadley.

For more information on Prime Minister Yoshida's intentional misreading of SCAP's directive on p. 33, see Al Alletzhauser, *The House of Nomura* (Bloomsbury Publishing Ltd., London, 1991). Nomura was perhaps the best representative of the "new zaibatsu" and Alletzhauser's study is particularly valuable for its historical insights into the birth and growth of this group.

The Fair Trade Commission (discussed on pp. 34 to 36) originally had seven members, all of whom were appointed by the prime minister. SCAP's goal in structuring it so was to make sure that the FTC members were not chosen by the bureaucrats—also an indication of where they suspected future problems worthy of FTC attention might lie. What the Allies did not count on was that ex-bureaucrats would become prime minister so often (as they did from 1957 to 1972). This undermined the whole structure of the organization.

Moreover, the original membership of the commission included one judge and one representative of the private sector. The bureaucrats deemed this unnecessary and had the latter two officers removed from the composition of the FTC. The remaining five seats were reserved for bureaucrats. To those foreign bankers and brokers who complain that the Antimonopoly Law is never applied to Japan's financial sector, it is instructive to note that eight of the FTC's past thirteen chairmen are "old boys" from the Ministry of Finance. Today the Commission's five seats consist of two graduates from MOF, one from MITI, one from the Justice Ministry, and one from the Ministry of Foreign Affairs. In other words, all former bureaucrats, and a majority from MOF and MITI. Professor Chalmers Johnson notes that by 1958 "it seemed to some that the FTC would approve anything short of piracy if MITI said it was necessary for Japan's rapid economic growth." Times have changed, but not so very much.

The comments on MITI's organization of cartels on p. 35 (for "cooperative behavior") and on the public interest not being served by free competitive order come from Chapter 6 of Johnson's excellent *MITI and the Japanese Miracle* (Stanford University Press, Stanford, Calif., 1982). His description and interpretation of the rise of Japanese industrial policy is strongly recommended for anyone interested in Japan's postwar "economic miracle."

The citation on p. 37 "No sooner had the Occupation ended . . ." comes from Professor Yoshinari Maruyama, "The Big Six Horizontal Keiretsu," in *Japan Quarterly*, Tokyo, April–June 1992.

The story of MITI's dealings with IBM on p. 41 comes from Johnson's *MITI and the Japanese Miracle.*

MITI Minister (later Prime Minister) Miyazawa's comments to Japanese legislators were quoted in Hiroshi Okumura's *Kaishime-Nottori-TOB* (Shakai Shisosha, Tokyo, 1982).

Chapter 3

The study of 873 listed companies on p. 48 and the role of the bank as credit monitor on p. 50 are both discussed more fully in Professor Paul Sheard's article "The Main Bank System and Corporate Monitoring and Control in Japan" in *Journal of Economic Behavior and Organization*, 11, Elsevier Science Publishers B.V. (North-Holland) 1989.

The idea of the banks as venture capitalist on p. 50 comes principally from Kenichi Imai, *Japanese Business Groups and the Structural Impediments Initiative in Japan's Economic Structure: Should It Change?* (Society for Japanese Studies, Seattle, 1990).

The description of the sogo shosha on p. 54 is from M.Y. Yoshino and Thomas B. Lifson, *Invisible Link* (MIT Press, Cambridge, Mass. 1984).

As for the comment on p. 55 that "On the whole, the shosha make very little profit on their business . . ." we should note that on average the shosha's profit margins are miniscule. On individual transactions, however, such as importing consumer goods and distributing them inside Japan, their profits may be enormous.

The quote on p. 56 is from Robert Ballon and Iwao Tomita, *The Financial Behavior of Japanese Corporations* (Kodansha International, Tokyo, 1988).

For the illustration on p. 57 showing how a shosha facilitates business with Japan we are deeply indebted to Professor Paul Sheard of Australian National University. His drawing makes an otherwise complicated-sounding transaction appear relatively simple. Our diagram is based on the one that appeared in "The Japanese General Trading Company as an Aspect of Interfirm Risk-Sharing" in *Journal of the Japanese and International Economics*, 3, 1989, pp. 308–322.

With regard to the shosha's practice of issuing and receiving trade bills on p. 57 (not so common a feature in the West), Professor Ballon points out: "Promissory notes (*yakusoku tegata*) are an age-old and ubiquitous method of payment, in particular among small/medium enterprises. The two centuries of Japan's seclusion (1632–1854) witnessed an extraordinary expansion of domestic commercial activities and the development of an elaborate system of payment based on trust. . . . One contemporary manifestation of this heritage is the promissory note." (From Ballon and Tomita.)

The analysis of the shosha as "a kind of quasi-insurance agency" and the quote on p. 58 are from Paul Sheard's "The Japanese General Trading Company as an Aspect of Interfirm Risk-Sharing."

Chapter 4

The quote on p. 62 is from Professor Maruyama's "The Big Six Horizontal Keiretsu," and the quote on p. 64 is based on interviews with Professor Maruyama.

The quote on p. 66 beginning "What the Japanese government . . ." comes from Ballon and Tomita.

The quote from Toyota Chairman Taizo Ishida on p. 70 as translated by Professor Paul Sheard appeared in "The Economics of Interlocking Shareholding in Japan," *Ricerche Economiche*, XLV, Paprile-Settembre, 1991, pp. 2–3.

Chapter 5

It is important to note in the discussion of Kanto versus Kansai on p. 76–77 that there are numerous cases of Mitsubishi and/or Mitsui firms working together with Sumitomo and/or Sanwa firms. However, the gross generalization that they would prefer to work with each other rather than with their Tokyo or Osaka counterparts is still accurate.

Chapter 6

Some of the background information for the section on labor and overhead costs as well as the quote on p. 120 were based on a series of personal interviews with Professor Shoichiro Sei of Kanto Gakuin University. Part of this material appeared as an article by David Russell, "A Lean, Mean Subcontracting Machine" in *Business Tokyo*, December 1990.

Too often the term *Kyoryoku-kai* on p. 122 is translated as "cooperative" group or association without further comment. While the term *kyoryoku* does mean cooperation, the real meaning of the expression in this context is clear: the supplier is expected to "cooperate" with the parent firm.

The brief quote from Professor Kenneth Courtis on p. 125 is based on a personal interview. Courtis, it should be noted, is one of the most consistently interesting observers of contemporary Japan, and certainly the most coherent among a tiny handful of truly visionary Japan-watchers.

Chapter 8

When we set out to interview Japanese subcontractors, we naturally intended to use their real names and the names of their companies. This proved to be absolutely impossible. The background of this situation may be interesting to some readers.

In 1990, the head of a group of small Japanese manufacturing firms published an article in the *Harvard Business Review*. In it, he described how subcontractors are organized into pyramids of vertical keiretsu and he compared their existence to Japan's feudal age, with the big parent companies acting like feudal lords, expecting total loyalty from their underlings, the subcontractors. Although the author was bold enough (perhaps foolish enough) to publish under his own name, he carefully avoided mentioning the names of real Japanese companies with whom he was doing business. Even so, representatives of major corporations called this executive within days of publication. He was warned in no uncertain terms that talking to the foreign press about the keiretsu was "bad for business" and that he should make sure that this publication was his last. If not, all orders to his many group companies would be terminated.

Stories like this get around very quickly in the world of Japanese subcontractors. The executive involved has a reputation for being unusually strong-minded and his firms are relatively independent, yet he could not ignore the warnings he was receiving. As a result, when we asked him for comments on the material we had uncovered, he politely but firmly refused to comment.

Consequently, when we talked to much smaller and far less independent companies in Tokyo, the ubiquitous response was "Don't use my name, the name of my company, or the name of our parent firm." Some said, "Don't even describe what it is we make here; they'll find out who you talked to and make things tough for us." Despite the changes the vertical keiretsu are experiencing as a result of the prolonged recession, there is still widespread fear that it is unwise to speak openly about life inside the pyramid.

Chapter 9

Professor Naktani's study of the benefits of group affiliation cited on p. 197 comes from his essay, "The Economic Role of Financial Corporate Grouping," in *The Economic Analysis of the Japanese Firm*, M. Aoki, ed. (Elsevier Science Publishers B.V., Amsterdam, 1984).

The quotation from Isamu Nakagawa on p. 203 comes from "Distribution Keiretsu: Electronics Stores Rebel" in *Tokyo Business Today*, Toyo Keizai, Inc., September, 1990.

Mr. Terada's story on pp. 203–204 comes from Tokyo-based writer Peter Langan. A version of this story appeared in *Business Tokyo*, March 1991.

The quotation from Jim Abegglen on p. 206 is from a personal interview. In addition, the authors wish to thank Mr. Abegglen for a number of insightful comments he made on the topics presented here.

Index

AT&T, 148
Abegglen, James, 205–206, 217
Aiwa, 151
Akai Electric, 53
Allianz, 205
Antimonopoly Law (AML), 33–36, 39, 63, 65, 213
Apple Computer, 148, 150, 208, 209
Aristech Chemical, 92
Asahi Breweries, 76, 98, 103
Asano, Soichiro, 24
Asano Bank, 25
Asano Cement, 25
Asano Kokura Steel, 25
Asano Savings Bank, 25
Asano Shipbuilding, 25
Asano Shipping, 24
Asano Steel Works, 25
Asano Trading, 25
Asano zaibatsu, 24, 25, 27, 28, 99, 101
Asset bubble, 129–131
Assigned directors, 43, 70–73
Ataka & Co., 53, 58, 69–70
Automotive industry, 116–127, 131, 133–142, 199–202, 204–205
    personal accounts, 176–192

Bank of Japan, 26, 34
Bank of Taiwan, 28
Bank of Tokyo (BOT), 91, 150
Banks (*see* Main bank)
Bell Helicopter, 86
Big Six, 9–11
    (*See also* Horizontal keiretsu; *specific group*)
Boeing, 137
Boone Co., 1
Boone Pickens, T., 1–2, 9, 201
Bridgestone Corp., 10

Bubble era, 129–131

C. Itoh & Co., 55, 92, 112
Canon Group, 101
CBS Records, 150
Central Electric Industries (Chuo Denki Kogyo), 15–17
Chiyoda Bank, 37
Chiyoda Fire and Marine Insurance, 136
Chrysler, 122
Chuba (Nagoya) airport project, 103
Chujiro, Fujino, 62
Chuo Denki Kogyo (Central Electric Industries), 15–17
CIT Group Holdings, Inc., 112
City bank (*see* Main bank)
Clover-kai, 107, 108
Coca-Cola, 195
Columbia Pictures Entertainment, 150
Commercial bank (*see* Main bank)
Compaq Computers, 200
Computer Technology Corp., 208
Continental Illinois Leasing, 106
Corporate balance sheets, 80–81
Courtis, Kenneth, 125, 216
Cray Research, 143
Cross-shareholding, 43, 49, 61, 66–70, 81–82, 98, 195
    merits, 68–69
    share disposal, 69–70

Dai-Ichi Bank, 26, 37, 38, 75, 82, 91, 109, 111, 113, 194
Dai-Ichi Kokuritsu Ginko (First National Bank), 26
Daiei and Ito-Yokado keiretsu, 9
Daihatsu Motor, 86, 135

Daihyo-in, 64
Daiken Sangyo, 101
Daimler-Benz A.G. Group, 92
Daiwa Bank, 77
Daiwa Securities, 16, 17
Dan, Takuma, 30
Dango, 207
Dell Computers, 200
Denki Kagaku, 111
Denki-ya, 123
Dentsu, 12
Deutsche Bank, 205
Distribution keiretsu, 115–116, 122–125, 129–
    130, 195, 211
  changes to, 203–205
DKB (Dai-Ichi Kangyo) Bank, 9, 48, 85, 91,
    108, 109, 111–112, 146
DKB (Dai-Ichi Kangyo) Group, 39, 73–76,
    81–82, 109–113, 193, 197
  main members, 14, 86, 101, 106–108, 110f.*
  presidential council, 63, 111–113, 146
  profile, 109, 111
  snapshot, 109
Dodwell Marketing Consultants, 14–15, 17
Dresdner Bank, 205

Eiho-kai, 135
Electronics industry, 116–128, 131, 133, 142–
    151, 200, 203–204, 211
  personal accounts, 169–176
Equity assets, 69
Excel Industries, Inc., 209–210
Export-Import Bank of Japan, 141, 150

Fair Trade Commission (FTC), 34–35, 62, 63,
    78–80, 97, 207, 213–214
Federation of Bankers Association of Japan,
    77
*Financial Behavior of Japanese Corporations,
    The* (Ballon and Tomita), 56, 66
First National Bank (Dai-Ichi Kokuritsu
    Ginko), 26
Ford Motor Co., 79, 116, 122, 138, 209, 210
Fuji Bank, 9, 37, 38, 48, 72, 73, 81, 99, 101–
    103, 146, 194
Fuji Electric, 111

Fuji Heavy Industries, 53, 139
Fuji-kai, 102
Fujisawa Pharmaceutical, 108
Fujita zaibatsu, 24, 27
Fukami (latent assets), 69
Furukawa, Ichibei, 24, 109, 111
Furukawa Electric, 111
Furukawa Mining, 24
Furukawa zaibatsu, 24, 27, 28, 111, 113
Fuyo Group, 73–76, 81, 99–103
  main members, 72, 86, 100f., 106, 108, 109,
    113, 141, 148
  presidential council, 63, 101–103, 146
  profile, 99, 101
  snapshot, 99
Fuyo-kai, 102–103, 107
Fuyo Kondan-kai, 102–103

General Electric (GE), 146, 148
General Motors (GM), 41, 67, 116, 122, 134,
    137–138, 205, 208
General trading company, 3–5, 10, 37, 43–
    44, 53–59
  default of, 58
  functions, 54–55
    trade credit, 55–58
  fund borrowing by, 59
  profits, 55
  (*See also specific company*)
Getsuyo-kai, 86, 93
Goldman Sachs, 96

Hakusui-kai, 97–98, 145
Hino Motors, 135
Hitachi Corp., 10, 11, 20, 31, 86, 101, 103,
    109, 113
Hitachi Group, 115, 124, 142, 143, 145–149,
    158, 200, 210
  snapshot, 145
Hitachi Shipbuilding, 31
Hitachi Zosen, 104
Honda Group, 140–142, 150, 151
  snapshot, 140
Honda Motor Co., 66, 79, 80, 86, 90, 93, 122,
    140, 141
Honshu Paper, 111

*The *f.* after a page number refers to a figure.

Horizontal keiretsu, 9–11, 13, 14, 75–113, 115
  cross-shareholding, 81–82, 98
  economic strength, 78–81
  identity of, 75–76
  Kanto versus Kansai, 76–78, 108, 215
  purpose of, 193–199
  survival of, 211
  (*See also specific group*)
Hoya, 108, 196

IBJ (Industrial Bank of Japan), 9, 10, 49, 53,
  103, 135, 139, 146
IBM, 41, 136, 148, 208, 209, 214
IHI (Ishikawajima-Harima Heavy In-
  dustries), 148
Imai, Kenichi, 50, 51, 214
Imperial Bank, 37, 83, 85
INAX, 93
Indonesia, 106
*Industrial Groupings in Japan: The Anatomy of
  the Keiretsu*, 14–15, 17
Intel, 200
Interlocking directorates, 61, 195
Intragroup financing, 43, 74, 195
Intragroup trade, 43, 61, 195
Invisible Link, The (Yoshino and Lifson), 54,
  214
Isuzu Motors, 41, 67, 86, 140
Itochu Shoji, 14, 43–44, 53, 55, 77, 92, 97,
  102, 106, 107, 112
Iwai zaibatsu, 27
Iwasaki, Yataro, 23–26
Izumi, 97

James Wolfensohn, 102
Japan Company Handbook, The (JCH), 15–17,
  78
Japan Industrial Bank, 139
Japan Industries (Nippon Sangyo), 31
Japan National Mail Steamship Company
  (YJK), 22, 23
Japan Radio, 103
Japan Storage Battery, 93
Japanese written language, 13
JCSAT satellite communications project, 112
Jidosha Denki Kogyo, 142
Jigyo bussei, 143
Jinmyaku, 85

JIT system, 176–178
Jitan, 160
Johnson, Chalmers, 35, 41, 214
Joint ventures, 71
JVC (Victor Co. of Japan), 144

Kaisha (Abegglen), 206
Kaisha Shikiho, 15
Kajima Construction, 79–80, 98
Kansai International Airport project, 103,
  107, 112
Kasai Kogyo, 142
Kawasaki Heavy Industries, 111
Kawasaki Kisen, 111
Kawasaki Steel, 111
Keihin Electric Express Railway, 72
Keiretsu, 7–8
  history, 19–42
    competition, 39–40
    economic reform, 33–36
    government intervention, 40–42
    keiretsu development, 36–37
    Meiji restoration, 21–24
  keiretsu debate, 205–207, 211
  keiretsu literacy, 13–14
  listing sources, 14–17
  structure, 8–9
  success of, 194–195
  in United States, 7, 207–210
  (*See also* Horizontal keiretsu; Vertical
    keiretsu; Zaibatsu)
Kigyo Keiretsu Soran (Overview of the In-
  dustrial Keiretsu), 78
Kin'yokai, 62, 88, 90, 93
Kirin Beer, 14, 76, 103
Kleinwort Benson Government Securities,
  101–102
Kobe Steel, 104, 108, 113
Koito Manufacturing Co., 1, 141–142, 201
Kubota, 101, 103
Kuhara zaibatsu, 27
Kyocera, 108, 196
Kyoho-kai, 135
Kyoryoku-kai, 122, 216

Large-Scale Retail Store Law, 130
Latent assets (fukumi), 69

Law Prohibiting Excess Concentrations of
  Economic Power, 36
Life insurance companies, 52, 68, 79
Lifson, Thomas B., 54, 214
Lloyd's Bank of California, 106

MacArthur, Douglas, 31, 32, 36, 213
McDonnell Douglas, 86
Maeda Corp., 103
Main bank, 9, 10, 44–53, 77, 79
  company affiliation process, 45–48
  economic power of, 48–49
  functions of, 49–53
    bankruptcy intervention, 51–53
    credit monitor, 50, 52, 53
    fund lender, 49, 50, 52, 53, 55–57, 74
    stockholder, 49, 50, 53
    venture capitalist, 50–51, 53
  history, 20, 38
  (*See also specific bank*)
Maneshita Denki, 144
Manufacturers' Hanover Trust, 112
Marubeni, 73, 77, 97, 101, 102, 107
Maruyama, Yoshinari, 62, 64, 214
Matsukata (Kawasaki) zaibatsu, 111, 113
Matsushita, Konosuke, 143
Matsushita Communication Industrial, 144
Matsushita Electric Industrial (MEI), 11, 61,
  66, 77, 112, 115, 143–145
Matsushita Electric Works, 144
Matsushita Group, 122, 124, 125, 134, 142–
  145, 147, 203–204, 210
  snapshot, 142
Mazda Motor Corp., 53, 61, 79, 80, 86, 98,
  140, 141
Meiji Mutual Life Insurance, 93, 141
Meiji restoration, 21–24
Microelectronics, 208
Ministry of Finance, 32, 44, 91, 101, 129, 213–
  214
Ministry of International Trade and In-
  dustry (MITI), 32, 34–42, 67, 116, 117,
  148, 150, 153, 203, 214
Ministry of Munitions, 117
Ministry of Posts and Telecommunications,
  148, 150
MISCO (Mitsui Information System Con-
  ference), 87

MITI and the Japanese Miracle (Johnson), 35,
  41, 214
Mitsubishi Aircraft, 31
Mitsubishi Bank, 9, 36–38, 48, 53, 65, 79, 90–
  91, 93, 99, 111, 141
Mitsubishi Cement, 93
Mitsubishi Electric, 93, 146, 200
Mitsubishi Group, 9, 74–76, 81–83, 88–92,
  94, 103, 149, 198, 215–216
  main members, 14, 37, 86, 89*f.*, 141
  presidential council, 62, 63, 88, 90, 93, 137
  profile, 88, 90
  snapshot, 88
Mitsubishi Heavy Industries (MHI), 11, 31,
  45, 90, 93
Mitsubishi Materials, 93
Mitsubishi Mining, 93
Mitsubishi Motor Corp., 86, 90, 92, 140, 141
Mitsubishi Petrochemical Co., Ltd., 62
Mitsubishi Real Estate, 90
Mitsubishi Shipbuilding, 31
Mitsubishi Shoji (Mitsubishi Corp.), 37, 43–
  45, 62, 91–93, 97, 102, 107, 112
Mitsubishi Steamship Co., 23, 24
Mitsubishi Trading, 28
Mitsubishi Trust & Banking, 93, 141
Mitsubishi zaibatsu, 19, 24–29, 75, 94, 104
Mitsui Bank, 25, 26, 37, 38, 48, 85, 87, 99,
  104, 109, 111, 150
Mitsui Bussan (Mitsui & Co.), 11, 25, 27–28,
  43–44, 83, 85–86, 91–92, 97
Mitsui Fudosan, 86
Mitsui Group, 74–76, 82–88, 98, 215–216
  main members, 10, 13, 54, 84*f.*, 108, 141,
    148, 150, 196
  presidential council, 63, 86–87
  profile, 82–83, 85
  snapshot, 83
Mitsui Liquefied Gas, 88
Mitsui Marine & Fire Insurance, 86, 88
Mitsui Mining, 67
Mitsui Oil, 88
Mitsui Petrochemical, 88
Mitsui Toatsu Chemical, 88
Mitsui Trust & Banking, 85, 87, 150
Mitsui zaibatsu, 19, 24–28, 30, 31, 66, 94, 104
Mitsukoshi, 88
Miyazawa, Kiichi, 41, 67, 214
Mori zaibatsu, 101
Morimoto Group, 93

Morimura Group, 79
Morita, Akio, 143, 150
Motorola, 148

Nakagawa, Isamu, 203, 217
Nakajima Aircraft, 139
Nakatani, Iwao, 197, 217
Nakayama Steel, 67
National, 124, 125, 142, 203, 204
NEC (Nippon Electric Co.), 12–13, 51, 97,
    98, 146, 148, 200
New York Stock Exchange, 91
Nezu zaibatsu, 101
NGK Insulators, 93
NGK Spark Plug, 93
Nichimen, 109
Nichirei, 73, 101
Nikko Securities, 93
Nimoku-kai, 86–87, 137, 196
Nippon Cement, 101
Nippon Express, 108, 113
Nippon Kangyo Bank, 109, 111, 113
Nippon Life Insurance, 17, 77, 104
Nippon Light Metal, 111
Nippon Mining, 31
Nippon Oil and Fats, 101
Nippon Sangyo (Japan Industries), 31
Nippon Sheet Glass, 68
Nippon Steel, 10
Nippon Unisys, 86
Nippondenso, 121, 201
Nishimatsu Construction, 103
Nishin Flour Milling, 73
Nissan Chemical Industries, 31
Nissan Credit, 139
Nissan Diesel Motor, 139
Nissan Fire & Marine Insurance, 139
Nissan Group, 138–142, 199, 201
    snapshot, 138
Nissan Life Insurance, 139
Nissan Motor Co., 20, 31, 53, 73, 86, 101,
    103, 122, 137, 138, 146
Nissan Real Estate Development, 139
Nissan Trading, 139
Nissan zaibatsu, 30–31, 101
Nisshin Flour Milling, 101
Nisshinbo Industries, 73, 101
Nissho Iwai, 102, 106–107, 109, 112, 113
Nissho-kai, 139

NKK, 73, 99, 101, 199
NOF Corp., 73
Nomura Bank, 104
Nomura Securities, 77, 104
Nomura zaibatsu, 27, 28
Noritake, 93
NSK, 73, 101, 103
NTT, 72, 145, 148, 150, 199

Ohbayashi, 108
Ohki Construction, 103
Oki Electric, 71–73, 99, 103
Okura zaibatsu, 24, 27, 28, 101
Olivetti, 148
Oriental Steamship, 25
Osaka Bank, 37
Osaka Chemical Group, 115
Osaka Toyopet, 137
Osano Group, 67

Panasonic, 142
Penta-Ocean Construction, 103
Philips, 143
Plaza Accord, 125–127, 129
Presidential councils, 10, 61–66, 79
    functions, 62, 64–66
    post-Occupation, 64–65
    proceedings, 61–63
    (See also specific council; specific group)
Production keiretsu, 115–122
    changes in, 199–202
    structure, 121–122
    subcontractor control, 118–121
        labor costs, 119, 216
        overhead, 119–121, 216
Promissory notes (yakusoku tegata), 215
Pyramid keiretsu (see Vertical keiretsu)

Real estate assets, 69
Rockefeller Group, 90
Roku dai kigyo shudan, 9–10
Sakura Bank, 9, 85–88, 150
Sanbio, 107
Sankin Contact Club, 112
Sankin Information Systems Research
    Group, 112
Sankin-kai, 112

Sankyo, 111
Sannet, 107
Sansui-kai, 107–109
Sanwa Bank, 9, 20, 48, 77, 103, 104, 106–108, 111, 146, 194
Sanwa Group, 73–76, 81, 103–109, 216
  main members, 67, 86, 101, 105*f.*, 113, 115
  presidential council, 63, 107–109, 146
  profile, 103–104
  snapshot, 104
Sanyo Group, 124, 142
Sanyo Life Electrics, 203
Sapporo Beer, 73, 101, 103
Sasagawa Group, 67
SCAP (Supreme Commander for the Allied Powers), 31–34, 36–38, 66, 213
Sei, Shoichiro, 120, 216
Seibu and Tokyu keiretsu, 9
Sekisui Chemical, 104
Sekisui House, 108
Sematech, 208
Shacho-kai (*see* Presidential councils)
Sharp Group, 142
Sheard, Paul, 50, 56, 58, 214, 215
Shibusawa, Eiichi, 26, 109
Shibusawa zaibatsu, 24, 26, 28, 38, 75, 109, 111
Shimadzu Group, 79, 93
Shimadzu Seisakusho, 93
Shiseido, 116
Shock absorber strategy, 126, 199
Shosha (*see* General trading company)
Showa Denko, 73, 101
Showa Kaiun (Showa Line Ltd.), 73, 99
Siemens, 143, 148
Six Big Industrial Groups, 9–10
SMEs (small- and medium-sized enterprises), 116–117, 129, 131, 153
Sogo shosha (*see* General trading company)
Somu bucho, 93
Sony Chemicals, 151
Sony Consumer Marketing, 151
Sony Corp., 10, 66, 87, 90, 112, 150
Sony Group, 124, 125, 134, 142–145, 149–151
  snapshot, 149
Sony Music Entertainment, Inc., 150
Sony Network Hanbai, 151
Sony Pictures Entertainment, Inc., 150
Space Communications, 90
STEP, 204

Strategic alliances, 208
Structural Impediments Initiative (SII), 8, 59, 129–130, 144
Subaru, 53, 86, 139
Sumikin Bussan, 16
Sumitomo Bank, 9, 17, 48, 68, 77, 96–99, 101, 104, 108
  bankruptcy intervention, 53, 58, 69–70
  credit monitor, 16
  fund lender, 51, 74
  history, 37, 38
Sumitomo Chemical Ltd., 11, 68, 98
Sumitomo Coal Mining, 74
Sumitomo Communications Industries, 97
Sumitomo Construction, 74
Sumitomo Copper and Steel, 31
Sumitomo Fire and Marine Insurance, 74
Sumitomo Group, 68–70, 74–76, 81–83, 94–98, 103, 112, 193, 216
  main members, 16, 17, 61, 80, 86, 95*f.*, 104, 108, 109, 141, 145, 148
  presidential council, 63, 79, 97–98
  profile, 94
  snapshot, 94
Sumitomo Life Insurance, 16, 17, 68, 74, 145
Sumitomo Marine and Fire Insurance, 16, 68
Sumitomo Metal Industries (SMI), 16, 17, 31, 68, 98
Sumitomo Shoji (Sumisho/Sumitomo Corp.), 16, 68, 74, 96–98, 102
Sumitomo Steel Works, 31
Sumitomo Trust & Banking, 16, 17, 68, 74, 79
Sumitomo Warehouse, 68, 74
Sumitomo zaibatsu, 19, 24, 26, 66, 94
Sun Microsystems, 143
Suntory, 77, 108, 196
Suzuki zaibatsu, 27, 28, 38, 104

Taisei Construction, 73, 101
Taisei Corp., 103
Taisei Group, 101
Taisho Marine & Fire Insurance, 86
Taiyo Kobe Bank, 85
Takarakuji, 111
Tanabe Seiyaku, 108
Tandy, 143
Tate (*see* Vertical keiretsu)
Technics, 142
Teijin (Teikoku Jinzo Kenshi), 104, 108
Terada, Yoshio, 203–204, 217

Texas Instruments, 146
Third-country trade, 54
Time Warner, 112
Toa Corp., 103
Tobishima Corp., 103
Tobu Railway, 73, 101
Toho Rayon, 73, 99
Tokai Bank, 86, 137
Tokai Group, 137
Tokio Marine & Fire Insurance, 93, 141
Tokyo Olympics, 76
Tokyo Stock Exchange (TSE), 11, 26, 44, 115,
    122, 145, 149
Tokyo Tatemono, 73, 99, 103
Tokyo Teleport project, 103
Tokyo Toyopet, 137
Tokyo Toyota Motors, 137
Tomen, 86
Toshiba Corp., 11, 87–88, 112
Toshiba Group, 13, 124, 136, 142, 146, 147–
    149, 200
    snapshot, 147
Toto, 93
Towa Real Estate, 136
Toyo Construction, 108
Toyo Keizai, Inc., 15, 78
Toyo Kisen, 99
Toyo Kogyo, 53
Toyota Finance, 136
Toyota Group, 1, 55, 115, 122, 134–142, 145,
    148, 196, 201
    snapshot, 134
Toyota Home, 136
Toyota Lease, 136
Toyota Motor Corp., 1, 9–11, 86, 103, 122,
    134–136
Toyota Tokyo Corolla, 137
Trade Association Law, 36
Trading company (see General trading com-
    pany)
Trust banks, 79
TRW, 146

Unisys Corp., 86
Unitika, Ltd., 108

Vertical keiretsu, 9, 11–14, 115–131, 133
    business fields of, 12
    criticism of, 125–131, 201
    distribution, 115–116, 122–125, 129–130,
        195, 203–205, 211
    hierarchy loyalty, 12
    importing exports, 127–128
    production, 115–122, 199–202, 216
    retail pricing, 130–131
    round-table discussion, 154–169, 216–217
    structure, 80
    survival of, 211
    (See also specific group)
Volker, Paul, 102
Volkswagen (VW), 137–138, 205
Volvo, 90

Walter E. Heller, 101

Yamaichi Securities, 53
Yasuda Bank, 26, 37, 38, 99, 194
Yasuda Fire & Marine Insurance, 73, 99
Yasuda Life Insurance, 99
Yasuda Trust & Banking, 72, 99
Yasuda zaibatsu, 24, 26, 75, 76, 81, 99, 101
YJK (Japan National Mail Steamship Com-
    pany), 22, 23
Yoko (see Horizontal keiretsu)
Yokogawa Electric, 73, 103
Yokogawa Medical Systems, 103
Yoshida, Shigeru, 33, 213
Yoshino, Michael Y., 54, 214

Zaibatsu, 19–26, 49, 66, 76, 213
    growth of, 27–29
    termination of, 31–33
    during World War II, 29–31
    (See also specific group)
Zenitaka Construction, 108

About the Authors

KENICHI MIYASHITA is a former senior editor of PHP, Japan's most respected publisher of business books and periodicals. He has written extensively on the business, economy, and history of Japan. Mr. Miyashita is a graduate of Tokyo University.

DAVID RUSSELL is an American journalist with more than a decade of experience in Japan. He has written and edited for both *Business Toyko* magazine and Nihon Keizai Shimbun (Nikkei), and is currently managing editor at *Tokyo Business Today*. Mr. Russell holds an M.A. in Japanese literature from Columbia University. Both authors live and work in Tokyo.